ERASED

Also by Anna Malaika Tubbs

The Three Mothers:
How the Mothers of Martin Luther King, Jr.,
Malcolm X, and James Baldwin Shaped a Nation

ERASED

What American Patriarchy
Has Hidden from Us

ANNA MALAIKA TUBBS

FLATIRON
BOOKS
NEW YORK

www.flatironbooks.com

Designed by Donna Sinisgalli Noetzel

The Library of Congress Cataloging-in-Publication Data is available upon request.

ISBN 978-1-250-87669-0 (hardcover)
ISBN 978-1-250-87670-6 (ebook)

Our books may be purchased in bulk for promotional, educational, or business use. Please contact your local bookseller or the Macmillan Corporate and Premium Sales Department at 1-800-221-7945, extension 5442, or by email at MacmillanSpecialMarkets@macmillan.com.

First Edition: 2025

10   9   8   7   6   5   4   3   2   1

In honor of my mother,
the children she raised,
and the children we are raising

CONTENTS

ERASED

INTRODUCTION

Let Us Begin, Again

Day six arrived. I scrolled through the "just checking in" texts, appreciative but also slightly irritated with everyone who thought they were more anxious than me for the moment we were waiting for. It was a Sunday morning in late August in Los Angeles, and on this particular day the heat was all-consuming. I was desperately craving an iced latte so we—my husband, son, and I—stopped at a café on our way to the park for a playdate. Sitting on a picnic blanket with a newly made friend, sipping my drink, watching my son run up and down and around a structure of slides and swings, I started to feel it again, a pain surging in my lower abdomen that would rise before it suddenly went away completely. I had been feeling this on and off for two weeks so I breathed through it, keeping my excitement at bay, and focused on what my midwife had told me: "A due date is only an estimate. Your baby is not six days late; the estimate you were given is just a few days off."

Just like we had done the first time, we left the sex of our baby a surprise. I wanted this decision to serve as a small reminder to others that we should stop making assumptions based solely on the number of X chromosomes a person has, and stop trying to place people into categories even before they are born. I have always been fascinated by the way sex dictates our lives and how it does so across the world, a fascination that led me to pursue degrees in anthropology, gender studies, and sociology.

Majoring in anthropology as an undergraduate, I explored how across cultures everything appears to begin with the categorization of a person's sex. My observation was that as a result of human reproduction and the early human belief that reproducing was the ultimate goal of humanity, historically people have been organized by common but not universal functions of genitalia. In other words, every culture I have ever encountered or studied has largely been defined by the role people can play in reproducing based on the body parts they are born with. Even though we are now aware that not everyone is born with only two options for reproductive organs (there are over thirty intersex variations), and that they may not want to reproduce, nor may they be able to, an assignment of sex is still the first distinction we make.

This distinction is only the beginning, however, because what comes next is a question of why, between two recognized sexes, one would be treated better than another, or why one would have control over the other. This question led me to pursue a master's in multidisciplinary gender studies because I wanted to learn more about different theories concerning the power dynamic of the sexes and how, to preserve it, the notion of gender became socially constructed. The creation of gender meant it was not necessarily body parts that could distinguish human beings but the different ways in which people were taught to act as a result of the category ascribed to them.

There are several theories concerning why this inequity came to be, and many studies that try to answer why, in most societies, men hold more power than women do. Some suggest that women have always been dependent on men because of vulnerability during pregnancy and men needing to hunt and provide while women carried, birthed, and cared for their offspring. However, recent research suggests that humans were egalitarian between the sexes up until the emergence of agriculture, when land and its resources came to be seen as something that could be owned and accumulated. Some theories argue that men have always been taller and stronger than women as well as more violent, while others show that girls and women started to get shorter than boys and men over time when they suffered from malnutrition because boys were fed more protein. Some have argued that the power women hold as the givers of life was seen as something men needed to control, while other studies have provided evidence that in many cultures women were revered for this ability, hence the honoring of female deities and the discovery of artifacts representing pregnant bodies. Despite variance in conclusions regarding the origins of what we call "patriarchy," most theorists agree on the following: discrepancies in gender roles have come to be as a result of a combination of both biological and social factors, gender roles have differed throughout the world depending on cultural beliefs like religion as well as other hierarchies like race, and gender roles are not fixed but are flexible.

This is why I decided to pursue a PhD in sociology. Despite the debated origins of patriarchy it was clear to me that it dictated our society, our behavior, and social relationships in the United States and that, vice versa, these things then continued to reinforce patriarchy.

Regardless, my decision to keep my baby's sex a surprise didn't keep anyone from guessing "what" they thought I was carrying, or from speaking about their guess with presumptions that conflated sex and gender. As I walked to a checkup weeks before, a stranger took it upon himself to roll down his window and yell "Someone's having a boy!" as he drove by. Who knows what he believed about differences between babies that theories claimed began even in utero. Perhaps he perceived me to be "carrying low," or he thought my bump looked more wide-set like a tire rather than sticking straight out. Whatever the reason, this stranger was in agreement with my husband and midwife, who were both also certain I was carrying another boy.

I, on the other hand, did not care, and I made no guesses. The only thing I felt was that this baby was going to arrive early, maybe even a whole month early. So when the weeks continued to pass and this definitely wasn't the case, I distracted myself by spending as much time as possible with my twenty-two-month-old and with my work.

My first book was released in February 2021 and, six months later, in August, I was still busy with virtual tour events as well as preparing for the TED Talk I was going to give in a few months. I was feeling grateful for the realization of my dream: writing books and speaking to audiences all over the world about them with a mission of helping people understand more about gender, race, and justice. Of course, I had imagined I would be traveling to all these places to speak to people in person. Though the pandemic changed that, I was actually able to connect with even more people through virtual platforms. Realizing quickly that people grew tired of hearing someone give a traditional book talk through a screen, I started doing fireside chats where a moderator would interview me about the book while leaving a little time at the end for audience questions.

My debut book stemmed from my doctoral research on three women by the names of Alberta King, Louise Little, and Berdis Baldwin, the mothers of MLK Jr., Malcolm X, and James Baldwin, respectively. In the book I make it clear that Martin, Malcolm, and James became who they were by following in their mothers' footsteps. As I had expected, readers often felt a sense of shock that they didn't already know these women's names before encountering my book, sadness that history had forgotten them despite how obvious their contributions were to their sons' lives and careers, and confusion as to how we had previously lost knowledge of their stories.

In almost every single one of the interviews I did I would be asked some iteration of the following questions: "How were these women erased?" "Why did this happen to them?" By month six of my tour and after dozens of conversations about Alberta King, Louise Little, and Berdis Baldwin, I still had a hard time formulating my response.

The answer is both so simple and also complicated because of all the ground one could cover. I would attempt to respond with, "It's a little something called patriarchy, and the way it intersects with things like racism makes it so that the further one is from being a white, straight, cisgender, able-bodied man, the less one's life will be valued. This is the case while the person is alive, and it will also be the case once the person passes away. Posthumously, their name, their stories, their contributions will not be protected, they will not be shared, they will not be highlighted and, instead, they will be erased." This is the simple answer, but each time I find myself wanting to say much more. I want to say that it should not be surprising at all that three Black women's lives have been kept from their due recognition if you understand how the story and system of patriarchy operates, especially American patriarchy. It is wrong, but it is not surprising. I want people to stop feeling so shocked when the apparatus operates exactly as it was designed to.

I want to say that the denial of these three mothers' existence is just one of countless symptoms of a system holding up a country founded on the premise that "[only some] men are created equal." I want to unpack the threat to American patriarchy that acknowledging the lives of Alberta King, Berdis Baldwin, and Louise Little poses in challenging the myth that there are any self-made men in this world at all; in bringing to light the ways in which other women, specifically white ones, have contributed to the degradation of their fellow women, especially Black women; and even in calling attention to the persistent lack of support for all mothers in our nation. I want to make the connection between the issue of not knowing these women's names and the overturning of *Roe v. Wade*, as one example, so painfully obvious that the system of American patriarchy, in all the ways that it exists, becomes tangible so we can put our hands right on it and completely tear it apart.

I want to recommend all the books that people need to read—*Women, Race & Class, This Bridge Called My Back, How We Get Free, Hood Feminism*, just to name a few—and I yearn for one contemporary book that can do what masterful authors like Isabel Wilkerson, Ibram Kendi, Clint Smith, Layla Saad, and others have done in framing structural racism in a straightforward, make-it-plain kind of way, including its history, the mechanisms of the system itself, and the connectedness between its many iterations—but for patriarchy in the United States, from an intersectional lens. This is not at all to say that racism and sexism are the same, but instead to make it clear that one cannot be studied without the other. If we are indeed experiencing a reckoning with racism like we never have before, as many have claimed in recent years, we must also confront the role patriarchy plays in fostering more inequality, oppression, and exclusivity in our nation.

When I say "American patriarchy" I am using it to not only describe a system that gives men access to power and excludes women from it, as the term "patriarchy" by itself typically denotes, but to also provide a more descriptive and accurate analysis of a particular patriarchal system that is centered on keeping power in the hands of people who fit the description of our "founding fathers," i.e., white men who believe in white supremacy and reap the benefits of capitalism. American patriarchy relies on putting white men at the top of the hierarchy and keeping power out of the hands of everyone else unless it serves the dominant group to include them, usually only temporarily, if so. At times it has served white men to include white women, for one example, but when the goal has been met, white women's power becomes vulnerable again. When this happens, white women react with shock, awe, and sadness that, let's say, the Supreme Court does not respect their bodily autonomy even though they voted for the politicians who allowed for the court to be filled with American patriarchs—a title I will use throughout the book in reference to individuals upholding systems in our nation that keep power solely in the hands of white men. While the definition of who can be described as a white man has expanded over American history to keep power away from other groups—Jewish, Irish, and Italian people are the examples race scholars often refer to—the rest of the social order that American patriarchy tells us we belong to has remained mostly the same since 1776, when the Declaration of Independence was signed. This is not to say that those opposed to American patriarchy haven't pulled off monumental feats in shaping our nation for the better since 1776; it is instead to bring our attention to the persistence of American patriarchy in its current state and to make clear what social order American patriarchs are still intent on fully restoring.

I do not aim to argue about whether the patriarchal system we find ourselves in is better or worse than those in other countries; I aim to make it clear what we are facing here in the US. In 2025 in the United States we have never elected a female president, we do not have universal parental leave, boys grow up believing the only feeling they can show is anger, by age six girls stop describing themselves as "brilliant" and believe it is a word better suited for the boys in their class, human sex trafficking continues to rise, women still do not make as much as men in the same positions, and jobs that have larger representations of women pay less. The list continues of examples that pulse with the heartbeat of American patriarchy. But believe it or not, these also extend far beyond the gender binary. Thus far, many have spoken about men's dominance over women in ways that suggest all men and all women are treated equally within their respective groups when it comes to patriarchal divisions.

I am not the first to argue that patriarchy is damaging to *all* those who live with it. It is not only women who suffer; men suffer too. People who live outside or between the gender binary, as well as people who are nonheteronormative, suffer because they challenge the power dynamic of man versus woman even more. All women do not suffer equally because of patriarchy; neither do all men, or all nonbinary people, or all nonheteronormative people. Our experiences of American patriarchy will vary, but it will damage each of us nonetheless. When American patriarchy is allowed to persist we continue to experience a maternal health crisis that severely impacts Black women; grown men of color are tormented by what "men should provide for their family" when at every attempt to do this they face insurmountable structural barriers; white women vote overwhelmingly, not once but twice, for a candidate who says he grabs women by the pussy; the pay gap is worse for women of color; gay couples are threatened by the constant possibility that their marriages will not be acknowledged; parents of nonbinary children are forced to move to other states just to feel safe; and white men account for an overwhelming majority of mass shootings in our country while other white men make money off the purchase of the guns that are used in those shootings.

American patriarchy is simple in the way that it spares none of us and complex in the different ways it affects us depending on how we identify and how we are perceived. No matter how much it hurts us, however, many have tried to play by its rules, aligning themselves with the dominant group rather than fighting the system, and those who uphold it, alongside others who have been excluded from it. In her masterpiece *Caste*, Isabel Wilkerson states:

> A caste system persists in part because we, each and every one of us, allow it to exist—in large and small ways, in our everyday actions, in how we elevate or demean, embrace or exclude, on the basis of the meaning attached to people's physical traits. If enough people buy into the lie of natural hierarchy, then it becomes the truth or is assumed to be.

But she leaves us with hope, reminding us that we can live differently:

> Once awakened, we then have a choice. We can be born to the dominant caste but choose not to dominate. We can be born to a subordinated caste but resist the box others force upon us. And all of us can sharpen our powers of discernment to see past the external and to value the character of a person rather than demean those who are already marginalized or worship those born to false pedestals.

This is why an in-depth analysis of the way patriarchy upholds the centuries-old American hierarchy that Wilkerson identifies so powerfully in her work is desperately needed, so that we can continue to untangle the many tentacles of the American caste system and perhaps, as a collective, can choose to take a different approach. I believe we can burn the book of American patriarchy and start anew.

I have a lot more to say than I have been able to provide in response to one question among many in the middle of a fireside chat. In this book I am going to get it all out there, if nothing else to finally relieve myself from that frustration and say everything I need to say. But I also hope it will serve a larger purpose. Ironically, despite how obvious patriarchy in the United States seems to me, I believe it has continued to persist because it is so ingrained in our way of life that it almost becomes unnoticeable. It has been written into our laws, taught to us generation after generation, reproduced in day-to-day conversations as well as in movies and TV shows, so that over time it just seems like the natural order. American patriarchs have even interpreted ancient texts through their lens to make their preferred organization of the country appear divine. The mechanisms of the apparatus have disguised themselves in different ways, and with this camouflage each of the injustices of the system then appears to be separate from the others, their connecting lines no longer visible. Those who sense American patriarchy operating might be told that their accurate assessments of an unjust system are now just feelings, because "progress has been made." Yes, the law that once stated that a man could beat his wife is no longer in existence, but the effect of that law still is. Yes, women are now allowed to participate in sports, but they must still wear uniforms that objectify and hypersexualize them, and if they go on to play professionally, they will be paid much less than their male counterparts. Yes, mothers can legally work in and outside the home, but they will have to figure that balance out on their own without complaining and without guaranteed support like childcare. Yes, the Harvey Weinsteins and R. Kellys of the world are starting to face repercussions, but it takes over one hundred pieces of evidence for this to even be a possibility. Yes, trans people are represented on TV more, but anti-trans violence has continued to rise. We have not come as far as we think, largely because many of us are not aware of a huge and inconspicuous enemy we all share. To take it down it has to be properly defined, mapped, and made obvious and visible in all its forms.

This accurate definition and mapping is my first goal. I hope that by showing what American patriarchy is, how it came to be, how it has persisted, and how it has disguised itself, this book can be a go-to tool for those of us who already understand that oppression is intersectional and who already know that without understanding patriarchy we cannot solve anything else. I also hope this is a book for those who may be new to conversations around American patriarchy, or at least think they are. I hope to bring into one place as many as I can of the different battles that are being fought against American patriarchy. I want to make the system of American patriarchy as painfully obvious to you as it is to me, so that it stops surprising and confusing everyone, and so the need to dismantle it becomes unignorable.

Here is the definition. American patriarchy is the guiding story and system of the United States, and it has been since the founding fathers drafted the Constitution. While patriarchy is present around the world, it is unique in the United States as a result of the heterogeneity of our population, which has been used to further build on a gender-binary divide. In the United States patriarchy places men in a higher position of the hierarchy of humanity and also organizes race, ability, class, and other identifying factors as reasons to separate some of us from the gender binary. The gender binary is already problematic and flawed as the first signifier of humanity but in the US it gets worse because, depending on your other demographic information, you may not even be considered fully man or woman by American patriarchs. We live in a country where we are told to compete for power by fighting for our right to be gendered. In the way we currently define gender, men are the holders of power. Women are to follow men and reproduce men's power through children. Men have power through money and land ownership and domination of women; they also experience a sense of immortality through their children. As long as power stays within their ever-growing, male-led family, they have accomplished their ultimate goal. This premise is already destructive in any culture, but in our American patriarchy, not everyone is believed to have a rightful claim to either of these roles because here, being a man or a woman does not depend solely on genitalia or reproductive organs; it actually depends on white supremacy and holding power over others. In the story that is American patriarchy, if you are not white, you are not fully considered man or woman, but more animal and inhuman. People of color are almost entirely separated from the protections of the problematic gender binary. Furthermore, many white people do not reap the full benefits of the system either because even if you are white and male but are not rich and dominant, you have failed at holding power over others, and therefore failed at the dictates of being a man. If you experience any disability, especially if you cannot reproduce, you are seen as unable to fulfill these roles. And if you do not desire to play these parts, you are seen as deviant and a threat to the system; you are not entitled to full inclusion in our nation either. Summarizing the foundational belief and organizing system of our country in this way may feel hyperbolic but the chapters that follow and the examples I discuss will make these assertions definitive.

Throughout American history, many have believed they have only one choice, in this order: assimilate as much as possible to the powerful white man first, the white woman second, and perhaps you will know what humanity feels like. But the reality is that there have always been other choices, other ways to define humanity, other ways to live. These other choices have purposefully been challenged and erased by a system that was made to seem unavoidable and, therefore, unbreakable. Fighting the erasure of the ways of living and being that depart from American patriarchy is the other goal of this book.

Even more important than it is for me to map American patriarchy so you can see it clearly is my desire to show you what American patriarchy has been trying to cover up. I visualize American patriarchy as a web stuck to all of us, keeping us within its grasp, one that you can feel tingling and bothering you but that you cannot remove no matter how many times you try to shake it off. Through understanding how it works, however, it becomes more visible and tangible; its rigidity becomes unignorable; we can put our hands on it and lift it up, first off ourselves and then off others; we can tear it to pieces, all with the goal of discovering what lies below it. Returning to Black women and mothers like Alberta King, Louise Little, and Berdis Baldwin, we see that they have been sharing their vision of a world beyond what white supremacist men have manufactured for centuries; they have been pushing for others to follow them all along. As people who could not accept the notion that they and their children did not deserve the same treatment as other human beings in their country, BIPOC people of all genders have pulled from ancient practices that predate colonialism not only to offer new imaginations of what is possible here in the US but also to prove that change through activism is doable and necessary. These moments of wisdom, power, and unwillingness to stay trapped in the web are what American patriarchs fear most and work their hardest to control and erase. Hence why many American patriarchs have focused on implementing book bans across our nation, as one example.

What is American patriarchy and what has it tried to erase? This book provides the answer through a road map of the system operating from the definition I offer above, rather than the incomplete one we had previously come to know. Our lack of fully understanding American patriarchy up until this point is what has kept us from defeating it, but I believe this book will be the key to exiting the maze and discovering our collective potential. We can defeat American patriarchy if we notice it at every turn and embrace what lies beyond it for us all. While many people are deliberately committing themselves to protecting American patriarchy due to a lack of understanding regarding how it hurts them too, there are more people who are feeding it without even knowing they are doing so. This book aims to open all our eyes. We cannot be delayed any further from the liberation that awaits us in an intersectional understanding and destruction of American patriarchy.

When I wrote my first book about three Black mothers who had been erased from history, I took on the challenge of piecing together their lives with very little to start with. I couldn't interview the women; instead I had to go digging for every single shred of evidence of their existence that I could find. This book, however, has presented me with the opposite issue. Sadly, American patriarchy exists in virtually everything we do and experience. It touches our lives even before we are conceived, it dictates how we will live, and it impacts our stories beyond our actual time on earth. There are endless examples to explore that are all related to one another. As a result of this magnitude, worried about how to tackle such a large subject, I decided what would be most helpful would be to use my own journey with American patriarchy as an organizing principle of the book.

My mapping of the system and the vision I offer to reclaim what has been kept from us stem from my mother's teachings and her legacy; my childhood of experiencing the different ways that countries are organized around the world after growing up nomadically abroad; my career as a storyteller with degrees in anthropology (BA), gender studies (MPhil), and sociology (PhD); the wisdom and writings of Black women and other BIPOC antipatriarchal activists, organizers, scholars, and their allies who came before me and walk beside me; my reflections as a mother of three and my hope that this country will experience groundbreaking reforms that move us from a sexist, racist, and capitalist organizing of people and into a transformative, community-oriented, humane society during their lifetimes. For these reasons, the book is broken into six parts that mirror my trajectory and lifelong journey of uncovering the true definition and magnitude of American patriarchy while also becoming fully aware of the power I possess to defeat it. In each part, I use stories from my own life and analyze people and moments in American history to reflect on the personal, the political, the societal, the historical, and their applicability to the present and the future. My hope is for readers to place themselves in the same stages of life that I discuss so that together we can reflect on the different effects American patriarchy has had on each of our lives, on our interpretation of events, on our opportunities and challenges, and on our responsibility to play our unique role in dismantling it so that we can live the full lives American patriarchy is currently withholding from us.

While the skeleton of the book follows a chronology of my own life, the body of it is more thematic, always keeping my intersectional perspective in mind. In the first part, I explore the primary component of American patriarchy: the story and the crafting of the narrative, for example, the lie that girls and boys are made to do different things, with boys holding more power. In the second part, I discuss how American patriarchy keeps people in "their place" through reminders of the social order and the imposing of explicit violence and punishment. In the third part, I move to a discussion of control and reproduction through an analysis of the roles of marriage and motherhood in upholding the system. In the fourth part, I discuss how the first three parts lead us to believe that the performance American patriarchy requires of us all is "natural" and unavoidable, while I reveal the mechanisms of the play we have been cast into. In the fifth part, I share my reflections on the ways in which American patriarchy will remain alive if we continue our current trajectory, before I offer hope for change in the sixth part of the book. In each part I also present the various people who have designed and maintained American patriarchy. These include the men who wrote the Constitution; the archetypal presidents whom we still honor and revere; the Supreme Court of the United States; many police officers; scientists and doctors who have also contributed to the notion of white men being the standard we should all aspire to; journalists and media correspondents who have contributed to the propaganda of American patriarchy; and founders at the forefront of our modern and future technologies who prioritize their own financial gain over the well-being of their users. I purposefully jump around time with different people in history in each part to make the point that no matter how much I was growing in life, I was always coming up against the same system as well as its architects and protectors. Similarly, as we have experienced incredible movements that ushered in social change throughout the history of our nation, American patriarchy has responded to each of these by trying to tighten its grasp; its upholders have invented new ways to maintain their desired social order. Still, however, the most beautiful thing about revealing what the system of American patriarchy is, and who the people who keep it alive are, is that you cannot avoid studying whom and what American patriarchy tries to defeat. In each part, as I make American patriarchy obvious, I also make it clear that we have had access to something different all along. As the full picture and cycle of American patriarchy has become visible to me through my own work and life experiences, I have also become better able to see the alternatives that I offer to you in the end. Trust that when we reach the conclusion, your vision will be clear too.

By the time the sun was setting on day six, my contractions had grown in intensity and were coming more frequently. I rocked my son to sleep with tears in my eyes knowing that by the time he woke up next he would likely be meeting his sibling. I kissed him and tucked him in before continuing to labor through the night in the same room where I did all my writing and my virtual talks. It was a space of creation for me in more ways than one, a room where I studied those who came before me and drew inspiration from the strategies with which they fought and where I also found joy, where I dared to envision and write about new possibilities for our world. In such a space, surrounded by the energy of breaking down barriers, disrupting the status quo, and focusing on freedom, I wanted my second child to breathe their first breath.

For the several hours my husband and I were alone, he held my hand through the waves until I felt I needed more support. Our doula, arriving by three a.m., showed me what other positions I could take to relieve the pain and held me up as I made my way to the bathtub. Our midwife arrived shortly after, reminding me of my strength and checking to make sure all was well. By 8:03 in the morning I was holding my daughter in my arms. My son joined us a few moments later, intrigued by his little sister. Despite the normal postpartum pains, I couldn't help but smile as I cuddled both of my kids. In my mind I thought of June Jordan's words, "children are the ways that the world begins again and again," and I wondered what new world had just begun with my baby, who had been with me in every conversation about Alberta King, Berdis Baldwin, and Louise Little, a baby who arrived by her rules rather than by someone else's calculations, and who was already defying assumptions, beautifully reminding us that people do not belong in previously drawn boxes. The world had indeed begun again.

Part 1

OUR SHARED
HUMANITY
AND ANCIENT
WISDOM

1

WE HAVE BEEN MISLED

◼

I n Clarkston, Washington, a blond-haired, blue-eyed girl grew up
in the predictable nature of her small town in the 1950s. On her
short daily bike rides she would pass the dress store, the diner,
the bank, the hardware store—that also carried canned food and
live bait—the library, the police station, and the jail, as well as the
beauty shop where her mom often got her hair done while the little
girl immersed herself in the world of *Look* and *Life* magazines
featuring the likes of Jacqueline Kennedy.

Her parents owned the town's title company and she loved visiting them at work. When she entered she would first greet her
mother, who was dressed in high heels and elegantly tailored business skirts; then she would peek around the corner of the secretary's
desk to see her father. He stood out as a big fish in a little pond as a
veteran of World War II, a lawyer, and a judge who sometimes was
paid for his legal services in cows, pigs, and other livestock because
his clients did not have much else to give.

As she watched her father, the little girl thought of the ways the
world revolved around him. It was he who sat at the head of the table
at every meal, moving only if his own father was visiting; he who
inspired reactions from everyone in town; he who at over six feet tall
could not be missed. Yet it was the women in her life whose stories

the little girl found to be more interesting, whose presence she found to be more intriguing and complex. Her mother changed her career once she married to work at the title company, but she was a trained laboratory scientist and nurse who could also cook divine meals, who was well informed on local and national politics and enjoyed campaigning for local candidates. Her paternal grandmother was a classical pianist and a wonderful storyteller who encouraged the little girl to be imaginative and to explore nature, and who also catered to her son. The librarian whom she saw multiple times throughout the week, Mrs. H, dressed in bold colors, and was well traveled and always ready with recommendations of books for the little girl to read. Mrs. H also shared her premonition that because of the little girl's beautiful eyes she would be lucky enough to grow up to marry a man who was tall, dark, and handsome. The little girl looked up to these women, but she could see that they all were confined by the small town they lived in, and she felt that over time they were all impacted by such limitations in ways the men in her life were not.

This girl, the youngest of four, could also see that although she had an inner desire to go to law school just like her father—and maybe even become a judge like him, one day—the only child her parents seemed to see as being capable of following in the revered judge's footsteps and carrying his professional legacy was her brother, the only boy in the family. She absolutely adored her big brother, but she did not understand why her parents' expectations of her differed from their expectations of him. During the Cold War era, being a lawyer was not something this girl nor her female peers should aspire to. She should instead know how to dress, how to organize a household, how to clean and cook—how to be like her sister, who was thirteen years older, had gotten married at seventeen, and had her first child by the age of eighteen.

My mom often told me about these experiences of hers growing up in Clarkston, many of which were happy memories filled with love and adventure that made her grateful for her upbringing. But she was also very cognizant of the ways in which boys and girls, men and women, were treated. She attributed many of her decisions to her desire to do more than what others believed she was "supposed" to do.

This seemingly simple story could describe the experiences of any number of women who were born in the 1950s, who were raised to see being married as the ultimate goal of their lives, having children their purpose, and witnessing from early on how boys would be favored above them. Magazines would tell them what clothes girls and women should wear to be both dignified and attractive. Their mothers would model the sacrifices that they believed were necessary, and that they were willing to make, to support their families. Even women who were single and going against the grain would themselves tell young girls they would be lucky to marry someday, knowing how difficult it was to live, make money, and have your basic needs met without a male partner. The treatment of their male siblings and peers would stand in contrast to them, signaling that boys had choices that girls did not, as well as expectations to provide for the women in their lives so that these women might depend upon and cater to them.

What my mother observed during her childhood was reflected across the country in the data of that decade. In the 1950s, about one in three women participated in the labor force. Seventy percent of employed women held clerical positions or worked in assembly lines or in service jobs. Twelve percent held professional jobs in nursing or teaching, usually before they were wed, and only 6 percent held management positions. During this decade, a mere 1.2 percent of women went to college. From 1950 to 1970, only 3 percent of all lawyers were women. Girls from white families like my mom's were caught in the cross fires of Cold War propaganda whose primary message was that the nuclear family was what made Americans superior to communists. The message was that democracy and freedom hinged on white women being able to enjoy tending to their homes and children in their delicate dresses while, on the other hand, Russian women were shown toiling in factories as their children spent their days in cold day-care centers. It is this decade that the term "MRS degree" is most associated with, when the media inundated women and girls with the idea that a marriage was the most important thing they could achieve.

Furthermore, starting in the 1950s, sex was viewed more than ever before as a key component of a happy marriage to keep the nuclear family together and husbands away from infidelity. Married women were tasked with holding "the state of the nation's morality and culture" through keeping their husbands happy in bed, as Miriam Reumann, the author of *American Sexual Character*, puts it. Unmarried women were viewed as promiscuous and seen as a threat to national security because they could entice married men and weaken their bodies through the transmission of venereal diseases. Young wives were faced with the pressure to always be available to their husband's desires despite the absence of effective contraceptives. The number of families with three children doubled during this time, while the number of families with four children quadrupled.

I begin with these small pieces from my mother's childhood stories because her upbringing not only played a role in her own feminism but would also eventually influence mine. Additionally, I begin here because what I have discussed thus far in brevity is the definition that many have reduced the entire system of patriarchy to. Books and even whole movements have been based on something like this: A white girl with certain privileges learns that although she is seen as being worthy of protection and holding importance as a future wife and mother, she is supposed to be content with this and never ask for more. Her ambition in life is supported so long as it contributes to the ultimate goal of marriage and mothering. She is not in any explicit danger, but the cycle of being dependent on men puts her at risk of future abuses, including the inability to choose whether or not she would become a mother. She wants to be able to dream for herself, to someday earn her own money, and to have access to the same opportunities as her brother, but is told repeatedly that simply because she is a girl she is not allowed to, and that choice over her own life will be limited.

This experience is certainly part of the problem with American patriarchy. But when we reduce it to this, when we say that girls just need to see themselves and be seen as equal to the boys in their life for things to change, when we believe everything will be rectified when women are able to earn their own money and pursue their own degrees, when we state that if women could think beyond marriage and motherhood they would be liberated, that if they could work outside the home, patriarchy would be dismantled, we do very little to rid ourselves of the problem. This centering of the experiences of white middle- and upper-class girls and women as the rallying cry for all has long held the reins in our shared fight against patriarchy, but has only exacerbated a culture of division and exclusion.

Thankfully, my mom came to understand this well. Instead of solely focusing on her own immediate experience of the issue and how it impacted her, she became interested in learning more, placing herself in the larger context, equipping herself with knowledge to not only question what she was noticing but also think about how others were impacted.

The first question she reflected on is the same one I will answer here in part 1: Were the rules fixed like this since the beginning of time, or were they created with a specific agenda? These lessons on gender are often presented as if they are simply the natural order of things, the way the world has always worked. With the remnants of the laws that were written to make them true no longer visible, the rules seem unavoidable and unchangeable; but the key word here is "seem," because one only has to look a little further back into Clarkston's history to know that much effort was employed in establishing a hierarchy that served white men and did away with any practices that might produce other results or distribute power differently. One place to begin is to consider how Clarkston gained its present-day name.

2

OUR STORIES CONTORTED
AND BURIED

◆

The image is familiar to most Americans. Two men and one woman are standing next to one another. The men are white; the woman is Native American. One hand is holding on to a large stick slightly taller than she is, and with her other hand she points with two fingers. The woman's face is stern. Behind her we see what at first looks like a hat but is actually a cradleboard that her child is sleeping in. The two men standing beside her hold their guns in the same way she holds the stick. The man in the middle wears a black hat and carries a telescope. The other man wears a fur hat and has a knife hanging from his belt. In reproductions of this image we typically see only these three primary characters: Sacagawea, Meriwether Lewis, and William Clark, but the original image also includes three other men, one of them being York, an enslaved Black man. There are many issues with the painting, including the erasure of York over the years, and these problems serve to illustrate the creation, uniqueness, and intersectional nature of patriarchy in the United States.

The painting encapsulates what Sacagawea has come to symbolize in American history: It shows that she is revered for her leading of Lewis and Clark on their expedition through the lands of the American West that were acquired in the Louisiana Purchase. It represents her as a grown woman who appears to not only be well respected by these two men and in control of her own choices, but who also seems to be at least thirty years old. Sacagawea was even honored in the year 2000 on a dollar coin with an imagined picture of her (modeled after a college-age student) and her baby. This Native American woman has posthumously been lauded for her decision to join the expedition and for being an asset to the expansion of the US in a number of ways. She shared her knowledge of Native foods with Lewis and Clark, she guided them through the terrain, she acted as their translator, she negotiated with tribes they encountered along the way; some say she even cooked and washed/mended clothes for the thirty men she accompanied on the eight-thousand-mile journey, all while carrying her infant on her back.

Her story has been used to celebrate a range of national aspirations from multicultural allyship to biracial marriages and women's empowerment, yet the story we have come to know and uplift is riddled with American patriarchy. This becomes clear when we investigate Sacagawea's life a little further, as well as question who the carriers of her story have been thus far; when we ask whose goals are being met when she is spoken about as a symbol of collaboration and patriotism.

Sacagawea was only twelve or thirteen years old when a Frenchman fifteen years her senior, Toussaint Charbonneau, bought her from the Hidatsa people after she had been kidnapped from her Lemhi Shoshone tribe. He called her one of his wives and just a year or two later she, a child herself, was pregnant. It was while she was pregnant that Charbonneau met two men by the names of Meriwether Lewis and William Clark.

Lewis and Clark had been sent by Thomas Jefferson to explore newly acquired territories, and with them they brought their own beliefs concerning nonwhite people. Using the Bible, the Declaration of Independence, and their own relationships with white women as well as their views of gender roles, they embarked on their mission, where they would encounter around fifty Native American tribes.

These tribes had their own ways of organizing their people, and their own beliefs concerning sex and gender. Women were often chiefs and warriors; in many tribes people were what is now termed "two-spirit," not fitting into categories of boy and girl and regarded as holy people, mediators, and healers. Among many other traditions that varied from tribe to tribe, such possibilities for women and nonbinary people were not accepted by their colonizers. In the tyranny of the European ethnic cleansing of Native Americans—that included tactics like taking children from their homes and placing them in Westernizing schools, where they were abused—there was an apparent need to eradicate any notion that stood against a white American patriarchal organization of society. Lewis and Clark even took it upon themselves to bestow the title of chief to men they felt should hold more power in tribes, by giving them coins and medallions to disrupt systems already in place.

Sacagawea was told that she would join the expedition to translate for Lewis and Clark. There was no choice, no question; as a teenager expecting a child, she was forced to accompany upward of thirty men across the country, something that would seem unthinkable for a white girl of the same age. She would not receive compensation, but the man who owned her, Toussaint Charbonneau, would be paid for her contributions to the mission. While on the already exhausting journey, she gave birth to a son whom she carried on her back for the duration of the two-and-a-half-year-long trip. Unlike what the famous image might lead us to believe, the men did not see Sacagawea as their equal. Lewis describes in his journal a scene where the travelers finally arrive at the West Coast and Sacagawea has to beg to be permitted to see a whale that has washed ashore. It did not matter how impossible making it to the destination would have been without her; she was still an indigenous creature living under the instructions of white men who, despite her skills, strength, and savvy, was still looked down upon not only because of her sex but, in her case, also because she was Native American.

Although the Lewis and Clark expedition started in 1804, it wasn't until one hundred years later that Sacagawea was given any credit for her contributions to a journey that would change the course of the nation. And even in the moment where she was finally recognized, she was still used for another cause, her story warped and reinterpreted yet again for someone else's gain. This time it was white women's suffrage.

In 1905, a statue of Sacagawea was unveiled at the Lewis and Clark Centennial exhibition in Portland, Oregon. Again appearing much older than a teenager, the bronze statue is of a woman who is reaching forward with her right hand, with a baby on her back. At its unveiling, Susan B. Anthony described the sculpture as "the first time in history that a statue has been erected in the memory of a woman who accomplished patriotic deeds." At a time when women were fighting for their right to have their voices heard through their vote, there was a need to point to women's additions to the nation that resembled the kinds of acts that men were recognized for. Women were kept from participating in traditional patriotism like fighting in war, so when the tale was found of a girl who traveled across the country through the cold and the heat alongside soldiers, and who jumped into the ocean to save documents and supplies when the men were afraid to, it seemed like a godsend. All that needed to be done was suspend any actual thought about the treatment of Sacagawea. First, she had not been treated like a human but instead like an object that could be acquired. Second, she was a being whose own desires were ignored, in the same way one might disregard the needs of a horse. Third, she was presented as a relic of a world that never existed, where

Native American women were seen as peers to white women and their stories could be exchanged with each other.

Sacagawea's story was "discovered" by the historian Eva Emery Dye, a suffragette on the hunt for a heroine who would help their cause. She needed to find a woman who had given her everything for her nation, but who also maintained patriarchal ideals of womanhood—birthing children, tending to the clothes, nursing men through their sicknesses, pleasing her husband whenever he wanted to be pleased—as evidence that women should be able to vote, but emphasizing that this right should not be accompanied by any fear of women forgetting their roles.

When Dye found evidence of Sacagawea in Lewis's journals, she wrote, "The beauty of that faithful Indian woman with a baby on her back, leading those stalwart mountaineers and explorers through the strange land, appealed to the world." Somehow a Native American teenager was again spoken about as a grown woman with control over her decisions, now to represent the struggles of white women. Dye and other suffragettes knew how powerful it would be if the statue were revealed on the centennial celebration of the Lewis and Clark expedition. It would make the statement that men could not accomplish great feats without the women who accompanied them, and it would serve as a reminder that the entire nation relied on the labor of women. The fact that Sacagawea was not treated with the dignity or protection that these suffragettes had was ignored for them to make their point, further dehumanizing Sacagawea by turning her into a symbol of female liberation, while also ignoring the fact that Indigenous women who were Dye's contemporaries were still being severely mistreated.

The reveal of the feminist statue would also ignore important details concerning the expedition. In addition to misrepresenting a young Indigenous girl's experience of forced labor and forced pregnancy by a white man, it would also obscure the role the expedition played in the eventual massacre and removal of Native people. While Sacagawea, Lewis, and Clark's journey was a relatively peaceful one focused on discovery, their findings provided the US government with detailed maps and key information on the tribes encountered along the way. The Lewis and Clark expedition is largely responsible for the success of "anti-Indian" policies and sentiment of the 1800s.

Clarkston, Washington, my mother's hometown, was named after Captain William Clark in the late 1800s, around the time when the American government started separating Native children from their parents and sending them to boarding schools. It is reported that in Washington alone there were fifteen such schools that stripped children of their culture and heritage, subjected them to corporal punishment, and in some cases left them to die. More recently, activists and scholars have fought for the stories of these boarding schools to become better known, for the history of their atrocities to be exposed and recognized. Pictures have emerged showing what Native children looked like before they were enrolled in these so-called schools, in comparison to pictures showing the changes forced upon their small bodies.

Many of these images are now accessible through a basic online search, and while you will find very different children in each search result, you will see commonalities in the transformations, the most obvious one being the creation of a clear distinction between the boys and the girls. The boys' hair would immediately be cut short, and if they wore any traditional jewelry it would be removed. The boys were also made to change from any traditional wear, which could include tunics, skirts, or wrapped cloth, into dark-colored cadet uniforms that consisted of collared shirts and pants. The girls would have their braids taken out and their hair pulled back into buns, and they were made to wear dresses usually accompanied with a white apron.

The studio photos taken at the boarding schools did not usually combine boys and girls in the same frame. But there is one set of pictures of four Pueblo children that stands out in my mind. The first was taken when the two boys and two girls entered the Carlisle Indian School in 1880, and the other was taken after their compulsory transformation. Beyond the change in their hair and clothes, in the first photo the boys are sitting and the girls are standing, while in the second picture the boys have been instructed to stand over the girls as if they were the girls' superiors and protectors. It is another symbolic restoration of what the people on the other side of the camera saw as the right way of doing things.

The story of Sacagawea and the way in which it has been co-opted to fit others' views of how the world should work shows how storytellers in positions of power can manipulate facts to fit their own mission. The painting many of us have seen shows Sacagawea in this unrealistic way because it came from the perspective of a white man, Edgar Samuel Paxson, who initially gained recognition as a painter for his depiction of George Armstrong Custer in the Battle of Little Bighorn. The sculpture of Sacagawea that was used for the suffragettes was created by a white woman, Alice Cooper. We are reminded that we must question what we are being told, by whom, and for what purpose. This is especially the case when thinking about the treatment of sex and gender in the United States. The first step in dismantling American patriarchy is a realization that what we are told is simply a story passed to us by those with power who aim to keep their power.

The larger mistreatment of Indigenous people across the United States before and during Sacagawea's time, and well into the decade when my mother was born, displays the lengths to which American patriarchs will go to erase any record of life being lived differently; groups being organized differently; and, especially, men, women, and nonbinary people being treated differently than they believed they should be.

The question my mother asked herself about the story she was being told was one that she could answer both by studying the history of how her immediate world came to be, as well as by looking beyond what her family had become accustomed to and questioning what was happening in real time. The fabrication of the story was not only a historic occurrence but a contemporary one.

My mom was born in 1952. In 1950, the United States proposed a plan to "solve the Indian Problem." The Bureau of Indian Affairs (BIA) provided a hundred thousand Native Americans packages to leave their reservations and move into cities where they could assimilate to white American culture and open space for the US government to eliminate reservations. The package for a man and his wife included a one-way fare plus forty dollars a week for a month. Families with children would also receive another ten dollars a week per child. The BIA declared these meager packages enough to sustain families until the husband earned his first check. The BIA advertised to Native American families the "opportunity" with films that showcased men welding, cutting hair, and even preparing meals in white chef outfits, while showcasing women pushing strollers through beautiful neighborhoods. Another ad showed a Native man with long hair, wrapped in a blanket, with the words: "Hunger & Cold . . . Stuck in Your Tepee?" while offering "relocation services" as "a way out."

Although families were promised jobs and better living conditions if they accepted, they all found themselves stranded in new cities with less than what they had started with. They were encouraged to depart from their customs only to find that they had been lured and tricked by a false promise that they would be better off assimilating to American patriarchy. A false promise that had also appeared when Native American men were told that they could prove their worthiness through their participation in World War II. Native Americans enlisted at the highest rate of any group, believing they would earn better treatment by serving the nation, only to find that upon their return their living conditions were made even worse. The further devastation of reservations during the war that ended in 1945 made the relocation packages of 1950 seem like the only way to gain a better life. Native Americans were told that their "Indianness" could be "washed away" over time the more they interacted with and acted like white Americans. The first individuals to relocate did so in 1952.

My mom likely did not realize the extent of the fabrication of American patriarchy when she was a little girl. She was not immediately aware of tactics that warped the story of Sacagawea, minimized the damages of Lewis and Clark, and removed children from their homes. Nor would she have known at first that even white women like herself who were intent on earning their right to vote and leveling the playing field with white men—in the case of the suffragettes—also played a role in hurting other women. If she knew about the treatment of Indigenous people during her childhood, she likely could have been convinced that the United States government was simply trying to help them. Her awareness would come over years of study, and would develop through her own personal experiences that would continue to open her eyes and mind even more as she came into adulthood. Her journey to enlightenment started with a feeling that something was not fair, and it grew with her desire to not only understand how it came to be but to commit herself to changing it, not just for herself but for everyone.

This is where we must all begin: with an acknowledgment of the injustices we have each experienced as a result of the limits placed upon us as soon as we consciously find ourselves in the hierarchy of American patriarchy. This must be followed by a burning desire to know fully how such imbalance has come to be, by seeking understanding of the history that has led to our current experience while also knowing that is not an ancient fabrication but a living one, rooted in colonization. We should all trace our own stories as far back as we possibly can to understand the extent of the many strategies used to uphold the falsehoods. Above all, we must know who and what are keeping the story of American patriarchy alive and why, from the storytellers to the sculptors, to the paintings and statues, to the landmarks and national memorials that we have been told represent our nation as it was, is, and always should be, lest we be brave enough to do something about it.

3

THEIRS WERE ELEVATED
AND ROMANTICIZED

✴

On October 31, 1941, it was finally complete. The audacious project of carving four sixty-foot-long faces with twenty-foot-long noses and eighteen-foot-wide mouths into a mountain had taken fourteen years. Four hundred people were paid fifty-five cents per hour to blast and painstakingly carve the faces that eventually would attract around three million visitors each year. Doane Robinson, a state historian credited with conceiving the idea for Mount Rushmore, wanted to create a tourist attraction that would bring more visitors to South Dakota. He envisioned the carving being of notable Western icons like Lewis and Clark, as well as a Lakota leader named Red Cloud and maybe even Sacagawea. He also thought it would be done on a smaller rock formation, known as the Needles. However, Gutzon Borglum, the Danish American sculptor who was recruited to bring the vision to life, had larger plans. Borglum wanted the monument to be on a mountain, to be one of a kind, and to be of national significance. He concluded that four US presidents should be honored, and that they should be presidents who, according to Borglum, represented the most important parts of American history until that point.

Mount Rushmore is still considered by many to be one of the

greatest American achievements. Those who worked on it felt such a sense of honor and were held in such esteem that in 2019, when a man named Nick Clifford passed away, countless articles across the world ran with headlines such as "Last Living Mount Rushmore Carver Dies at 98." Clifford, who started working on the site in 1938 when he was only seventeen, was the youngest crew member at the time. Before he passed he said, "Mount Rushmore was the greatest thing with which I was ever involved. It tells a story that will never go away—the story of how America was made and the men who helped make it what it is today."

I agree with Nick Clifford's statement that Mount Rushmore tells a story about the United States, but I am not sure we would have agreed on the tone of said story. His would probably be one of triumph and celebration; mine would be one of violence and tragedy. Regardless, the creation of Mount Rushmore, as well as a look at the men carved into it, are necessary and illustrative for our understanding of American patriarchy. Knowing what George Washington, Thomas Jefferson, Abraham Lincoln, and Theodore Roosevelt believed and/or represented, particularly when it came to patriarchy, is a useful starting point. Although Washington served as president in 1789 before Jefferson, I want to begin with the latter not only because of his relationship to Clarkston, Washington, but mostly because of what may very well be the most quoted document in American history.

In 1776, Thomas Jefferson drafted the Declaration of Independence to explain to the world why the colonies were seeking to separate from Great Britain. The famous words read,

> We hold these truths to be self-evident, that all men are created equal, that they are endowed by their Creator with certain unalienable Rights, that among these are Life, Liberty and the pursuit of Happiness. That to secure these rights,

Governments are instituted among Men, deriving their just
powers from the consent of the governed.

The Revolutionary War had already begun and Jefferson was
adding fuel to the fire. The hypocrisy of the Declaration has been
discussed and studied at length ever since its words were first published, for in a fight against the named tyranny of the British monarchy and the quest for freedom, Jefferson meant for his words to
apply only to white men.

Three groups in particular were notably excluded: Native people
and Black people altogether, as well as white women. I will discuss
the omission of Black people in depth in the following chapter and
will focus on Jefferson's dismissal of white women here because
gaining a deeper understanding of Jefferson's and his peers' sexism
allows us to understand the experiences of women like the suffragettes and even young white girls born in the 1950s like my mother.
It also gives us a deeper understanding of their dehumanization of
Black people and the way Black people were represented as being
neither man nor woman.

Thomas Jefferson influenced US history in a myriad of ways, as
a lawyer and as a philosopher, a governor, the primary author of the
Declaration of Independence, one of the founding fathers, secretary
of state, vice president, and the third president of the country, who
sent Lewis and Clark on their expedition. In these roles he produced
foundational and formative documents for the trajectory of our nation. Jefferson was all the titles listed above *and* he was also an American patriarch who saw himself as superior to women and baked
his views into the formation of a new country, both by completely
ignoring their existence, like he did in the Declaration, and by rele-
gating them to the domestic sphere in other publications and letters.

Jefferson's sexism can be clearly seen in the way he spoke to
and about his daughters (the ones he acknowledged, at least) about

their hygiene, what they should wear, how they should spend their time, and what they should aspire to be in life. He once wrote in a letter to one of his daughters, "A lady who has been seen as a sloven or slut in the morning will never efface the impression she has made, with all dress and pageantry she can afterwards involve herself in." If it wasn't strange enough that a father was shaming women whom he saw as messy or promiscuous in a letter to his child, he also stated, "Nothing is so disgusting to our sex as want of cleanliness and delicacy in yours." In addition to holding strong convictions concerning women's clothes and hygiene, he regulated his daughters' daily schedules to make them the best wives and mothers they could be to their future husbands and children. From his point of view, the best wives and mothers could cook, clean, and produce needlework, and they also should play instruments and practice drawing to tutor their children in such things. Jefferson's daughters' days followed a strict schedule to create room for these "essential" skills. Looking solely at the parallels between my mother's observations of the women in her life and the dictates that Jefferson laid out could lead a modern reader to question that a century and a half had transpired between Jefferson being president and my mother being born.

Depending on how they dressed, how clean they were, how trained they were to be wives and mothers, white women in Jefferson's eyes were either ladies or deemed "slovens" or "sluts" if they failed in any of the above. Regardless of the category he put them in, he believed women were meant to stay at home and not concern themselves with the matters of men, such as receiving an education beyond their wifely duties, getting involved in politics, or voting. He once said, "Our good ladies, I trust, have been too wise to wrinkle their foreheads with politics. They are contented to soothe and calm the minds of their husbands returning from political debate. . . . It is a comparison of Amazons to Angels." The Amazons he refers to here were the women he encountered in France who were emancipated and oversaw their own Parisian salons. He was deeply concerned that France would someday be run by women and that this would lead to catastrophe. He made it one of his personal missions to ensure that women in America would not consider such possibilities of independence for themselves.

Following the end of the Revolutionary War, there were many questions about how the new independent nation would organize itself and concerns about establishing rules and guidelines that could keep a country in order, according to a select group of white men, while upholding ideals of liberty and independence. Divisions among the states were frequent, small rebellions were emerging everywhere, women had become more involved in affairs outside their home to help support the Revolution, and Black people who were enslaved had contributed valiantly to the fight. All these things made men like Thomas Jefferson and George Washington, among their colleagues James Madison, Alexander Hamilton, Benjamin Franklin, John Adams, and others, concerned about losing the fruits of the war they had fought. They had been fighting to gain their own power over others, and they would not stand to lose that power to their wives or to the human beings they viewed as property. They needed to establish order for the entire country, as well as order in individual households, by setting forth rules that they would be in charge of upholding.

These men discussed at length what requirements should be in place for people to be eligible to participate politically in the government they were forming. As the late historian Mark E. Kann summarizes it,

The American founders aspired to create a republic of men. Their problem was that a democratic distemper infected the men of their time, resulting in disorderly conduct. . . . The founders addressed the problem by employing hegemonic norms of manhood to stigmatize and bring into line disorderly men, reward responsible men with citizenship, and empower exceptional men with positions of leadership and authority. One result was that their republic presupposed and perpetuated women's exclusion from politics. . . . The founders' original intent, then, was to create and sustain a republic based on male governance and female subordination.

We must keep this premise of American patriarchy in mind as we proceed: The United States was formed with the goal of fabricating a system that would put white men in power, keep white women under control, and exclude everyone else. The goal was never hidden or complicated, and we should no longer waste time or energy wondering how everything that came after the Declaration followed this central tenet. Every law they instituted, every speech they gave, every punishment they declared when someone countered them, every document they wrote all serve American patriarchy by design and not by simple coincidence.

The way they decided to structure the United States would mirror the way they believed all systems should operate, with mature and strong white men at the helm, mentoring younger white men who needed direction, providing for their female dependents, and keeping in line those whom they saw as their nonhuman slaves and Indigenous counterparts. The person who could represent this to the best extent became the first president of the nation.

Referred to as the "Father of His Country," George Washington not only became revered as a hero by persevering through hardships in the war and leading his troops to victory at the Battle of Yorktown, he also came to symbolize the ideal American man and in many ways the embodiment of American patriarchy. To this day, biographers who have written about his life, mostly other white men themselves, speak about Washington as if he were some kind of god, often commenting on his physical strength and his attractiveness. One of the few women to write a biography of Washington, Alexis Coe, has brought it to modern readers' attention just how strange it is that male historians have had so much to say about George Washington's physicality, especially through their seeming obsession with his masculine "thunderous thighs." Modern patriarchal men are often obsessed with historical patriarchal men whom they find inspiring, to whom they return and study repeatedly to keep their patriarchal practices alive by romanticizing them.

Washington's sexism was far less explicit than Jefferson's. In fact, although Washington has been extensively studied, it is difficult to find much in written or spoken form about his beliefs concerning women. Instead, he simply chose not to mention women in his speeches, and he had no issue with the lack of attention paid to women in the Constitution when he signed it. This serves as a reminder that not all believers in patriarchy profess their stance in the same way; some will proudly declare that women should be treated as less than them, while others will just allow women to be treated that way without them having to say anything about it. Whether overt or covert, sexism keeps patriarchy alive.

Washington's covert sexism did not come from a lack of activism on the part of women who wanted political inclusion. Abigail Adams, John Adams's wife, communicated her political views with her husband, Thomas Jefferson, and George Washington through letters she exchanged with each of them. In one letter to her husband, as drafts of the Constitution were being considered, she said, "In the new Code of Laws which I suppose it will be necessary for you to make I desire you would Remember the Ladies, and be more generous and favourable to them than your ancestors. Do not put such unlimited power into the hands of the Husbands." To this request her husband replied with a scoff, "As to your extraordinary Code of Laws, I cannot but laugh. . . . We know better than to repeal our Masculine systems." Again, these words show that the "masculine system" we still confront today was by no means a mistake, and it did not come to be because women were not yet aware of the injustices they faced. When women like Abigail Adams voiced their discontent, their husbands and male peers felt even more justified in upholding and even worsening the limits placed upon them.

In the end, the Constitution did not guarantee women the same protections and rights as men when it was first written, and it still doesn't guarantee them. The US is one of the few countries left in the world that doesn't guarantee in writing women's equal rights. As for John Adams, he would go on to become the first vice president and second president of the United States when George Washington resigned from office after two terms.

Before moving on to Abraham Lincoln and Theodore Roosevelt, we must pause because what we have learned about Thomas Jefferson and George Washington is essential in our mapping of American patriarchy. There was an opportunity at the early formation of the United States to do something new and continue the Revolution when it came to the meaning of freedom and independence; there were voices calling for ideas that differed from English common law, which stated such things as "The very being and legal existence of the woman is suspended during the marriage." The founding fathers instead chose to not only maintain English patriarchy but worsen it with their own additions. For example, the Declaration of Independence was adopted in 1776, and in 1777 all states passed laws to take away women's right to vote. The white men of this time were making a clear statement that we can find in their correspondence and speeches, and even see in the absence of direct mention of anyone other than themselves: the new nation they were forming was for them to rule with the same fervor, wit, and ruthlessness with which they won the Revolutionary War; they would leave no room for anyone to stop them. They were intentional in establishing their desired hierarchy, a republic of white men, and in designing a system that would keep such a hierarchy in place for as long as possible. This is the country we have inherited, with every patriarchal strategy they carefully paved into the roads. I will delve into these strategies in later chapters, but what I want to make obvious in part 1 is the unapologetic intention and narrative with which our nation and government were built.

More than sixty years passed between the presidencies of Washington and Lincoln, but not much had changed for white women, as they were still not given the right to vote. Although suffragettes would later quote Lincoln in a 1910 campaign, "Lincoln Said Women Should Vote," it turns out the words they referred to were originally meant more as a mockery of the women's movement in a letter he wrote in 1836. The full quote reads, "I go for all sharing the privileges of the government, who assist in bearing its burdens. Consequently I go for admitting all whites to the right of suffrage, who pay taxes or bear arms, (by no means excluding females.)" Lincoln was well aware that the only women who might even be eligible to pay taxes for themselves were widows who had chosen not to remarry, and that no woman was allowed to join the militia. Therefore he did not intend to actually support women of his time, but instead to draw attention to his opinion that women were not carrying the same "burdens" as men that could earn them the right to vote or be heard.

Not only did Lincoln find the idea of women participating in government to be funny, there is extensive evidence that Lincoln was uncomfortable even being in conversations with women. Michael Burlingame, a historian, quoted a contemporary describing Lincoln as "very awkward, and very much embarrassed in the presence of ladies." The late David Herbert Donald, a Pulitzer Prize–winning biographer, wrote that Lincoln "was extremely awkward around women . . . At his store he had been reluctant to wait on them, and at Rutledge Tavern he was unwilling to sit at the table when a well-dressed Virginia woman and her three daughters were guests." While there is no evidence that he was against women or that he ever did anything directly harmful to women, he was also not an advocate for women. Instead, he perpetuated the commonplace belittling of women of his time and he clearly saw them as less capable and possessing less value than men. He once wrote, "Thank God for not making me a woman," which stemmed from an old prayer that men would often speak to express gratitude that they were not "women, slaves, or boors."

One of the most revealing discussions connected to Abe Lincoln and women comes from a study of his marriage to Mary Todd Lincoln, perhaps the most controversial First Lady ever to hold the title. Following from the notion that the president of the United States was meant to reflect the expectations of how men should conduct their home, the same was true for First Ladies. Those in the role are supposed to reflect the ideal woman who manages the home while her husband works, reflects beauty standards of her time, and plays instruments or speaks other languages in order to represent her husband well and tutor her children. She hosts events for guests, decorates their home, and can be her husband's confidante and private adviser but will not get any credit for her ideas and must keep herself from voicing her opinions publicly, especially if these are different from her partner's. She is not paid for her efforts because these are all things women are simply expected to do, and to do happily.

Mary Todd Lincoln was different, and has even been ranked as the worst First Lady by many scholars. She has been described as crazy, rude, loud, spiteful, dismissive, corrupt, unrefined, and jealous, based on rumors that she was delusional, plagued with constant headaches that some referred to as "feminine madness" or the result of a "menstrual" disease, and that she abused her husband. Lincoln's law partner called her a "she-wolf" and a "female wildcat." No matter what it is that she did, these titles and descriptions are soaked in sexism and misogyny. There is no record of Lincoln standing up for his wife or offering a different perspective that would allow others to know more about the early tragedies she suffered, like losing her mother and her children. Burlingame argues in his book *An American Marriage: The Untold Story of Abraham Lincoln and Mary Todd* that Abraham Lincoln was "seduced" by Mary and then forced into the marriage to protect her honor. While I do not know Mary Todd Lincoln's full story, it is evident that the treatment of her during her life, and posthumously, represents the belittling of women of the nineteenth century, the critique they suffered when they were viewed as unable to play their part, and the ways they were dismissed, blamed, and misunderstood, especially by their male contemporaries.

Lastly we have Theodore Roosevelt, who became the twenty-sixth and youngest president in American history in 1901 at the age of forty-two. His presidency is often spoken about as a progressive one—he was an environmentalist; he believed private wealth should not be allowed to accumulate without regulation, and that the government had a responsibility in leveling the playing field between the rich and the poor. When it comes to women he was more progressive before and after he assumed the presidency than he ended up being while in office. As an undergraduate at Harvard, he wrote a thesis where he advocated for equal rights for women: "Viewed purely in the abstract, I think there can be no question that women should have equal rights with men." Regarding marriage, he said, "There should be the most absolute equality preserved between the two sexes. I do not think the woman should assume the man's name. The man should have no more right over the person or property of his wife than she has over the person or property of her husband."

All this sounds great and promising. However, once he was elected president, he felt other matters were more important to address, and women's right to vote was not at the top of his agenda. He also believed that the women's rights movement would be more successful if women made sure that they still fulfilled the roles they were meant to in their homes. This was similar to what Eva Emery Dye, the suffragette who usurped Sacagawea's story, believed. In summary, his personal stance was that women should be able to vote even though he wasn't willing to champion this while serving as president, and he also felt strongly that women must prioritize their role as wives and mothers above everything else. Passionately in opposition to birth control, he was pleased by white women he met who had given birth to large families. In one particular case he was delighted to meet a voter and his wife who were happily raising their seventeen children. He was disappointed with leaders of the suffrage movement who dismissed their womanly duties and instead were displaying what he saw as disorderly conduct that degraded the morality and duty of their sex.

Roosevelt had already served as president for eight years, but in 1912, when he disagreed with his successor William Taft's policies, he formed a third party in order to challenge Taft's reelection. He chose to take up the banner of women's rights to gain additional support, as women could now vote in some states. Regardless of his support for women's suffrage pre and post his presidency, the reality is that Roosevelt did not see the cause as important when he had power to do something about it, and he still believed that women's primary duty was not to themselves but to their husbands and children.

Thomas Jefferson, George Washington, Abraham Lincoln, and Theodore Roosevelt differed in several ways, but they also shared important commonalities, one of those being that they were all American patriarchs. In these four men in particular we see different ways in which patriarchy can operate. Jefferson intentionally left women out of the Declaration of Independence because he fervently believed in the superiority of men. Washington wasn't vocally against women's rights, nor did he voice his opinions on women as openly as Jefferson did, but he simply accepted the gender roles as they were and happily stepped into his position as the head patriarch of a new nation that aspired to be a republic of and for men. Lincoln was known to be uncomfortable around women and even thought the idea of women's suffrage was something trivial that could be made fun of; he also did not appear to care about disparaging representations of his own wife. Roosevelt, the most forward-thinking of them all on women's rights, was not willing to use his presidential platform to speak in support of women, only willing to lift the banner of women's suffrage when he needed their votes. He, like the three men before him, believed women should first and foremost be in charge of domestic duties, including reproducing and caring for their children.

Over one hundred and thirty years spanned the signing of the Declaration of Independence and the end of Theodore Roosevelt's presidency, and yet another fifty-some years would pass before my mom was born, but unfortunately the patriarchy the founding fathers created held strong. Yes, women were able to vote before my mom's time, but they were still largely being told to uphold the same expectations of women before them. In other words, the story of American patriarchy, the belief that white men should rule and white women should follow, remained the same. Furthermore, the Voting Rights Act was still years away from being realized. This brings me to the other common denominator these presidents shared, something Gutzon Borglum, the sculptor of Mount Rushmore, also fervently defended: a belief in the supremacy of white people over all others, especially over Black people.

When Borglum was called to create a monument in South Dakota, he was in the middle of working on what was referred to as a "shrine to the South," honoring Robert E. Lee and Stonewall Jackson, complete with a Ku Klux Klan altar, at Stone Mountain. He worked in Atlanta for ten years and became heavily involved with the KKK, attending their rallies and serving on Klan committees. A number of issues stalled Borglum's work on his ode to the fathers of the Confederate states, including infighting between members of the group that originally hired him, the Daughters of the Confederacy, which pushed Borglum to abandon the project and take his skills and beliefs about Black people to his envisioning and carving of Mount Rushmore instead.

Washington and Jefferson were both slaveholders, and while many have come to see President Lincoln as an ally to Black people because of his issuing of the Emancipation Proclamation, Lincoln too believed in white supremacy. One way of understanding Lincoln is to think about the following words written by Borglum to his dear friend the Grand Dragon of the Realm of Indiana, Klansman David "Steve" Stephenson of Indianapolis: "While Anglo-Saxons have themselves sinned grievously against the principle of pure nationalism by illicit slave and alien servant traffic, it has been the character of the cargo that has eaten into the very moral fiber of our race character, rather than the moral depravity of Anglo-Saxon traders." Here is a statement similar to the stance President Lincoln took in his remarks to and about Black people of his time: Slavery was wrong but the character of Black people was the larger problem. Lincoln actually wanted Black people to leave the country when they were emancipated, not stay and demand equal rights in the nation they had built. And President Roosevelt celebrated those who he believed rose above their lesser race, like Booker T. Washington, but in thinking about Black people as a whole he felt that "as a race and in the mass they are altogether inferior to the whites."

Yes, Mount Rushmore tells "the story of how America was made and the men who helped make it what it is today." It is a story of American patriarchy, one that depends not only on sexism but also on unrepentant and unabashed racism.

4

TO JUSTIFY DEHUMANIZATION AND STOP US FROM

◼

On December 21, 1848, two people boarded a train in Macon, Georgia, as they began their journey to Philadelphia. They were traveling together but laws, particularly slave codes, made it so that they needed to sit in separate cars. To others on the train everything seemed relatively normal even though one member of the pair was ill. In their eyes, a white man with an injured arm and bandages on his face had boarded the train with his dark-skinned slave. They were traveling north for the white man's treatments. Not only was he in a cast and facial wrappings, the white man also appeared to be hard of hearing. He sat down in the comfortable, clean, and airy "whites only" car without acknowledging a fellow passenger's attempts at conversation about the weather while his devoted slave, assured that his "master" was comfortable, proceeded to the crowded "negro" car to find his seat.

On a surface level the traveling pair symbolized differences in the life experiences of Black men versus white men, most notably when it came to their free will. On their four-day journey, the white man was congratulated for having a "very attentive boy"—another slaveholder even offered to buy him and take him back down South, while another person mistook the enslaved man for their runaway and threatened to capture him. At each stop the Black man was degraded and sent away to eat and sleep where he would not be seen and where conditions would be subpar. The white man, on the other hand, traveled in luxury, staying in the nicest rooms with pity taken upon him for his injuries. The only outward imposition on his agency after he was cordial to his Black companion came in the form of advice from a fellow white man to never thank one's slave, saying:

> I assure you, sir, nothing spoils a slave so soon as saying "thank you" and "if you please" to him. The only way to make a nigger toe the mark, and to keep him in his place, is to storm at him like thunder and keep him trembling like a leaf. Don't you see, when I speak to my Ned, he darts like lightning; and if he didn't I'd skin him.

In other words, one of the two travelers was seen as a human being with rights to live freely and make their own decisions, to be treated with dignity and care; the other was either infantilized at best or completely dehumanized.

What the people they encountered on their travels were unaware of was that this duo was relying on the assumptions of their time, the prejudices of their contemporaries, and the dictates of the status quo to do far more than to take a trip north for medication. They were heading to Philadelphia in search of freedom from it all, to release the chains of captivity that bound them, and to escape the cruel, inhumane practice of slavery. This quest was not solely for the liberation of William Craft, the Black man. It was also for his wife, an enslaved woman named Ellen, who, in preparation for the journey, had agreed to cut her hair to neck length, sew herself a pair of men's trousers, and wear a hat and glasses to conceal her identity. The couple knew that if Ellen were to pose as a white man she would be required to sign documents on behalf of her "slave" in order to travel, but because both of them had been restricted by law from learning to read or write, they wrapped her arm in bandages and feigned an injury. The dressings on her face would further cover her identity, and when she was greeted by her "master's" dear friend upon boarding the train with "It's a very fine morning, sir," she pretended to be deaf for several hours for fear that he might see through her disguise.

This true story of Ellen and William Craft reveals far more than the unequal treatment that white and Black people received. It invites us to examine the layers of oppression that exist when considering not only sex and gender but also race, it showcases the arbitrariness of categorizing human beings based on sex and skin color, it calls our attention to the many ways in which both gender and race are performative social constructs, it highlights the cruelty of slavery, and, perhaps most important, it explains how the most assured road away from American patriarchy is by following where Black women and nonbinary people, those who have been cast the furthest from power as it has thus far existed in the United States, are pointing.

Ellen and William were born in 1826 and 1824, respectively, as John Quincy Adams's presidency began. You will recall that Abigail Adams, John Quincy Adams's mother and John Adams's wife, had urged her husband to "remember the ladies" in the formation of the new rules. Although her husband mocked the notion and dismissed her, Abigail Adams continued to advocate for women's rights and also stood in opposition to slavery. She was still someone who believed Black people should be treated differently than white people, something that was evident in her review of Shakespeare's *Othello*, where she wrote, "I could not separate the African color from the man, nor prevent that disgust and horror which filled my mind every time I saw him touch the gentle Desdemona." Yet her stances against slavery placed her in opposition to many of her contemporaries. I mention that here to show that it is always an option to stand against the norm, especially when the norm is wrong, and it is always valid to revisit history and question those who accepted injustice rather than simply excusing their actions as "products of their time."

Abigail Adams greatly influenced her son's politics. Although women were not allowed to vote and the emancipation of enslaved people was still many years away, John Quincy Adams's stances hinted at the potential for change. Most notably, while leading a movement against a gag rule forbidding citizens' petitions to Congress against slavery, he defended women's right to have their voices heard, citing examples of women's political involvement from ancient times to the American Revolution. He argued that women played an essential public role in society as a natural outgrowth of their private role in the home. John Quincy Adams also defended before the Supreme Court fifty-three Africans who had taken control of the *Amistad*, the ship transporting them. Surprisingly, the court ruled in favor of the enslaved men and women in 1841, stating it was "the ultimate right of all human beings in extreme cases to resist oppression, and to apply force against ruinous injustice." Despite this win, slavery continued in all its injustice, leaving people like Ellen and William Craft and countless others who resisted slavery each day to take matters into their own hands. Seven years after that Supreme Court ruling, the Crafts began their journey.

American patriarchy relied on enslavement for its survival. Ellen and William Craft were not included in the definitions of "men" and "women" that the founding fathers or the other men on Mount Rushmore lived by; they were seen as something else entirely and in a different way than Sacagawea and other Indigenous people. On the one hand, Indigenous people in the US were often viewed as being able to assimilate to white culture eventually because if they did there would be more land available to white people; this is why colonizers tried two methods of erasing Native people and culture: assimilation and genocide. Relocation, boarding schools, and marriages, especially between white men and Indigenous women, all pertained to assimilation. In the case of Black people, however—who were brought to the nation as slaves or who were born into slavery, and were told they had no claim to the land, but who fueled the economy with their blood, sweat, and tears—neither their assimilation nor elimination was beneficial to white people. The line could not be blurred with them; white men raped slaves and slaves were forced to nurse white children, but slaves could not be seen as people, especially during antebellum times. Even someone who stood in opposition to slavery, like Abigail Adams, could not stand the thought of a Black Othello and a white Desdemona intermingling. This need for separation carried forward into the sharecropping era post–official slavery, and is especially evident in the "one-drop rule" that said you were Black if you had any Black ancestry, a code of the land that did not apply to Native people.

There have been many attempts by so-called scientists and researchers to prove that whiteness is superior to Blackness, and to claim that one drop of Black blood made a person less worthy of living with dignity and agency. The most notable example of this comes in work done by the founder of anthropology in the US, Samuel Morton. Morton wrote an entire book comparing around one hundred human skulls, in which he argued that, based on his unrepresentative sample and measurements, the Caucasian race had relatively larger "internal capacity." Therefore, he concluded, whites had "the highest intellectual endowments." Others went further by arguing that anyone with African ancestry was more akin to an animal and perhaps was not a human being at all. What we have not paid enough attention to, however, is how a denial of a gendered identity that fit the way white men defined themselves and their female counterparts was employed to solidify a belief in the lack of humanity of Black people.

Slaveholders relied on both implementing strict categories of gender for themselves and their female relatives, then stripping away access to these categories for slaves. In other words, white patriarchs relied not only on assigning and ascribing to men and women specific roles and characteristics, they also needed to find ways to exclude slaves from these as a way of justifying their extreme tactics of oppression.

Here is where the performance of gender in the play that is American patriarchy becomes plain to see. Without reducing the unfathomable courage the Crafts possessed to face potentially horrendous, and even fatal, consequences were they to be caught, the story seems almost too easy. How could a haircut, articles of clothing, some bandages, and a little acting give two people who were enslaved a path to their freedom? The answer is that putting people into a ranking system of race and gender is unsophisticated to begin with. So arbitrary are these categorizations that they have been redefined and restructured multiple times over American history to include people when it benefited white men with power and to exclude others, which in and of itself defies the notion of there being a "natural order." Books like *Stamped from the Beginning* by Ibram Kendi and *Caste* by Isabel Wilkerson take readers through detailed histories of how race came to be, and here I will briefly focus on how a woman who was considered a slave but whose skin color was light not only exposed the senseless dehumanization of her people but also highlights the undeniable manufacturing of American patriarchy.

The Crafts' story displays how white women were still treated as inferior to white men, but also showcases the incredible disparity that existed between white women and Black men as well as white women and Black women. Ellen Craft knew she could not pass as a white woman and expect to escape with her husband because white women did not have the same rights as white men. As we've learned in the story that is American patriarchy, white women were presented as their husbands' dependents made to live within the confining rules of their time; they were not seen as authoritative figures. And it would not have been customary for a white woman to travel with her male servant.

White women were supposed to be docile, obedient, well mannered, ladylike, fragile, innocent, and chaste, in need of guidance and protection. They were first the property of their fathers, and when they married they became the property of their husbands. We see this play out even in the way last names work. The historical reason why women took their husband's last name is that the English common law that we reviewed stated that through marriage a woman's separate identity from her husband no longer existed. In many ways, a white woman's identity disappeared through marriage and her life became entirely about her husband. Dictates like those found in the *Ladies' Book of Etiquette*, first published in 1860, told them how to dress, how to sit, how to eat, how to speak, all in ways that reflected the aforementioned characteristics of their sex. Chapter titles included "Bridal Etiquette," "Conversation," and "How to Behave at a Hotel," and the book is filled with commentary like the following:

> Many a wife, thus commencing, has laid the foundations of future fortune, at least independence, to her husband, by keeping his mind at peace, during his progress up the steep ascent to professional, or clerical, or literary fame.

In antebellum America, to be a man meant to be the strong leader and provider of the household, knowing your wife's and children's worth were based on you. To be a woman meant to be submissive, supportive of your husband's aspirations, and a means through which to carry on his name.

So where did people who were enslaved fall within these gendered delineations that were represented as both natural and divine, but that we know were fabricated? Some abolitionists tried to use this same question for their cause, leaning fully into such divisions to expose the tyranny of slavery, saying that slaveholders were not doing their part as patriarchs if they were mistreating their dependents, which not only constituted their wives and children but should also include their slaves. Abolitionists even referred to slavery as the "patriarchal institution" to expose how it misaligned with what society claimed to hold as a standard of operation where men led their households, dependents were well provided for, the chastity of women was protected, and marriages were respected. These abolitionists believed that showcasing the stark contrast between what leaders of the nation claimed were their values, and their actions toward humans who were enslaved, would result in the eventual illegality of slavery.

What became even clearer through the abolitionist patriarchy argument, however, was that slaveholders did not see or speak about the people they enslaved as human beings at all, having intentionally removed their identities, especially gendered identities, to justify abuses against them. Enslaved women were seen as promiscuous and incapable of sexual self-restraint, in direct opposition to "ladylike" white women. Enslaved men would be punished if they tried to protect their female counterparts, thus removing the role of protector from their experience. But perhaps most notable of all was that being Black stood in direct opposition to the law that applied to white people. For slaves, children carried the status of their mother rather than their father. By this I mean that laws were written to ensure that any child born to an enslaved woman would be seen as a slave, no matter what. This not only encouraged the rampant sexual abuse of slaves; it also made it so that unions between enslaved people were completely disregarded. In our study of the creation of American patriarchy this fact must be clearly understood: One of the most effective strategies employed in dehumanizing Black people was, and continues to be, any attempt to exclude them from a gendered social order.

This is the reason why respectability politics still exists to this day. Being human has come to mean fitting into prescribed roles that are largely gendered and heteronormative. Fitting into the patriarchal organization of society is seen as a path to being treated with dignity and respect, to no longer being cast away as an outsider. The thought is that if we can dress the part, sound like them, and walk like them, follow their belief systems, shed our ways, maybe we will finally be given the chance to live freely. We need only memorize the lines and stage notes that guide even our smallest movements, and perhaps we too will fit into the story. For an enslaved person whose life depended on the whims of slaveholders, for a woman like Ellen and a man like William, who could be forcibly split from each other at any moment, who wanted children but feared they would be robbed of them as soon as they were born, disguising themselves and following the script of patriarchy was worth the risk.

For this plan to have even the slightest chance of working, Ellen needed to embody the role of someone who could go almost completely unquestioned, who could get away with breaking the made-up rules like not signing for his property, who might surprise someone if they didn't engage in conversation but who would be given the benefit of the doubt, and who could come and go on trains and in and out of hotels and restaurants as they pleased, seen as being in charge of their own choices without having to answer to anyone else.

Ultimately, it would take a mastery of a book she had been forced to study all her life; it would require a brilliant performance. Ellen knew her character well because her survival had already depended on it long before she cut her hair and sewed her pants. She had picked up the knowledge she needed to turn white patriarchy into her escape by serving those who called themselves her masters. They were the characters in the book. She knew how they acted in social settings, what drinks and foods they liked, what phrases they used, how they carried themselves; she knew how they sat and what they

wore. She had been forced to learn the needs and wants of her oppressors from the moment she was born, to examine them down to
the smallest of details because they relied on her to do so. Once fluent
in their ways, with the story of American patriarchy memorized, she
transferred it beautifully into her four-day journey as a white man.

After an epic voyage filled with close calls and constant danger
were they to be caught, Ellen and William Craft triumphantly arrived in Philadelphia on Christmas Day. They started taking classes
to learn how to read and write as soon as they could. They were
given assistance by the Underground Railroad network and were
able to get on their feet. Two years later, when the Fugitive Slave
Act was passed, however, when people were being forcibly returned
to their supposed owners even if they lived in a free state, their liberty was in jeopardy again. Unable to risk staying in the US, they
boarded a ship to England. There they had five children and continued to be involved in the abolitionist movement from afar. In
an emotional full-circle moment, after twenty years abroad, they
returned to the US to open a school for newly freed Black people in
their home state of Georgia.

The details of this couple's valiant escape became known when
William published his account in the book *Running a Thousand
Miles for Freedom* in 1860. While Ellen's thoughts and experiences
are certainly included, the publication of a book written from William's perspective brings up more information for us to consider
in our larger discussion of American patriarchy. It would not have
been customary for a woman to publish her writing at the time,
and Ellen was also in charge of caring for their five children. In
letters she wrote, emphasizing her pride in her domestic responsibilities, she recalled how desperately she and William wanted their
marriage to be legally protected, and how grateful she was that her
motherhood and bond with her children would not be stolen from
her. She connected her freedom to her ability to bear and raise her
children in peace, something she had been told she was not entitled

to in the United States. She was also an activist, a seamstress, a tutor, and a lecturer. Ellen Craft was a woman who tried to find balance amid all the layers of her identity and the stories American patriarchy had told her about them, stories that were told differently abroad.

Ellen Craft's life teaches us that when we speak about the plague of American patriarchy, we need to acknowledge the ways in which we all must collectively battle our common enemy while also recognizing that we have been hurt differently by it. We will be more effective if we all challenge patriarchy together *and* we cannot erase the different experiences and histories of oppression we bring to the fight. We can neither forsake one another nor speak for one another. Instead we can use our different perspectives to call attention to the production of American patriarchy, to its malleability and ultimate breakability.

Ellen Craft was a student of American patriarchy, and she used her examination to create a new path she once only dreamed of having for herself and for her family. Her life highlights how Black women are the most astute observers of American patriarchy as a result of being violently excluded by it historically, named by law as direct opposites of white men but forced to live dangerously close to them. While respectability politics remains an issue to this day, and we can at times find ourselves caught in the traps of attempts at assimilation, more often than not, Black women have shown others paths to transforming systems and challenging long-held assumptions to create a world that is more equitable, and to leave space for new ways of living.

As a little girl, my mother may have found the ending of Ellen's story to be confusing, perhaps even disappointing. Wasn't motherhood limiting? Wasn't it problematic to tell women and young girls to aspire to marriage and domesticity? After her incredible feat, why would Ellen be so fulfilled with raising her kids while her husband gained recognition through the publication of his book? This is what brings us back to the problems that arise when our confrontation of American patriarchy is solely based on the experiences of white women. Ellen Craft represents the revolutionary nature of reclaiming roles that have historically been seen as domestic, having been controlled by American patriarchs, and transforming them into positions of freedom and power, another clue about the role of perspective and narrative. Her roles as a wife and a mother were inextricably intertwined with her fight for emancipation. For a Black woman to be able to raise her children without fear of being violently separated from them countered the dominant narrative and the entire system that our sexist, racist, capitalistic nation relied on; for a Black man to be seen as an educated husband, father, and provider cut the strings of the puppet show American patriarchy forced us into. Doing away with American patriarchy does not necessarily mean doing away with family or doing away with motherhood, but means reframing the story around them and considering how they can both be transformative, something my mom would learn later on, when she birthed her own children.

5

WRITING A DIFFERENT STORY

■

One of the greatest gifts my mom ever gave me was her reflections on her own life in memoir form. In early 2021, telling me she wanted to start writing her own story and explore getting it published, she asked if I would be willing to be one of her editors alongside a writers' group she had joined. Without hesitancy I accepted. She had lived an epic life thus far, and I knew people would find her accomplishments inspiring just like I always had.

That little girl who wanted to become a lawyer not only succeeded in putting herself through law school, she traveled the world inspiring other women to do the same. She became a fearless activist for women's and children's rights both in the United States and abroad, working on projects ranging from teaching law students in Mexico, Sweden, and Estonia to helping rewrite the rule of law in Juba, South Sudan, to organizing female law students in Dubai, to advocating for victims of domestic abuse, to doing talks about her life experiences around the United States.

Her awareness of injustice only continued to grow when her education took her farther away from her more homogenous hometown. She learned how the oppression of women differed depending on factors such as race and class, and she became keenly aware of her privilege. She staunchly believed that fighting for women's rights was inextricably linked to all other forms of oppression, and she did her best to become educated in ways to combat them. She also became a mother herself, birthing and raising two daughters and one son to break the boxes others might try to force upon us. She took pride in her motherhood while also continuing her work abroad; some projects allowed for us to travel with her, others meant that she had to be away from us for long periods of time. While I'm sure it was difficult to make those decisions, her dedication to her work gave me endless inspiration, especially because of her understanding of interconnectedness across all human beings.

I always use my mom as an example when I am asked about how we should approach fighting oppression together across different groups, how women can come together without erasing the experiences and voices of the most marginalized among us, how we can see one another's pain and know the ways in which there are both similarities and differences, how we can be allies and ultimately much more effective at tackling the root cause of all our problems, and how maybe together we can write new rules that are considerate of our unique experiences. My mother's allyship was something I, growing up, didn't even realize was so unique, something I didn't know others struggled to understand. My mother was a white woman with a Black husband and Black children, and through both words and examples she told me that she knew about unfairness in the world, but she could never tell me what it would be like to be a Black girl, she wouldn't pretend she could walk in my shoes, but she insisted she would walk beside me, learn with me, and do her part to make sure this world became a place that was worthy of me. She taught me to see the rules of the status quo as breakable, to follow my instinct if something seemed wrong and unfair, to not believe people if they did not see my potential, and to celebrate all the ways I could rewrite the story that others would tell me I needed to follow, just like she had done in her own life.

In deciding to write about her experiences in narrative form from her own perspective, she brought attention to the power of storytelling, something she always reminded my siblings and me of in each of the countries we traveled to. Whole nations relied on stories passed from one generation to another about the way they thought the world should work, and it was clear that voices with more power were louder than others, sometimes seeming like the only ones you could hear.

This practice is, once again, both simple and complicated. Simply put, stories are what dictate our lives, but the way they turn from narrative into practice is through tactics of control that can be difficult to track. The first part of this book is dedicated to understanding that American patriarchy relies on a specific story about two genders, a story that conflates sex with gender and tells us that other genders outside the binary do not exist; it says that performing according to the dictates of our gender is how we can claim our humanity; it tells us that one gender is more valued than the other, that one gender should be in power while the other should be controlled, and it also tells us that not everyone is entitled to these problematic categories.

The story my mother encountered was one that had been passed down at least since the signing of the Declaration of Independence. It was one that was crafted by white men that they used to not only suppress white women but also to fuel their own ruthless imperialism, seen especially through their abuse of Indigenous people and their attempts to eliminate Indigenous culture through forced-assimilation tactics and genocide. Not only was the story used to determine the future but it was also placed on the past to distort events that already took place, making them seem like they too fit into the order of things, such as the manipulation of Sacagawea's life and the need to keep American patriarchs alive through statues and even a carving that covers fifteen thousand square feet. The story of American patriarchy has also been used to grow xenophobia during times of war, by painting a picture of American people who followed the dictates of gender as thriving while describing other populations as decaying as a result of their disruption of the rules. The story also communicated that the disgusting and cruel practice of slavery was permissible because Black people did not fit into white men's notions of "man" and "woman." The story has been told so often that even in a fight against American patriarchy, many have been unable to avoid reinforcing the notion of white women being the only real women when they base their strategies on white women's experiences alone.

Yes, we have learned the story in the first part of this book, and we have also learned that by seeing American patriarchy for what it is at its core, a script written by someone else that we are each told to follow, it becomes obvious just how fragile it is. The made-up system of American patriarchy has tried to rob us of wisdom, choice, truth, and recognition, but we have learned in this section that the people of this land have not always organized themselves in such an unsophisticated way. There have been countless voices speaking in opposition to American patriarchy since the nation's founding. Even the founding fathers were aware that they had to force people to follow certain rules by writing them into law. They made intentional decisions to exclude women as well as the people whom they deemed their slaves. Haircuts and clothing changes were enough to expose the lie and the lack of its supposed naturalness. The knowledge of its being so delicate is what has driven those who think they benefit most from it to employ every weapon in their arsenal to protect and shield it. The scariest of these has come in the form of violence, punishment, and consequences for those who stand up to American patriarchy, as well as rewards and protection for those who uphold it. The more you are invested in

American patriarchy and the way it keeps people in the places to which you have relegated them, the more you will do, whatever it takes, to hold them there so that they cannot fight, so that they cannot unite, so that they cannot expose the vulnerability of it all. This is where we will move to in the next part.

After just finishing a full draft of her memoir, my mom got sick and sadly passed away unexpectedly in December 2021, just a few months after my daughter was born. They never had the chance to meet each other in person, but I am honored to be the link between them. I look forward to sharing my mother's writing with my kids and maybe, someday, with the whole world. It is a special gift to inherit the awareness and bravery my mother passed to me, the knowledge of the power of stories, the fighting spirit that not only makes me challenge the script but also encourages me to burn it through my career, through this book, and through my own motherhood with the fire my mother instilled in me from birth. May the flames only continue to rise with each generation.

Part 2

OUR
INTUITION
AND
SELF-DETERMINATION

6

THROUGH VICIOUS REMINDERS

■

I was born in July 1992 in Albuquerque, New Mexico. My mom was teaching law at the university at the time while my dad was completing his law degree. Growing up with two experts on the American legal system as my parents, I became aware of the supposed rules of our nation, the fact that they were not fixed, and the ways in which they applied differently to people. In other words, depending on who you were, consequences for your actions would be very different. These differences in each individual's relationship to the law of the land depended on identifying factors like their sex, skin color, social status, and even their comfort or lack thereof with English. Outside explicit language that directly imposes different treatment in the United States based on factors like race, such as Jim Crow laws, we also witness the spectrum of enforcement when we see discrepancies in sentencing or changes in behavior on behalf of authorities when someone is aware of the law as opposed to when they are not. Hence why understanding how the law works holds immense power, because the more one knows about the "rules" that dictate our lives, the more one might gain the ability to use them in their or their community's favor. It is this view of law and policy, this understanding of them as being open to interpretation and subject to editing, that drives many to pursue careers as lawyers or politicians. They might be interested in upholding things as they are or, like my parents were and taught my siblings and me to be, they are interested in reshaping the laws in place in order to engender more equity and justice.

With similar motivations, a girl born thirty-six years before me came to believe that she could make a difference for her country through law and policy too. In July 1956, Erma and Albert Hill welcomed their thirteenth child into the world. They were farmers in Lone Tree, Oklahoma, only one generation removed from slavery—Erma's father and grandparents as well as Albert's grandparents had all been enslaved. With their Baptist faith, Erma and Albert raised their children to be hardworking, to cherish their freedom, and to believe that God had given them each a unique purpose in life. They did their best to shield their children from racism so that their kids could walk through life with their heads held high.

From the lessons her parents instilled in her, Anita, the youngest of the family, went on to earn a degree in psychology from Oklahoma State University and a law degree from Yale University. She was a shy girl in personality but bold in her belief in herself and what she could accomplish in life. She knew she was brilliant, and she had the potential to leave an impact on the world, hopefully one that would honor her family and improve conditions for her larger community.

From her birth in the 1950s through the beginning of her career in the 1980s, Anita Hill lived through key moments in American history, such as the modern civil rights movement. She saw firsthand how Black people continued to fight to be recognized and treated as human beings in their country while white supremacists continued to try to exclude them from basic human rights. The sentiment that Black people were more akin to animals was still used to justify abuses against us and was still especially concerned with keeping Black people from a gendered social order even after slavery was abolished. In the horrific act of lynching, it was commonplace for mobs to cut off parts of Black bodies that signaled their gender as a way to further declare Black bodies as "other." Black men were castrated, Black women's breasts were severed, and pregnant Black women were hanged before their babies were cut out of their abdomens.

In addition to such torture, new tropes were introduced to blame Black people for the social ills their community faced, describing them as violating the rules of the white gender binary. Black women were described as promiscuous jezebels or emasculating sapphires, or as the mammy who was only concerned with pleasing her white family, without any needs of her own or any obligations to her own children. The "welfare queen" stereotype was then used to shame Black women for having children at all. Black men were described as animalistic and dangerous mandingos or brutes, or were depicted as lazy and unwilling to provide for their families and reliant on women to do everything for them. Such tropes fueled the rise of "misogynoir," a term coined by writer Moya Bailey to refer to prejudice against and hatred of Black women. Misogynoir not only dehumanizes Black women and justifies white supremacist violence, it also divides Black people from one another and adds to the fabrication that Black women are the ones keeping Black men from being treated as men.

This context is critical in our understanding of the evolution of American patriarchy, especially concerning Anita Hill, who, after finishing law school and joining a firm in Washington, DC, left to work in the US Department of Education's Office for Civil Rights in 1981. There she served as a legal adviser to the assistant secretary, a man named Clarence Thomas.

Anita Hill had done everything in her power to avoid the tropes that she confronted on a daily basis as a Black woman in America. She was well educated and accomplished, yet she still presented herself with a practiced elegance and femininity. In the early 1980s, she was reaching new heights in her career, making her family proud with degrees and a job her enslaved ancestors could only dream of. She had taken a different route from her own mother in her decision to wait on getting married and having kids. In many ways, she was breaking barriers for women, especially women of color in her field. But her boss was making it difficult for her to fully enjoy her accomplishments and focus on her work. He constantly made her feel uncomfortable. He would approach her to talk, not only about her professional responsibilities but also about sex. He would describe pornography in detail, he would talk about pubic hair, he would ask her to go on dates with him no matter how many times she turned him down. She did her best to change the subject or avoid conversation with him when possible.

After a while, it seemed Thomas was getting the message. The harassment dwindled, but when he was made chair of the Equal Employment Opportunity Commission in 1982 and she followed him, excited to do even more work to make our country more equitable, the unwelcome sexual remarks resumed. Eventually, Hill could no longer tolerate the discomfort. She chose to take a risk and try to rebuild her career elsewhere. In continuation of her groundbreaking accomplishments, in 1989 she became the first tenured Black professor at the University of Oklahoma. Feeling thankful that she no longer had to deal with Thomas, and relieved her career could move forward despite walking away from a position she had worked hard for, she was moving on with her life.

In 1991, her old boss was nominated for the Supreme Court of the United States, and Hill was called in to tell her story. Reluctant at first and worried about risking everything she had achieved, she convinced herself that she needed to tell the country what she knew about Thomas, who was now being given the opportunity to hold one of the most powerful positions in our nation. At the hearings, Anita Hill, thirty-five years old at the time, testified to a judiciary committee made up of fourteen white men and led by then senator Joe Biden.

Dressed in a perfectly fitted blue blazer with gold buttons, her hair straightened and her makeup precisely done, she spoke bravely and eloquently as she faced the men in front of her. But it did not matter how prepared she was, how intelligent she was, how well dressed she was, or how closely she followed the script. Not only did they not believe her, and not only did they demean her with their questions, they also felt that the things she alleged Thomas had said and done were "not so bad." It was clear that these men did not see any issue with Thomas's actions, which were considered by the committee to be acceptable behavior for men at the time but were especially permissible toward a Black woman. In their eyes, Thomas was following an American patriarchal order as closely as he could while still being Black, but Hill was not. In one of the most famous instances of American patriarchy, Thomas was confirmed as a Supreme Court justice, while Hill faced extreme backlash for coming forward, and the majority of the public believed she was lying. The overarching sentiment was that she wanted to ruin a Black man's career and that she was interrupting national progress regarding racial equity to do so. Put differently, a Black woman was being blamed for delaying racial equity simply by coming forward with her truth.

Through Hill's story several points become clear. First, in a country where sexism reigns supreme and patriarchy is the protected social order, women are subject to the whims of men who see them as lesser and will remind them of that no matter how far they get in life; no matter their degrees or accomplishments, they will be told that they should serve the role of pleasing the men around them. Theory concerning sexual harassment tells us that it is entirely concerned with power and perpetrators needing to assert it, especially when they believe their power is being threatened. In the United States, straight, cisgender, and typically white men tend to hold power over others, hence why women, nonbinary, nonwhite, and nonheteronormative people are the most vulnerable. Women are vulnerable to sexual harassment in the workplace, especially in industries that are male-dominated and where men are less likely to face repercussions. When men find themselves in a larger culture that represents women as inferior, submissive, and secondary to men, they bring these sentiments with them to their interpersonal interactions, especially in professional settings women were never supposed to enter, according to patriarchal beliefs. Sexual harassment is one of many "consequences" people are subjected to when they challenge the gender roles assigned to them; women who dare to enter male-dominated fields like Hill did are one example.

Hill also faced repercussions for speaking up and declaring her truth as a Black woman because, as we've learned, Black women are seen by our larger culture as bringing on sexual advances by their very nature, leading white men to call her a liar and tell her that what she described was not worthy of punishment. She faced further consequences for speaking up against "one of her own." As a result of the heinous oppression of Black people as a whole, Black women have often found themselves having to put their needs aside to protect their male counterparts, or they have been told they have to choose between being women and being Black.

This forced "choice" has been imposed on us by white feminism that wrongly tells Black women we cannot distract from a feminist fight by including race in our strategy—again, because race is seen as not fitting neatly into our gendered social order. It has also been enforced by Black men with internalized racism and sexism who want to be treated as humans themselves and are therefore assimilating in order to play their role in the gendered order. The late visionary bell hooks wrote about this in her book *We Real Cool*, where she explored the difficulty some Black men have in loving and affirming themselves as a result of American patriarchy, and how this translates into their inability to love, support, believe, and protect Black women. Instead of loving Black women, these Black men have at times replicated the hatred of Black women that has been normalized on a national scale. Some of the ways such hatred can take form are seen in sexual harassment, sexual assault, and domestic abuse. As victims of oppression themselves, there are Black men who may be completely unaware of how patriarchy influences their actions, who feel robbed of the power they were told men should hold, and believe Black women are culpable for their disadvantages. They blame and punish Black women for keeping them from experiencing full manhood and, therefore, full humanity. Tricked into thinking that they are suffering as a result of not maintaining the "natural" gendered social order, they attempt to assert their humanity by abandoning Black women as their equals and by reproducing American patriarchy in their own ways through intimidation and violence. Regarding this, hooks writes:

> This blaming ignited the flames of a gender war so intense that it has practically consumed the historical memory of black males and females working together equally for liberation, creating love in family and community. It has practically destroyed beyond recognition the representation of an alternative black man seeking freedom for self and loved ones, a rebel black man eager to create and make his own destiny. This is the image of the black male that must be recovered, restored, so that it can stand as the example of revolutionary manhood.

Revolutionary manhood frees all men from the constraints of sexism and misogyny that have also victimized them for far too long, that have kept them from expressing vulnerability, that have left them unprotected and uncared for, and that refuse to let them acknowledge their individuality. It highlights the freedom in store for everyone who is willing to break from the power struggle of American patriarchy. For men of color, in particular, who will never enjoy the full supposed benefits of the system like their white counterparts do, because they were never meant to be included, revolutionary manhood is the only road to truly taking control of one's own destiny by creating something new. We see revolutionary manhood when men become aware of the reasons they might actively cause harm or the ways they ignore and passively allow it to grow and, with this realization, do their part to weaken patriarchy's grasp in all its forms. Revolutionary manhood consists of knowing that fulfillment for men does not rely on the suppression of others.

In addition to sexism and racism, another factor that contributed to the mistreatment Anita Hill experienced from Clarence Thomas, from the Judiciary Committee, and from the American public was a lack of acknowledgment, analysis, and language about sexual harassment and the power dynamics of identity that make it possible. Viruses that go unnamed, unstudied, and therefore undetected are allowed to fester and grow. They make it so that even the people being overcome by sickness cannot fully describe what they are experiencing; all they know is that something feels wrong. The person causing it feels justified by an environment that says it is natural, normal, and without need of being treated or challenged. In the end, only 29 percent of Americans believed Anita Hill after she testified, and many saw her act of courage as an unnecessary distraction at best and an attempted "lynching" of a Black man at worst. Millions of people were angry with her for speaking up at all, and they wanted her punished for it. In 1996, she left Oklahoma State after the university continued to receive calls for her resignation even years following the confirmation hearings.

There were many who attempted to keep Anita Hill in her place by castigating her. This theme of punishment and consequences sets the stage for the second part of this book. Building on the narrative of American patriarchy, we now examine the "rules" that are in place to systematize it and guarantee patriarchy's longevity by ensuring that those who challenge it will face punishment.

I ask: How is violence employed as a tool to maintain the fabrication of American patriarchy, especially when such violence is protected and even justified by our laws and lawmakers? Take the Supreme Court of the United States, which bears the closest resemblance to its original form of all the operations of the government's three branches. While the Declaration of Independence broke political ties between the colonies and Great Britain, and the Constitution outlined how a new government would function to serve the patriarchal purposes we have already examined, the Supreme Court was to be the primary guardian and interpreter of said Constitution. Therefore, to see how patriarchal punishment operates on a national level and how this trickles down into our daily interactions with one another, understanding the makeup of the Supreme Court becomes essential. The ideals of the founding fathers that we examined in part 1 are living on through the Supreme Court of 2025. Yet we should not be dismayed, because when we are able to trace that rope we will then be able to cut it. And each time someone brings our national attention to that connecting thread, like Anita Hill did, the unraveling of its strands is accelerated.

By the age of thirty-six, Anita Hill had left an indelible imprint on the world. Despite the ways in which others tried to silence her or remind her of her "place," her story does not end in defeat. Her words traveled on wind blowing at the base of a kindling fire, enough to build on what others had started before her, and to raise a louder alarm. Hill was able to continue teaching, now at Brandeis University; she has become a sought-after speaker all over the United States as well as abroad and has authored books and numerous articles about race and gender issues. Survivors of sexual harassment and other forms of sexual violence, watching Anita Hill stand for and with them, started to feel more able to stand too. Even women who looked completely different from Hill saw the power in what they shared with her. The definition of sexual harassment became clearer, charges against perpetrators increased, and women across the country felt called to enter the political arena after feeling enraged by the patriarchy on full display during Clarence Thomas's hearings.

In 1991, the year Anita Hill became a household name, there were only two female members of the United States Senate. But in 1992, women across the country, inspired to change the face of those in charge, ran for office and won. That year voters elected four women as senators and twenty-four women as representatives to Congress. In the tug-of-war, the side of justice gained more power. As a result, the year 1992 was deemed the "Year of the Woman," a name that signified that change was on the horizon and that a better nation was being formed, slowly but surely. Not only was I born that year, so was a young woman named Chanel Miller.

7

AND HEINOUS VIOLENCE

✦

She is wearing a red jumpsuit with a bow tied around her midline. Her hands are on her hips, evoking the statue of the little girl who stands facing the bull of Wall Street. Her metaphorical bull is a painful journey through our legal system as she is asked to recount an event that changed her life forever, one that shot her to fame and that she wishes she never had to experience. The photo is part of *Time* magazine's 100 Next List, where people of note recognize emerging leaders they have something in common with. This specific recognition comes from Christine Blasey Ford, a professor and psychologist who endured a harrowing experience similar to that of Anita Hill in 2018 when she testified that Supreme Court nominee Brett Kavanaugh had sexually assaulted her years before his confirmation hearing. Like Anita Hill, Ford was courageous enough to speak, with the entire world watching her, about what happened thirty-six years prior. Although Kavanaugh was still confirmed to the Supreme Court, to sit alongside Clarence Thomas, Ford added a megaphone to the rallying cry of survivors. She later used her platform to shine light on twenty-seven-year-old Chanel Miller when she wrote, "Chanel will make many more beautiful things. She will make the world a better place, and she will make all of us a bit better."

Before Chanel Miller became known by her name, she was re-ferred to as Emily Doe or "unconscious intoxicated woman" in a trial against Stanford University student-athlete Brock Turner. What began as a spontaneous decision to go out and have fun with her sister one night became a nationally known case that put the layers of American patriarchy on display once again. One moment, Miller was enjoying herself at a party just ten minutes from her home, drinking freely and dancing without a care in the world. The next, she was lying on a gurney. She could feel pine needles in her hair, her hands and elbows were bandaged, she couldn't find her underwear. Nurses were measuring various abrasions on her body. They swabbed her vagina and anus, they smeared her genitals with blue paint to find yet other abrasions, she was instructed to spread her legs so that a picture could be taken of her injuries, and she was asked to sign papers that referred to her as a "rape victim." She couldn't piece together what had happened to her; she didn't know where her sister was, or how she had traveled from the party to this facility. This was just the beginning of both the physical and emo-tional pain, as she not only tried to fill in blanks in her own memory but would later have to convince a jury of what she had suffered.

In the months after she woke up to that nightmare, she would discover the details of the heinous attack she had experienced. She would learn that while she lay unconscious, Brock Turner, a nineteen-year-old student and star swimmer, had pulled off her clothes, penetrated her with objects, and thrust himself against her behind a dumpster. She would find the courage to face her per-petrator and testify against him in court, reading a statement that rang in the ears of survivors and their allies everywhere: "You took away my worth, my privacy, my energy, my time, my safety, my intimacy, my confidence, my own voice, until today." She would also learn how such cycles of violence are allowed to persist when decision-makers not only seem to protect offenders, especially if they are white men, but also punish victims, especially when they are women of color.

The defense attorney, Eric Multhaup, questioned Miller about her drinking and her choice of outfit on the night of the attack. Brock Turner's father, Dan Turner, wrote a letter to encourage a shorter sentence for his son in which he stated that incarceration was a "steep price to pay for twenty minutes of action out of his twenty-plus years of life." And the judge presiding over the *People v. Turner* case, Aaron Persky, was more concerned about the severe impact punishment would have on the perpetrator's life than how a lack of justice being served might impact the survivor and all others who were following the story closely. Eric Multhaup, Dan Turner, Aaron Persky, and Brock Turner are four white men who believed their needs and desires outweighed those of Chanel Miller and people like her. Despite witness statements, clear medical evidence, a powerful survivor's testimony, and a guilty verdict, Brock Turner served only three months in prison for his crime when the possible maximum sentence for the detestable acts he committed was fourteen years.

While Chanel Miller's identity was concealed during the trial and sentencing, a few years later she bravely revealed her name, her face, and her story. She powerfully documented her experiences in her book, *Know My Name*, where she explains why she needed to reclaim her identity beyond Emily Doe. Her words had already traveled across the planet when her victim statement went viral, but no one knew who she was until she took the risk of stepping into the spotlight. Readers learned that she was a shy girl, a college graduate, a talented artist and writer; she loved her parents and her little sister; and she was Chinese American. The revelation that she was a woman of color made the insufficient sentencing of her attacker something that felt tragically familiar, adding yet another layer to the injustice.

Her story cannot be fully understood without considering the long history of violence against Asian women in the United States, specifically concerning stereotypes used to justify sexual violence against them. We have discussed how American patriarchy frames Black and Native American women as dirty, animallike, promiscuous, and separate from the virtues of white femininity. We have seen how such representations not only reduce these two vastly diverse groups of people into monoliths but also have been used to justify rampant abuse against them. However, the history of sexual oppression of Asian women in the United States is a little different. Historically, Asian women from varied ethnicities have been looped together and presented as hyperfeminized, sexualized, and fetishized, seen as docile subjects whose purpose is to serve and obey. It is not that they are seen with the same humanity as white women within American patriarchy, but more so as dolls and fantasy playthings, still without needs or minds of their own.

These dangerous representations date back to the nineteenth century, when white missionaries and military personnel traveled across Asia, mostly East Asia, and recorded their observations of different groups, often describing Asian women as submissive and exotic. Such observations then translated into views of Asian women as sexualized beings who carried the potential of corrupting white men. The Page Act, the first US immigration law based on race, was passed in 1875 to prohibit the importation of free laborers as well as women brought to the United States for "immoral purposes," and it was used primarily against Chinese women in the assumption that they lacked moral character.

Then in the twentieth century, as a result of American wars and military bases in China, Japan, the Philippines, Korea, and Vietnam, interactions rapidly increased between American soldiers and Asian women who served them as they cleaned or cooked on base or who were sex workers in surrounding communities. Soldiers either brought some of these women home with them as brides and/

or they grew accustomed to seeing Asian women as their sexual subjects. In both of these roles, Asian women were expected to be subservient, either as prostitutes or as obedient wives.

Women of Asian descent also confront pressures as a result of being seen as members of the "model minority" group. If they have achieved higher socioeconomic status and are perceived as assimilating well to the hegemony of our nation, they are then expected to refrain from causing any trouble or challenging the status quo. They are divided from members of their shared ethnic communities who are working class by messages that portray them as innately gifted, hardworking, polite, successful, and law-abiding. This discourages any potential collective action or cries for help when violence occurs. Scholar Shamita Das Dasgupta argues that there is stigma associated with sexual violence in South Asian communities in particular because of the model minority myth, which keeps women from seeking help when they experience violence as they try to protect their adherence to American patriarchy.

Violence against Asian women in the United States has taken extreme forms and has been further perpetuated by representations of Asian women in popular media as well as in pornography, where Asian women are disproportionately portrayed as subjects of rape; Asian female bondage is a grossly popular subgenre. For many, especially Asian female historians, activists, and scholars, Brock Turner's attack was yet another reminder of the dehumanizing lack of regard for Asian women's humanity, bodies, and autonomy. Asian women are often blamed for their own victimization when images of them as being innately passive, immoral, and subservient go unquestioned and unexamined.

Whether subconsciously or fully aware of their biases, the men who together hurt, questioned, and doubted Chanel Miller while protecting and caring for Brock Turner felt justified in their acts largely because she was Asian American. They carried with them beliefs about the role she was supposed to play and the rights Brock

Turner inherently possessed that she did not. Unfortunately, this brings many other criminal moments to mind.

A recent gut-wrenching example took place in March 2021 when Robert Aaron Long, a twenty-one-year-old white man, shot and killed eight people at three spas in Atlanta. Six of the victims were Asian women. Long told investigators that he killed them because he was a "sex addict" and the spas were a "temptation" for him that he wanted to "eliminate." Long blamed his victims for tempting him and igniting his desire to have sex with them. Instead of finding help for himself, he punished the people whom he saw as sexual objects. The disregard for these lives did not end there, but continued when the county police response to the tragedy reportedly minimized the atrocity and displayed a lack of understanding of the gendered and racial politics of the murders. Captain of the Cherokee County police department Jay Baker was reported as having spoken about the killings with shocking levity, alleging that the shooter was having "a really bad day" and that he had acted as a result of that. Baker also made statements about how the killing spree was not motivated by race but instead had more to do with the supposed sex addiction.

Follow-up reporting now suggests that Baker may have been only quoting the perpetrator himself rather than putting his own spin on the murder spree. Regardless, whether these opinions were Baker's or a repetition of Long's testimony, they display a misunderstanding of the ways in which gender and race are intertwined. This is unfortunately representative of many others' views, especially other white men in leadership roles, and continues to hold us all back from reducing sexual violence, one of the most dangerous and ruinous products of patriarchy. If we cannot grapple with the factors that perpetrators of sexual violence count on when they treat another human being as an object without agency, factors that include racism, classism, and other iterations of oppression, we will continue to fail to stop them. In the past chapter we discussed how sexual harassment can be viewed as a form of punishment often employed against women who threaten a man's sense of power, and we saw how senators at the time of Anita Hill's hearing, as well as the general public, further punished her by calling her a liar and invalidating her experiences by minimizing their severity. In the cases of Chanel Miller and the victims of Robert Aaron Long's killing spree, we now see how rape, sexual assault, and sexual violence are also forms of American patriarchal punishment and manipulation that aim to reify the desired status quo. The punishment is then legitimized by authorities, who stand on the side of the wrongdoers and make their actions seem acceptable while finding a way to deny the motivation of the act as well as its harm.

The Rape, Abuse & Incest National Network (RAINN) estimates that an American is sexually assaulted every sixty-eight seconds, and that every nine minutes that victim is a child. RAINN also states that 82 percent of juvenile victims are girls and 90 percent of adult victims of rape are women, and that nearly 60 percent of perpetrators of sexual violence are white men. These numbers are alarming, and when we consider the additional barriers to reporting that women of color face, including biases that others hold against them, the problem is likely much worse than what the data shows for these groups. Sexual violence has ripple effects that extend far beyond the act, including a higher likelihood of depression, drug usage, and suicide for survivors. Yet the damage has been allowed to persist because it is dependent on American patriarchy, and American patriarchy is dependent on it. This is why it matters who our lawmakers and upholders of law are, because they are the ones who decide who gets to have power over others and even who gets to have power over themselves and over their own bodies.

In 1991, Clarence Thomas was still given one of the most powerful positions in our nation despite his mistreatment of Anita Hill, largely because white men saw nothing wrong with him sexually harassing a Black woman. In 2018, he was joined by fellow perpetrator Brett Kavanaugh, despite powerful and detailed testimony by Christine Blasey Ford as well as another allegation against him from a woman named Deborah Ramirez. Despite her fear of the retaliation she might face after coming forward, Ford testified in front of the world about a night when she was of high-school age when Kavanaugh thrust himself against her, held her down, tried to take her clothes off, and covered her mouth to silence her screams. Ramirez confirmed Kavanaugh's sexually aggressive behavior with her own story of being assaulted by him at a party in college when he took off his pants and thrust his penis in her face, forcing her to touch it, without her consent, before she pushed him away. Yet, once again, Kavanaugh still became a primary guardian and interpreter of the Constitution with the power to shape our nation for the rest of his life. Someone who commits such acts holds clear beliefs about his superiority over women and his right to take from them whatever he wants, whenever he wants. This kind of person is invested in maintaining the hierarchy that is American patriarchy because it both feeds and fits his view of himself and others like him being more important and worthy of the highest place in the social order.

When the highest authorities of our nation hold such views of women, including the president who nominated Kavanaugh to begin with and bragged about grabbing women by the "pussy," it becomes clear how American patriarchy has persisted. It has not been a mistake to put perpetrators in positions of power; it has instead been done intentionally to keep things as they are. From the president, to Supreme Court justices, to judges, to police officers, to fathers, to boys in college and high school, to strangers walking around with guns, many men believe they are entitled to do what they please to women and that they are in fact obligated to enforce the social order whenever the opportunity arises. When women ignore men, when women refuse men, when women stand up and fight, and when women name the injustices they have experienced, they are often met with cruelty to remind them where they belong. Even women who are simply going about their days are subject to potential punishment for being "temptations" in a nation where a white man having a "bad day" is enough reason to take another's life, or a woman's choice of clothing is an invitation to attack her.

At times it may feel like we lose no matter what we do. But I am reminded of Audre Lorde's words in her essay "The Transformation of Silence into Language and Action" when she refers to her realization that as a Black woman she was never meant to survive in "the mouth of this dragon we call america," that most of us were not meant to survive. She writes, "The machine will try to grind you into dust anyway, whether or not we speak. We can sit in our corners mute forever . . . and we will still be no less afraid. . . . It is necessary to teach by living and speaking those truths which we believe and know beyond understanding. Because in this way alone we can survive." She continues by explaining that we are being taught to respect fear in order to stay put, rather than using that fear as motivation to create new realities through our words and actions. She also emphasizes the importance of bridging our differences with the aim of defeating the dragon, the machine, together. Yes, Kavanaugh was still appointed, but Ford's courage and the response she received from the nation pointed to a changing landscape. Most of the public believed she was telling the truth, and she turned her fear into words and action to unite with others, like she did when she shined a light on Chanel Miller.

In 2019, Miller read a poem at the women-honoring *Glamour* Awards, where she reminded her listeners of what we should and should not focus on when it comes to sexual violence:

I don't give a damn / What you were wearing / I don't give a damn how much you drank / I don't give a damn / If you danced with him earlier in the evening / If you texted him first / Or were the one to go back to his place.

She continued,

But I do / give a damn / How you're doing / I give a damn about you being okay / I give a damn if you're being blamed for the hurt you were handed / If you're being made to believe you're deserving of pain. . . . I will always, always give a damn about you / The way you gave a damn about me.

The first part of this poem refers to all the many reasons people find to punish women, to try to tell them that the victimization they experience is their own fault and that it is completely acceptable. But the second part presents our nation as it should be, a place where we care, where survivors are not punished, where we do not send women the message that they deserve pain, but instead that they are just as worthy of being okay, of having their needs and well-being considered and respected.

May her words continue to ring in our ears as a reminder of how we move forward. We must give a damn about the right things, we must see every instance of sexual violence as stemming from someone's desire to keep another in "their place," we must recognize that none of us are safe, we must transform our silence and fear into language and action, and we must change the faces of those in positions of authority who set the stage for the entire country. The dangers of being led by American patriarchs are present not only in public places, such as in our workplaces, on the street, or at parties, but tend to be even more ruinous within our own homes.

8

WE HAVE BEEN SUBJECTED
TO THEIR RULES

✴

I distinctly remember reading about Chanel Miller's story and being in awe of what one of my contemporaries was willing to do on behalf of our entire nation. Chanel was asking us all to shift our mindsets around the codes we were taught from a young age that put the onus on girls and women for any attack boys and men might subject them to. This shift is necessary not only when speaking about assaults on behalf of strangers; it is sadly even more relevant when discussing the closest of our relationships. In many families and in marriages to this day, women are often seen as needing instruction by men and unable to control their own decisions and lives.

American patriarchy tells women that they must rely on close relationships with men and follow the guidance of men, lest they be seen as rebels in need of punishment. Throughout history we have seen the lengths to which communities have gone to castigate women who did not fit into this accepted way of life. The most famous example of public castigation came in the form of witch trials, the Salem witch trials being the best documented. Women could be executed for following Satan if someone else said they did, and most of the victims of the trials were considered outcasts, largely because they were not in traditional relationships with men and/or because they were not seen as women to begin with. The women who were killed were usually poor, elderly, or widowed, and according to researcher Kali Nicole Gross, many of the women believed to be witches were Black. Their deaths were used to set an example that virtuous women of God should stay in line to avoid such fates and to solidify the message that women were more virtuous when they were in close relationships with men who could guide them and issue consequences as they saw fit.

Over time literal witch hunts became less popular as a way to keep women in "their place," and other tactics arose to chastise them were they to rebel against the made-up dictates imposed on their sex.

In the 1800s, a growing number of women who wanted to be independent and speak for themselves were sent to asylums. Since a woman was not supposed to possess the capability to think for herself and have her own ambitions, women who rejected their "natural" state of domesticity, caretaking, and servitude were viewed as insane. Fathers and husbands often had their daughters and wives institutionalized until they could conform to more feminine behavior. Some women were diagnosed with made-up disorders such as "uterine derangement" if they did not accept their roles and if they were seen as being overly emotional or distracted from their destiny of bearing children and caring for their husbands.

One woman, named Elizabeth Packard, was forced into an asylum by her husband in 1860 when she stood up to him. In 1864, she spoke about her experience publicly to advocate for all those she had met while institutionalized, as well as for women she did not know across the country who were also being denied freedom. The women she met in the overcrowded wards had ended up there for different reasons, some punished for simply reading novels, others for talking back to their husbands. They were experimented on with various treatments that included being put in straitjackets, made to ingest chloroform, and even subjected to a procedure known as a clitoridectomy, which consisted of cutting off a woman's clitoris.

To be released from such torture, a woman needed to submit to the comportment those who had brought her there desired from her.

Other men took matters into their own hands and, rather than having the women in their lives institutionalized, they punished them behind closed doors. For centuries, English colonial culture has given men the power to control women's lives, especially through familial relationships such as fathers dictating the lives of their daughters, husbands dictating the lives of their wives, and even brothers dictating the lives of their sisters. When these relationships turned violent and even lethal, there were no protections in place for young girls and women because there was nothing criminal about hurting a woman if it was done by someone who was in a role to protect and guide her.

Domestic violence, including verbal, physical, emotional, psychological, and sexual abuse, has been justified and ignored largely because of antiquated beliefs like those reflected in the following quote: "The husband cannot be guilty of a rape committed by himself upon his lawful wife, for by their mutual matrimonial consent and contract the wife hath given up herself in this kind unto her husband, which she cannot retract." These words were written by Sir Matthew Hale, an English judge and lawyer who lived in the 1600s. While he has long been gone, his sentiments about women and their lack of rights in close relationships with men still feel eerily current. In addition to his views concerning the impossibility of marital rape and his feelings that men should be wary of women who claimed they had been raped, he also accused women of witchcraft and sentenced them to death. Even more terrifying, his words were recently brought to our current discussions of womanhood by Supreme Court justice Samuel Alito, who spoke of Hale as a "great" and "eminent" source of inspiration. In his effort to treat women like objects without rights of their own, Justice Alito called upon Hale's words in order to argue against a woman's ability to choose what she would or would not do with her own body.

Once again we see how those in charge of our laws at the highest levels are playing the biggest role in attempts to keep women in "their place." It wasn't until 1871 that Alabama became the first state to make it illegal for a man to beat his wife, and not until 1920 that all then-existing states made it illegal. It may sound surprising that Alabama led the way on this feminist front, but it makes more sense when we consider that the case that made it illegal for husbands to beat their wives in 1871 concerned two emancipated slaves. This fact has caused some scholars to argue that it was not necessarily a feminist take to make "wife-beating" illegal initially, but instead that it had more to do with continuing state control of the Black family unit. Margo Mahan writes that "wife-beating laws that threatened to punish black men, in the midst of socio-legal norms that kept black women vulnerable to white male violence, helped to restore a southern way of life that simultaneously controlled the labor and degraded the status of black families." In a sense, it was another way to keep Black men from doing what white men had a right to do and to once again assert the superiority of white men over others. To this day, Black and Latino men receive harsher sentencing than white men do for all forms of violence across the country, including in cases of domestic violence, when instead we should see equal punishment for perpetrators across race lines.

Despite the fact that by 1920 it was illegal for men to abuse their wives, several decisions throughout the 1900s point to the inadequacy of changing the laws while applying them differently across each case in a way that actually maintains American patriarchy. For example, in 1966, beating as cruel and inhumane treatment became grounds for divorce in New York, but only if the plaintiff could establish a sufficient number of beatings had taken place, in effect saying that a few times was justified but that abusers should not get carried away. In the 1970s, married women who left their husbands due to battery were denied welfare based on the argument that they could have stayed and had access to their husband's salaries. It wasn't until 1990 that some state laws required judges to consider any history of spousal abuse before determining child custody or visitation rights. Up until 1976, all states deemed spousal rape to be legal, and it wasn't until 1993 that it was declared illegal across the country.

Even after these changes, victims of domestic and intimate partner violence have continued to be left unprotected. Many are too afraid to leave or seek help out of fear of experiencing even worse outcomes. Those who survive and do leave, despite barriers in their way, find that their claims are often not taken seriously or believed, the dismissal of their experience another mechanism of keeping them in place.

Again, the reason why abuse exists in the first place is a person trying to assert their power over another. In a patriarchal system, it is usually men who try to maintain their power over women, especially those in close contact with them such as their wives, daughters, and sisters. Domestic violence takes different forms and is allowed to continue in a nation where men believe they are entitled to control women, where men believe they are being robbed of their manliness if women speak for themselves or act with their own agency, where men for centuries were told there was no such thing as abusing their wives because wives were theirs to do whatever they pleased with. Women are not believed or taken seriously where men's words are taken as the truth and left unchallenged, especially by the powers that be. A harrowing example of the cycle of control and punishment women can face in their homes, then on a local level, then on a state level, then on a national level and back, comes in the Supreme Court case *Jessica Lenahan (Gonzales) v. United States*.

On June 22, 1999, Jessica Lenahan, a Latina and Native American woman from Pueblo, Colorado, was panicking. Her daughters had been kidnapped by their father and her estranged husband, Simon

Gonzales, who had verbally, physically, and sexually abused Jessica for years. Jessica had courageously separated from Simon and was able to get a restraining order against him that required him to stay at least a hundred yards away from her, her children, and their home. While the restraining order brought her temporary relief from anxiety, she quickly realized it was not enough to protect her and her children. Simon continued to harass them; he broke into the house, changed the locks, and stole her things. His reign of terror persisted despite the fact that she carried the restraining order with her at all times and called the police department to report the violations. Due to Simon's other run-ins with the law, including an incident involving road rage and another where he trespassed at a police station, a judge gave Jessica full custody of their children, allowing Simon only a few weekend visits.

Three weeks after this decision, however, Simon violated the restraining order once more and kidnapped their three daughters on a day that was outside his scheduled visitation. Despite Jessica calling the police immediately and telling them about the restraining order and her worry for her children's safety, she was told there was nothing they could do. She was instructed to wait until that night and told she could call again if her daughters still weren't back by then. At 8:30 p.m., Simon finally answered her calls and informed her he was at an amusement park with their daughters in Denver. When Jessica called the police with the information, they simply replied with, "At least you know the children are with their father."

This rude and dismissive statement points not only to the gendered disrespect Jessica was treated with but also to the discrimination she faced as a Latina woman. Jessica was coming up against sexism as well as stereotypes used to objectify Latina women, such as a belief that they have "too many" children and that their reproduction should be monitored and even controlled. In the horrific history of forced sterilizations in the United States, women of Latina origin have been targeted disproportionately. Cases are as recent as 2020, when Immigration and Customs Enforcement (ICE) doctors performed unnecessary and invasive gynecological procedures on women at a detention center in Georgia without their consent. A whistleblower alleged that ICE doctors went so far as to perform hysterectomies on these women. In another example, in 2013 it was discovered that doctors sterilized nearly 150 women, most of whom were Latina, without their consent while they were incarcerated in California prisons between 2006 and 2010. As a result of US economic and military policies that created instability and dependence on the United States in countries such as Mexico, Guatemala, and El Salvador, masses of people were forced out of their countries seeking better conditions up north. This influx of people led to the perpetuation of dehumanizing stereotypes that also include the "spicy Latina" and sexualized Latina maid tropes. In American patriarchy, Latina women from very different countries and backgrounds are looped into one group and are problematically represented as freeloaders who are meant to serve us, sexualized women who should stop having children, and foreigners who are unworthy of being protected, despite the fact that many Latinx people have lived on this land since before the US was founded.

By midnight, the girls still weren't home; they'd been gone all day. Jessica pleaded with police officers to do something to find them but they continued to ignore her. At 3:20 a.m., Simon showed up at the police station, shooting a gun he had purchased that same day. The police fired back, eventually killing Simon. When they examined his truck they found the bodies of Jessica's three slain daughters in the trunk.

In a statement Jessica made to the Inter-American Commission on Human Rights (IACHR) she said,

So why did the police ignore my calls for help? Was it because I was a woman? A victim of domestic violence? A Latina?

Because the police were just plain lazy? I continue to seek answers to these questions. . . .

Had I known that the police would do nothing to locate Rebecca, Katheryn, and Leslie or enforce my restraining order, I would have taken the situation into my own hands by looking for my children with my family and friends. I might have even bought a gun to protect us from Simon's terror. Perhaps if I had taken these measures, I would have averted this tragedy. But then I might be imprisoned right now.

Jessica sued the police in a case that went all the way to the Supreme Court, which in 2005 ruled that she had no due-process right to the enforcement of her restraining order. This shocking ruling came in a 7–2 vote. The only two judges who dissented from the majority and who stood in Jessica's favor were Ruth Bader Ginsburg and John Paul Stevens. The message the Supreme Court sent with its disappointing decision was that Jessica and her daughters were not owed any protections, that police are not obligated to shield survivors from their abusers, and that the immeasurable loss Jessica suffered was acceptable by their standards.

Jessica refused to give up. With help from the American Civil Liberties Union, she took her case to the IACHR, which, in a landmark decision, found that the United States violated the human rights of Jessica Lenahan and that the government, including the Supreme Court, was responsible for the violations against her and the deaths of her children.

Tragically, her story is representative of many victims of domestic abuse whose tormentors take the lives of their children as the ultimate punishment. In a disturbing report by Jerry Mitchell of the Mississippi Center for Investigative Reporting, thousands of similar cases were found across the nation, and these grew in number during the pandemic. Author, advocate, and survivor Kit Gruelle writes that if "men cannot destroy women through homicide they will destroy them through killing their kids." This punishment continues for the rest of their lives with each day that passes as they painfully try to live with the trauma of losing their children.

What are victims of domestic abuse to do when law enforcement does not protect them or believe the danger they describe finding themselves in? What should they do when they need to protect not only themselves but also their children? As Jessica Lenahan stated, had she known she wasn't going to get help from the police, she would have taken matters into her own hands, even with the awareness that she would likely face imprisonment. Sadly, she is correct in this assumption; we only need to look at the data surrounding women and incarceration in the United States to substantiate her feelings.

The United States incarcerates more people than any other country, and between 1980 and 2020, the number of incarcerated women in our nation grew by more than 475 percent. In 1980, it was estimated that 26,326 women were incarcerated, and by 2020, that number rose to a staggering 152,854. In 2017, more than a quarter of the women who were incarcerated had not yet had a trial, and 60 percent of the women in jail that year had not yet been convicted of any crime. Many were simply "stuck" there for being unable to afford their bail. Studies have found that the majority of women in prison in the United States are victims of domestic violence, and that their "criminal acts" were necessary for their survival. Many of them have acted in self-defense and then been subsequently punished for doing so.

The group Survived & Punished draws attention to such cases through their advocacy work and campaigns to have domestic violence survivors released from prison. Primarily working with women in New York, California, and Illinois, Survived & Punished demands the commutation of sentences of all criminalized survivors. On their site, they publish the stories of the women they advocate for, women like Betsy Ramos. Betsy has been behind bars for over twenty years for second-degree manslaughter.

She is now in her early sixties, is fighting cancer, and is HIV-positive. In 1998, Betsy was arrested when police officers came to her home with a warrant for her abusive boyfriend, Jose Serrano. Jose told her to tell them he wasn't there, which she did out of fear for her own safety. When officers entered her home using force and found Serrano, he resisted arrest. He grabbed one of the officers' guns and shot before the other officer shot him back. Jose Serrano and Officer Anthony Mosomillo both died that day, but it was Betsy who was charged with Mosomillo's death.

The commonality between witch hunts, the institutionalization of women against their will, the physical abuse of women at the hands of men who claim to love them, the killing of children as an additional means of control, the inaction of police officers, and the punishment of women who act in self-defense as a final desperate measure is the goal of keeping power in the hands of men and forcing their subjects to conform. Women might be deemed insane, they might lose the ones they hold most dear, they might be put behind bars, and/or they might lose their lives. Even scarier is the fact that these outcomes will be normalized by American patriarchy and all those who have been appointed to protect it by any means necessary, namely the Supreme Court.

In the history of our nation we have yet to witness an anti-patriarchal Supreme Court. We must understand this fact in order to no longer be caught off guard by their largely patriarchal decisions. Our current court, despite having the most diverse slate of judges in American history, is still majorly made up of American patriarchs who have shown repeatedly that they intend to keep the status quo. Regarding the current Roberts Court with its strong six-justice conservative majority, we have briefly discussed Clarence Thomas, Brett Kavanaugh, and Samuel Alito. In the following chapter we will discuss two others who, whether they would openly admit it or not, believe in maintaining American patriarchy no matter how dangerous it is for us all.

9

AND THEIR HATRED OF

◼

n 1981, shortly after President Ronald Reagan was inaugurated, Anne Gorsuch was appointed the administrator of the Environmental Protection Agency (EPA). This appointment was historic: It was the first time in United States history that a woman would run the agency. Hailing from Casper, Wyoming, one of seven children, she was accustomed to breaking gender barriers. Her career up until that point was filled with impressive accomplishments, including graduating from college at nineteen, then receiving her Juris Doctor degree at the age of twenty-two and becoming the youngest woman admitted to the Colorado bar at the time. In 1975, she was elected to the Colorado House of Representatives, where she was voted Outstanding Freshman Legislator. Although women's groups supported her candidacy, once she was elected, Anne Gorsuch made it one of her missions to end the Colorado State Commission on Women, and she also stood passionately in opposition to abortion rights. When President Reagan appointed her, she planned to take her talents and conservative leanings to a national level.

Only two years after she began in her new position, the EPA was in shambles. People were fired, dozens of political appointees resigned, and one deputy administrator was even sentenced to prison. Believing that states were better custodians of resources, Gorsuch slashed the EPA's budget by 22 percent, relaxed federal regulations on businesses, made it easier for corporations to use pesticides, and helped to reduce the number of cases filed against polluters. Many accused her of trying to dismantle the EPA, and she became the subject of critique by mainstream media platforms. A 1983 *Newsweek* article, "Ice Queen Under Fire," described Anne Gorsuch's tenure:

> Bad intentions alone are never enough: it takes incompetence and arrogance as well to seriously weaken in two years what it took a decade to build. Behind the public demeanor—the forceful intelligence even her enemies have come to respect, the "Ice Queen" [is] a two-term Colorado legislator with virtually no environmental experience at the head of one of the most sensitive agencies in the federal government.

In addition to reducing the budget and loosening restrictions, Anne Gorsuch was also cited for contempt when she refused to turn over documents to Congress concerning how the EPA mishandled a $1.6 billion Superfund waste. Gorsuch stated later that the White House instructed her to withhold the documents.

After a short tenure and in the midst of scandal, she was forced to resign. Although Gorsuch was once seen as a rising conservative star, her record had now been tarnished as the entire nation watched, and this was something her fifteen-year-old son was incredibly disappointed about. He wanted to become a lawyer like his mother and one day hold a national position like she had, but he would keep her experience and his chagrin over it in mind. "You should never have resigned," he told her. "Why are you quitting? You raised me not to be a quitter. Why are you a quitter?"

This son, Neil Gorsuch, went on to earn a bachelor's degree from Columbia University, his JD from Harvard University, and a PhD in law from the University of Oxford, where he was a Marshall scholar. Just like his mother, he was driven and a conservative, especially when it came to women's rights. In his career he would serve as a law clerk, a law professor, and a judge on the Tenth Circuit, where he would hear numerous cases in which he would establish a reputation for himself as standing in opposition to women's freedoms. In *Hobby Lobby v. Sebelius*, he and his colleagues ruled that a corporation could deny coverage of contraceptives to its female employees if it conflicted with its owners' religious beliefs. In *Strickland v. United Parcel Service*, he went against his colleagues and wrote a dissent against a woman who claimed workplace discrimination when she was held to higher performance standards than her male colleagues even when she exceeded them in sales. In *Weeks v. Kansas*, in which a woman alleged she was fired in retaliation for speaking up against gendered workplace discrimination, he denied her right to proceed with her claim, saying she had failed to cite relevant precedent, even though he was aware of such precedence.

In 2017, his hard work would be rewarded with the ultimate prize when President Donald Trump announced him as his pick for the next Supreme Court justice, who would fill the space left by Justice Antonin Scalia. Scalia advocated for originalism in our interpretation and application of the Constitution. He, like other American patriarchs, believed the Constitution was a fixed document that should be used and analyzed as the original founders intended. He was proudly antiprogressive: He voted against protecting equal pay; he thought Black students did not belong at elite schools; he wanted states to have the ability to outlaw gay sex, which he compared to bestiality; he wanted to overturn *Roe v. Wade*; and he believed that women were rightfully not protected by the Constitution. Trump promised his followers a nominee who would continue Scalia's legacy and he stayed true to his word with Neil Gorsuch. At the time, Gorsuch was the youngest nominee to the highest court in the United States in more than twenty-five years. This was intentional; Trump chose someone who would have the power to influence decades of decisions.

Then on September 18, 2020, a national tragedy opened up another opportunity for Donald Trump and his supporters. Only forty-six days before the presidential election that would see Joseph R. Biden temporarily replace a man who did everything in his power to hurt women by limiting access to reproductive healthcare, slashing funding to family planning programs, revoking protections against workplace harassment and sexual assault, stating that pregnancy is an "inconvenience" to employers who shouldn't have to pay women as much as their male counterparts, Justice Ruth Bader Ginsburg passed away after a long battle with pancreatic cancer. It was one thing for Trump to have control over a seat that had already been filled with a bigot. It was devastating for a space to be open that was previously filled by a woman who became a symbol of breaking gender barriers and fighting to dismantle sexism in the systems of our country, as she did in the *Jessica Lenahan (Gonzales) v. United States* case from our previous chapter.

In the 1970s, when Anne Gorsuch was fighting to take down the Colorado State Commission on Women, Ruth Bader Ginsburg was establishing the first law journal in the United States devoted to gender equality issues. A few years later she founded the ACLU's Women's Rights Project, and then wrote the first textbook on sex-discrimination law. She fought staunchly against sex discrimination and successfully argued six landmark cases before the US Supreme Court. From her earliest cases to those she saw as a Supreme Court justice, she advocated for reproductive healthcare, pregnancy benefits, and equal pay. Her stances were not only pro-women, they were also usually pro-immigrants, and pro-minorities in ways that are rare to find on the Supreme Court. For example, she challenged Trump's decision to overturn the Deferred Action for Childhood Arrivals (DACA) ruling, fought to protect voting rights for all groups, and stood for LGBTQ+ equality. In contrast to originalist judges, who want old laws to be immutable, Ruth Bader Ginsburg saw the Constitution as a "living document," meaning it could and should change with the times, hence the reason why amendments are possible. Due to her countless liberal rulings and the fierceness with which she argued for them, Ruth Bader Ginsburg became an icon, affectionately referred to as the "notorious RBG."

RBG was not perfect. When it came to women's rights, she was largely concerned with white feminist issues. By this I mean that she based many of her decisions on the notion of achieving equality between men and women without considering the fact that not all men and women are treated the same in our country. Some scholars refer to this as "sameness feminism," and show how the assumption of sameness among all women obscures and can even worsen the experiences of poor women, women of color, and queer women who have other layers of marginalization to overcome. Furthermore, RBG spoke about people of color derisively more than once, such as when she called Colin Kaepernick's national anthem protests "dumb" and "disrespectful." She also had a mixed record on tribal law and the rights of Indigenous people. In one case, *City of Sherrill v. Oneida Indian Nation of New York*, she delivered a blow to the Oneida Nation by saying that even though their land was taken from them illegally, there was nothing that could be done to honor their sovereignty over it because too much time had passed. She concluded that they were required to pay taxes to the city. These are all valid criticisms of her record, and we can still acknowledge that she was one of the most effective antipatriarchal advocates in all of American history. She served on the court for twenty-seven years.

When Ruth Bader Ginsburg died, Donald Trump moved quickly, throwing decorum out the window as he often does. Only three days after the legend herself passed away, he offered someone else her seat. Amy Coney Barrett was also a woman, but she had more in common with Anne and Neil Gorsuch, greatly differing from Ruth Bader Ginsburg, largely because of her religious views and the church she had been a member of since she was a little girl: the congregation People of Praise.

People of Praise was founded in South Bend, Indiana, in 1971, by Kevin Ranaghan. On their website they describe themselves as "a charismatic Christian community," saying, "we admire the first Christians who were led by the Holy Spirit to form a community. Those early believers put their lives and their possessions in common." When Amy Coney Barrett's name rose in notoriety as Donald Trump rushed to fit into forty-three days a nomination process that, on average, takes about three months, People of Praise came under national attention and scrutiny. Although Barrett never mentioned her affiliation with the Christian community publicly, and although People of Praise moved swiftly to erase any online record of her ties to the group, journalists were able to find extensive evidence of her questionable relationship to the community and its founder. In their investigations, records of controversies and scandals with People of Praise also emerged.

While it would be unfair to say that the following characterizes all members of People of Praise, it is crucial to know that some previous members have stated that the group allowed for the abuse of women by their husbands. Others state that Kevin and his wife, Dorothy Ranaghan, created a sexualized atmosphere in their home where they housed dozens of people throughout the years and performed strange acts in front of their children and other adults such as Dorothy rocking on top of Kevin in their TV room. Another former member of the community stated that Kevin Ranaghan had full control over her finances and that she was asked to hand over her paycheck to him so he could decide how it would be spent. Amy Coney Barrett and her mother both served as "Handmaids" in the community, a title that the community states signified female leaders, although all the official positions of leadership are filled by men. In 2021, four people who say they endured sexual and physical abuse while they were members of People of Praise published an open letter calling for reforms within the faith group.

It is easy to see why Amy Coney Barrett might try to hide her affiliations to People of Praise, especially reports that state she lived with the Ranaghans for two years while she attended law school. Aside from Barrett's unusual relationship with her faith group, her record as a law professor and her rulings on the Seventh Circuit Court of Appeals are even more concerning. In multiple cases she ruled in favor of perpetrators of violence rather than victims, and she showed little care for Black people, gay people, transgender people, immigrants, and the poor. In 2006, she also signed an ad that urged the overturning of what she called the "barbaric legacy" of *Roe v. Wade*. These are the stances that made her Donald Trump's first choice as he left a legacy of tilting the Supreme Court of the United States even more heavily toward the right. His hope was that Barrett would be just as reliable a conservative, right-leaning vote as Ruth Bader Ginsburg was for the left. Nearly a week before Election Day and only thirty days after she was nominated, Amy Coney Barrett took her constitutional oath at the age of forty-eight, administered by Justice Clarence Thomas.

In summary, the Supreme Court of our nation has been intentionally stacked with protectors of American patriarchy. This is not a hidden fact but one that they and those who appointed them proudly flaunt and stand by. Clarence Thomas, Samuel Alito, Brett Kavanaugh, Neil Gorsuch, and Amy Coney Barrett are intent on keeping us all in "our place"; therefore, their rulings should not come as a surprise to any of us. They remind us that although it was white men who wrote the Constitution to establish an American patriarchy, it is not only white men who have become its protectors. We have briefly discussed through our exploration of

Clarence Thomas how Black men at times try to align themselves with white men to reap what they see as the benefits of American patriarchy, but there is no one who has aligned themselves more with white male supremacy than white women. This does not apply to all white women, by any means, but we will never dismantle patriarchy in our nation without challenging the white women who are contributing not only to their own oppression but to maintaining a specific order for us all.

Professor of history at UC Berkeley Stephanie Jones-Rogers writes that white women can be called "co-architects of the system," from the times of slavery to today. Jones-Rogers studies the system of slavery, which, as we have discussed, is inextricably intertwined with American patriarchy. A glaring example of the "co-architect" identity being one many white women are proud to hold came on January 6, 2021, when the US Capitol was attacked by a mob of Donald Trump's supporters who believed that he had been robbed of the presidency in the 2020 election. Many women were present at the riots, wearing their MAGA hats, and many more cheered on the insurrectionists from back home. Images of these women reminded me of pictures from the early 1900s of white women proudly wearing their Ku Klux Klan uniforms. The fact that there is a problem with white women becomes even more obvious and troubling when we look at voting data. Even though the GOP has been warned that they will alienate women if they continue to assault our health and reproductive freedoms, if they remain hostile to care policies that include paid leave and childcare, and if they continue to bolster candidates with histories of committing sexual harassment and assault, white women have largely remained steadfastly committed to Republican policies and candidates. When the rest of us witness this, it becomes clear that many white women are more motivated to align with their race, and the potential for them to hold power over others through upholding white supremacy, rather than aligning with their best interests when it comes to health, safety, and agency.

It also appears that many white women fear what might happen to them if they stand in opposition to the men in their lives, especially when it comes to politics.

Although Trump was temporarily voted out of office in November 2020, he had accomplished what he promised, especially in relation to the Supreme Court, the final authority on every legal decision in the United States. Donald Trump appointed the most Supreme Court justices since the president we began this chapter with, Ronald Reagan, leaving his first presidency with three of the youngest, most antifeminist, and most conservative originalists he could find. All three believe that the Constitution should be applied in the way the founding fathers intended, to protect white men, their power, and their views of the world above all. This is the court Donald Trump has happily returned to after winning reelection. It is also the court he will try to strengthen further by replacing already conservative judges with younger ones. The message for everyone else is loud and clear: Stay in "your place" or face the consequences. The highest court of the land will enforce the order the majority of them believe in.

In this chapter, we have seen how women like Amy Coney Barrett unapologetically do their part to protect American patriarchy, and we also have seen how they pass their commitment to the cause on to their children, as in the case of Anne and Neil Gorsuch. In his book *A Republic, If You Can Keep It*, Neil Gorsuch, discussing the role of judges in maintaining our constitutional order, explains why originalism is the way we should interpret our founding documents. In it you can find the opening statement he gave at his confirmation hearing, where he declared, "There's no question on whose shoulders I stand," thanking his mother for exposing him to her line of work.

10

OUR CONTINUED RESISTANCE

◆

I started part 2 of this book with Anita Hill, showing how her life impacted my own even before I realized it. I believe it is possible she knew her testimony would not keep Clarence Thomas from being confirmed, but that she hoped it might do something larger: It might serve as a signal, among others, of the immense need for change regarding sexism in our country; it might bring more attention to our nation's leaders, as nine out of ten Americans tuned into the hearings, and watched carefully as Thomas was confirmed; it might lead to ripple effects that encouraged others to join her in the fight; it might make it so that little girls born in 1992, the Year of the Woman, would receive more protections than Hill was afforded; and perhaps, one day, they would also do what they could to challenge the system that Hill came up against.

It would be years later that I recognized the connections between my passions and Anita Hill, partly because I spent much of my life abroad. Shortly after I was born, my parents accepted jobs outside the US, which would take us on a nomadic journey for the following decade. We traveled to Dubai, Sweden, Estonia, Mexico, and Azerbaijan before returning, and in each place I observed different people, different beliefs, different systems of government, different organizations of society, and different ways to keep such organizations in place. As a child I wanted to fit in and be as much like the other kids I met as I could be, so in each place I learned to study the guidelines, to adjust to my environment, and to figure out the rules. In each place I became a student of the status quo. Over time I became more aware of what I was doing, and the practice fascinated me.

My understanding of the United States, my home country, was complicated. Depending on where we lived, I heard different interpretations of our culture and our democracy. Some thought the US was progressive, others saw it as backward and hypocritical, and my parents approached it with both pride and critique. It was not until I returned as a teenager that I was able to apply my skills to observing our nation and begin to learn where I fit in as a Black girl.

The year that I moved back to the United States was the same year that the movie *Mean Girls* was released. I remember watching it and feeling amused by the way it communicated how teenage girls acted and the way it presented how an American high school was organized. There was a hierarchy in place where white girls competed for the attention of white boys, and people of color and nonbinary people were stereotypically categorized. *Mean Girls* was just one of many ways I started to learn about the social order of the United States. Reproducing the social order through the stories we share is the first part of maintaining patriarchy, as we examined in part 1. The other part relies on keeping people in "their place" through rules and reminding them through words and actions of where the power lies.

Part 2 of this book has focused on this notion of keeping us all in "our place." I became aware of these strategies both small and large when I was a teenager, because young girls in the US are taught to do what we can to avoid such reminders of our supposed inferiority. For example, we are told how to dress appropriately or to have a male with us if we want to feel safe. These are small ways of explaining to us that it is our responsibility to follow codes of conduct in order to avoid consequences. We hear the message that if something happens to us, it is either the standard or our fault, because our victimization is normalized by American patriarchy. When a man catcalls a woman walking down the street it is an assertion of his power, whether he realizes that consciously or not; he is reminding the person he is yelling at that they are in a weaker position than him. When someone sexually harasses another person, it is also an assertion of power. The same goes for sexual violence outside and within our homes, and for other forms of domestic violence. The reason such horrible things exist, and overwhelmingly affect women and girls, is the imbalance of power that American patriarchy feeds upon for sustenance and simultaneously force-feeds us through the messages we hear from a young age. These types of incidents and attacks on our personhood are not separate from one another; instead, they are individual instances of the same overarching issue.

Beyond reminding people of "their place," believers in American patriarchy sustain the system by punishing anyone who tries to speak up against such reminders. Even if the person in charge of the punishment isn't directly involved in the initial transgression, they defend those who they feel are in alignment with the system that they would like to maintain. We see this in the friends who stand by those trying to assert their power, in family members who condone the imbalance of power within our family systems, and in law-enforcement authorities who do not believe or protect those who come forward in their pursuit of justice. Even worse, we have seen countless examples of law-enforcement officers further magnifying the violence.

It is not a conspiracy theory but a fact that several groups have been targeted by police violence and mass incarceration throughout American history in order to maintain American patriarchy. The practice of policing came to the United States from England, originally associated with the monarchy and keeping the king's orders. The US is technically antimonarchical, but as Thomas Paine once wrote, here "the law is king." The law is what tells us who has rights, who is protected as well as who is excluded; police officers are in charge of enforcing such dictates of inclusion and exclusion.

During times of slavery, officers were mostly occupied with making sure enslaved people were aware that they were not protected under the law, that they were meant to be wholly controlled by it. Some scholars have stated that modern policing began in 1838, and before this time those in charge of policing were better known as slave patrollers. The shift to what is considered more modern policing came as a result of having more groups to control: A rise in immigration during the Industrial Revolution meant policing of foreigners and the need to keep them from voting or becoming citizens; a rise in prostitution meant policing of "promiscuous" and "deviant" women who were viewed as trying to corrupt the traditional family unit, and less about policing the men who sought them; a rise in robberies meant policing of workers and the poor rather than providing assistance or balancing of resources. As time went on, law enforcement in the United States became decentralized, falling under local control, and, unlike their counterparts in other countries, American police officers were allowed and encouraged to carry their own guns. Even in places that did not have formal police, white men brandishing weapons became vigilantes who also targeted Indigenous people and Mexican people, in the example of the Texas Rangers, and California vigilantes lynched Chinese immigrants.

The police became more of a military unit in the early 1900s when August Vollmer, the chief of police in Berkeley, argued that police officers were in charge of "conducting a war, a war against the enemies of society." Vollmer is now known as the father of modern policing in the United States, credited with training officers to be experts in conquest and occupation of the "enemies" living on

American soil who did not align with American ideals and ways of living. Black people were enemies, nonbinary people were enemies, immigrants were enemies, poor people were enemies, workers striving for their rights were enemies; the list goes on. Vollmer was a proud member of the American Eugenics Society, which strongly believed certain humans were superior to others. He also believed that "undesirables" and people with disabilities should be prohibited from reproducing. He once wrote, "Why not make an effort to prevent such defectives from reproducing their kind? Preventing the socially unfit from multiplying [is] . . . vital to national welfare and would greatly reduce crime statistics." We will discuss the politics of reproduction more in part 3.

Even more terrifying than police officers upholding American patriarchy is the role the highest court of our nation plays in protecting it. Many have felt increasingly surprised by the things our Supreme Court has voted for, but I believe this surprise has come as a result of most people not understanding how the Supreme Court works or how patriarchal our Supreme Court currently is. I did not pay much attention to our Supreme Court justices until recent years, myself, which can be seen in my lack of awareness of them when I was in high school. A few years after my family returned to the United States, my parents decided they wanted to travel abroad again, and they sent me to boarding school. They found a small school in Indiana because my siblings were there for college and my parents wanted me to be close to family. One of the first interesting facts I was told when I got to the school was that Chief Justice John Roberts was an alumnus. While that sounded cool, I had no idea what that meant or who he was. I definitely did not know how differently he and I saw the world. I didn't know that the chief justice was the one who presided over the court and supervised the process of selecting the cases the court would hear; I didn't even know that the court decided which cases they would hear at all and which ones they would completely ignore. The chief justice supervises public sessions and hearings as well as private discussions of the cases, and this all-powerful role is a lifetime appointment.

I did not know all this in high school, but I grew to learn how influential Chief Justice John Roberts is and how he and his colleagues are at the helm of maintaining the organization of our country. While he has earned a reputation for surprising us from time to time, siding with liberal judges as when he preserved DACA in 2020, Roberts is one of the six Republican appointees on the court. Ever since Donald Trump flipped RBG's seat, Roberts now helps almost to guarantee that issues challenging American patriarchy, i.e., those that attempt to change power imbalances in our nation, will lose. This became clear when the six conservative justices ruled that affirmative action in college and university admissions violated constitutional equal protection but did not challenge legacy admissions. It also became clear when they ruled that civil rights laws must sometimes give way to religious objections when the owner of a wedding website did not want to celebrate the marriage of a same-sex couple. There are many more decisions I could name, but the one this court will be most remembered for is its overturning of *Roe v. Wade*.

On June 24, 2022, the country woke up to the news that a woman's right to an abortion was no longer protected. Within a year of that decision, 22 million women of reproductive age found themselves living in states where abortion was completely unavailable or severely restricted. The overturning of *Roe v. Wade* and the many state decisions that followed shocked people. Across the nation Americans wondered how it was possible that the highest court of our land, and governors across the country, did not believe in a woman's agency or her right to make decisions concerning her own body. But I hope that after reading part 2 you feel the same way I do: Absolutely nothing was surprising about this decision to overturn *Roe v. Wade* in 2022 when we look at the makeup of the justices. They did what they said they would. This plan was never covert, but one that was actually spoken about openly and followed accordingly. The shock and awe surrounding the leak, and the fulfillment of overturning the legality of a person's decision to have an abortion on a national level, makes it clear that many of us need a lesson on the system we are actively participating in, either by voting for Donald Trump and those like him, by not paying attention to the decisions of leaders even before they are elected and appointed, or by being oblivious to the connections between all the many iterations of punishment for those who do not follow the script of American patriarchy.

I might not have understood the power of the Supreme Court when I was in high school, but I do remember the constant debate surrounding women's rights, particularly concerning sexual assault and abortion, once I went to college. Stanford is a liberal campus where concepts like consent are spoken about often, but my female peers and I were aware of social dictates that told us it would still be our fault if something happened to us, like what happened to Chanel Miller. We knew that if we found ourselves in situations we did not want to be in, we would be told it was because we had dressed a certain way, or we had too much to drink, or we were being flirty, or we had simply made the wrong decision. In this way we were still conscious of our value compared to our male peers, and we knew differences in treatment existed across race. We were also aware of a national tug-of-war concerning our rights to bodily autonomy. In 2010, when I was in my first year of college, state houses across the United States turned red. That year, the GOP filled 680 seats in state legislatures across the country. Several scholars say that was the year that *Roe v. Wade* started to fall. Although the recession of 2008 had ended, Americans were still hurting, and Republican candidates presented themselves as alternatives to the Democrats who controlled the White House. With more Republicans elected, attempts to restrict abortion grew. Some state leaders went even further, saying they would reward people who helped to enforce limits on abortion, giving everyone further permission and motivation to police and punish women.

While access to abortion is not solely a women's issue, the fight over it is indeed about controlling women. Taking away our right to make choices concerning our own bodies is the apex of making us know that we do not exist for ourselves and that we hold no power. In the context of keeping us in "our place" and punishing us if we stand up, being forced to carry through pregnancies no matter the circumstances that led to them, no matter the viability of the fetus, no matter the risk a woman might face if she is to carry a child to term, is undeniably related to everything we have discussed in part 2. For the sake of clarity, I repeat: The founding fathers believed women should be controlled, surveilled, and reminded of the need to submit to the men in their lives in order to fulfill their purpose of being sexual subjects and/or birthing children to continue the legacy of the great men they were attached to. Forcing women to have children is perhaps the ultimate goal of a patriarchal system. It does not matter if she is raped, a victim of domestic violence, or too young, and it definitely does not matter if she has other priorities in her life, if she changed her mind, made a mistake, or even if her own life is at risk. To a believer in patriarchy, she is not the one who gets to make the decision.

While *Roe v. Wade* was a win for women's rights in the United States, one that was tragic for us to then lose in 2022 through *Dobbs*, it was also insufficient when it comes to all our reproductive needs, especially with the ways these needs differ across groups. In our country's history we have seen countless examples of people in power trying to force women to have children, but we have also seen people in power trying to restrict other women from having children at all. Any form of reproductive injustice is a way to maintain the hierarchy that American patriarchy relies on. Women who are seen as women are encouraged and forced to reproduce, while women who have historically been viewed as existing outside American patriarchy's definition of womanhood, especially once our laws changed to treat them as human beings rather than property, have met barriers to their reproduction. These barriers have included forced sterilization as well as a lack of access to nondiscriminatory healthcare and more.

Kathryn Kolbert, the attorney who argued the landmark Supreme Court case *Planned Parenthood v. Casey*, in which *Roe v. Wade* was reaffirmed in 1992, again, the year I was born, says we must demand more from our nation beyond our right to access abortions. A change in our system would also mean universal early childhood education for every child and universal paid parental leave; it would address the maternal health crisis and the systemic racism in our healthcare systems; it would allow for more research and intervention to be available for infertility and understudied illnesses like endometriosis; all people would have access to healthcare at all stages of our lives; contraceptives would be available over the counter; students in every school across the country would have access to quality sex education; abortion would be affordable and available in every state without bans or barriers; and the abortion pill would be easily accessible. Kolbert argues for our need to pass a gender-equity constitutional amendment "that would guarantee to all persons the ability to make decisions not just about abortions, but about pregnancy, and marriage, and sexuality, and parenting," that would permanently alter the United States Constitution. Kolbert believes that this kind of monumental change is possible if we can remember that "coalition is queen," and that we can unify our fights to not only address the inequalities of sexism but also to address the added attacks on women's, children's, and all human rights when we also consider layers of racism, homophobia, genderism, and more. The lack of each of these changes that Kolbert and others have highlighted contributes to keeping our current power imbalance in place. Again, they are all connected, and we must remember this as we fight to restore our access to abortion. *Roe* was just the floor, and it did not serve all our reproductive needs.

In part 2 we have come to see that American patriarchy, with the punishments it hands out to those in opposition to it, has tried to keep us from experiencing justice, fairness, and security, but through our collaboration and recognition of each other we have and can continue to push back. I came to better understand how our country operates as I moved through college and pursued my graduate degrees. But the experiences that taught me the most about the organization and hierarchy of our nation came in my interactions with children, first when I was a teacher and college counselor, and later when I became a mother myself. One of the darkest ironies at play in American patriarchy is the fact that we live in a country that removes women's autonomy over their bodies and forces them into motherhood, yet does very little to support or celebrate mothers. I could see this in the ways the parents of my students struggled to provide for their kids at times without resources like guaranteed paid leave. I could also see how mothers were desperately trying to balance their jobs and their parenting without resources that I knew existed in other places where I've lived. For example, in Sweden children can attend preschool from the age of one, and parents can take leave to care for a sick child, but in the United States it seems that women are overwhelmingly expected to carry their needs and their children's needs with virtually zero support built into the fabric of our nation and its systems.

When I started writing my first book on motherhood as I was becoming a mother myself, it became painfully obvious to me that experiences of motherhood in the United States are controlled by American patriarchy at almost every turn. American patriarchy is set on trying to rob mothers of their power, and this begins long before a woman might conceive. I am certain that our reproduction is controlled because it is the starkest reminder of what we are capable of: a metamorphosis of ourselves and our nation, the creation of something new.

Part 3

OUR
CAPABILITIES
AND
STRENGTH

11

THEY HAVE TAKEN OUR POTENTIAL

■

I am a mother of three children, whom I birthed within four years of one another. I nursed my firstborn for fifteen months and by the time he was weaned, my daughter was due seven months later. She nursed for twenty months, and by the time she was weaned, my last born was due just a few months after that. I have been pregnant or nursing or both, without any breaks, since January 2019.

I tell you this just to emphasize my hyperawareness of what one body can do, and to explain how motherhood made me even more aware of my capacity and power than I ever was before. The power of my physical body, in constant metamorphosis for more than half a decade, is surpassed only by the knowledge I have gained of my capacity to expand my heart and mind to not only do everything I did before other human beings fully depended on me but also to keep these children alive and thriving. I view myself as an unstoppable force who deserves unending appreciation and respect for all I do and give on a daily basis. This view is what allows me to be the best version of me that I can be; it allows my children to have a mother who is whole, who takes care of herself so she can take care of them, who gives herself grace so she can extend that same grace to them as well, who feels confident in her intuition and supports them in listening to theirs. I wish this was the norm in our nation, but these feelings stand in direct opposition to what American patriarchy wants women, especially mothers, and especially Black mothers, to have about themselves.

Thus far we have discussed how American patriarchy at its core is simply a story written in the 1700s that says there are two recognized groups of people in our nation: white men and white women. It tells us that white men carry more value than white women, and that everyone else is a part of another category. Members of this supposed "other" category face varying forms of dehumanization, objectification, and animalization in order to sustain the status quo of American patriarchy. Even white men and women can lose the protections the system provides them if they act in ways seen as contrary to their group, and members of the "other" category can at times enjoy certain privileges if they try their best to assimilate to the hegemony and do their part to maintain the social order. We have reviewed how American patriarchy and those who believe in maintaining it rely on keeping everyone in their ordained place through reminders of power imbalances and punishments for those who object to them. Now we move to the subject that perhaps American patriarchy fears most because it challenges everything American patriarchs want us to believe. Seen as holding the most potential to tear the system down is women's ability to carry children, because in and of itself it challenges the entire premise of men being more capable than women.

Adrienne Rich, a mother, lesbian, poet, and essayist, summarized this poignantly in her book *Of Woman Born: Motherhood as Experience and Institution*:

The one unifying, incontrovertible experience shared by all women and men is that months-long period we spent unfolding inside a woman's body. . . . We carry the imprint of this experience for life, even into our dying. . . . The makers and sayers of culture, the namers, have been the sons of mothers. There is much to suggest that the male mind has always been haunted by the force of the idea of *dependence on a woman for life itself*, the son's constant effort to assimilate, compensate for, or deny the fact that he is "of woman born."

Rich dives into a profound exploration of womanhood and patriarchy stemming from her own experiences with motherhood in the United States. She distinguishes between "the potential relationship of any woman to her powers of reproduction and to children, and the *institution*, which aims at ensuring that that potential—and all women—shall remain under male control." This book was one of the first scholarly explorations of the experience of motherhood, and of what motherhood symbolized for all humanity and the organization of our society in particular. Rich made the claim that patriarchy came as a result of men grappling with the knowledge that women have the potential to do something they will never be able to do, that they themselves could not exist without women, and they have formed an institution with this in mind: an institution that tries to deny, at every turn, the power of women, and that seeks to control it entirely and by any means necessary. Even for a person who is born female and does not identify as a woman, and even for women who have no interest in having children or who experience infertility, our potential relationship to carrying children always symbolizes a lack in cisgender men. Therefore, while I largely discuss how this weaponization of our biology has impacted girls and women who might become mothers, it is important to note clearly that not all people with the ability to have children identify as girls and women, and not all women are able to, nor do they desire to, have children.

American patriarchy takes women's power, ability, and potential and strategically makes them our weakness as well as the things that leave us most vulnerable. It is for this reason that girls and women are taught to hide any evidence of their undeniable strength, beginning with our period. Every girl in the United States is taught from a young age how to hide the fact that she is, or will someday be, a menstruating human. Even before a girl arrives at puberty she already knows to be secretive about it, to not speak openly about it; many girls are taught to fear it, and they dread the day it will begin. Confused by what menstruation is, because girls are rarely taught about their bodies in affirming ways, they meet their periods with embarrassment and shame. While this view of periods being unclean and impure is present across the world, there are several cultures that celebrate a girl's first period with ceremonies honoring the meaning and strength of the menstrual cycle. In the Americas many Indigenous people are trying to return to the traditional treatment of periods that they practiced before their violent encounters with white settlers. But sadly, the US as a whole presents menstruation as a bad thing and teaches girls that it is something negative.

In my own experience, even though my mother and older sister told me I could talk to them about anything concerning changes like getting my period, I still felt nervous about approaching them, largely because I heard messages outside my home of it being something grotesque and me needing to hide it. We've been sold products sprayed with harmful chemicals to mask the "smell"; the emotions we confront during our cycle have been used to further the message that we are in need of control and incapable of leading; and although recent research has shown there are many benefits associated with periods, the focus on them has overwhelmingly been a negative one. This has all developed over centuries of excluding from activities and gatherings women who were menstruating, keeping them from positions of leadership, and even sending them to asylums to treat their "unpredictable" emotional reactions. Much of the stigma surrounding menstruation has come as a result of "medical experts" professing beliefs that periods made women weak, as well as them ignoring women in their studies, which keeps us from understanding women's bodies or trying to find ways to make the experiences of women easier.

Periods have also been used to further sustain the hierarchy of American patriarchy, especially by creating another barrier for people living in poverty and for people who have been imprisoned, for example. Period products are not free in our nation; they are not available in public restrooms like toilet paper. Instead they are treated as luxury items despite the fact that every menstruating person needs them in order to participate in society. According to the ACLU, American teenagers who live in poverty are often unable to attend school when they menstruate because they do not have access to pads and tampons; people who are homeless are prone to infections because they are forced to improvise with things like paper towels, or they use pads and tampons for longer than the recommended time. Women who are incarcerated have to beg and bargain for access to menstrual products. In a horrifying example, a Department of Justice investigator found that correctional officers at a prison in Alabama withheld necessary menstrual items to coerce prisoners to have sex with them. Remember, American patriarchy is concerned not only with keeping power in the hands of men, it is also invested in maintaining other forms of discrimination beyond sexism. In this case, the classism of American patriarchy becomes painfully obvious by displaying that in order to participate in our nation you must have the money, and that basic necessities like menstrual pads are not going to be provided.

This control over the power of a woman's body extends far beyond period-shaming and using periods as a way to exclude certain groups to maintain the larger structure. Another example of how women are taught to hide something they might be able to do that men cannot is the control of breastfeeding. The ever-changing sentiments around breastfeeding throughout American history alone are difficult to keep track of, but they show how popular

opinion shifts around natural processes in order to serve the dominant group and divide others from it. In the early 1900s, people in
the United States began considering breastfeeding as "low-class"
and even hypersexual, as especially inappropriate for high-class
white women. Women who were seen nursing in public would be
shamed and could even be arrested for committing a crime. The
first law that exempted breastfeeding from public indecency of-
fenses was passed in New York in 1984, but it wasn't until 2018
that a woman's right to breastfeed in public was protected by law
in all fifty states, and although it is now a protected right, it doesn't
always keep safe women who choose to nurse their children. In
2006, a mother by the name of Emily Gillette was escorted off a
Delta Airlines plane when she refused to cover up her breast while
nursing her daughter. She was sitting discreetly by the window
next to her husband when a flight attendant offered her a blanket
as a cover but when Gillette turned down the offer, she was forced
to get off the flight. Many women still report being harassed when
they breastfeed their children in public, either by people who believe it is not appropriate or by others who see it as an invitation
to talk about a woman's exposed body. Both of these reactions are
indicative of the need to exert control over a woman's agency and
ability, and follow historic patterns of seeing breastfeeding as inappropriate or sexual.

Breastfeeding also presents an example of something others have
used to not only control women but to divide us from one another.
In the question of how parents might choose to feed their newborn
children, a slew of controversies have arisen over the years where
all parents but especially moms, by virtue of them being primary
caretakers, feel like they are judged no matter what. After World
War II, views of breastfeeding started to change slightly: It became
the more educated and high-class thing to do in order to encourage
women to return home to their children and abandon pursuits of
work outside the home. Now, it was less privileged women who

did not have the luxury of staying with their children who would face commentary regarding their inability to mother well. Despite it being encouraged among women of privilege, breastfeeding in public was still frowned upon, however. Therefore, mothers who nurse are often judged for doing so in the open, while also being told they should nurse for two years without support in place to do so. Others tell them they are nursing their children for too long if they want to continue nursing past one year.

Mothers who do not nurse hear constant messages that they too are doing something wrong by not offering their children the healthiest option; they are judged when they cannot produce enough milk, and/or they feel there is something wrong with their bodies. These mixed messages around lactation, an ability unique to the female body, are intentional and are meant to make women feel they cannot win no matter how hard they try. Sadly, this becomes a source of division between women, who then take it upon themselves to judge the actions of another person rather than the societal factors feeding those judgments. Some women internalize the embarrassment of nursing in public and try to keep others from doing it; some women judge others for using formula instead of breast milk even though we do not live in a nation that supports breastfeeding even by allowing mothers to stay closer to their children rather than returning to work as fast as possible, for example. And it is a reminder that we do not live in a nation that believes in the agency and choice of women, so each of us feels empowered to tell others what we think about their decisions concerning their bodies and their babies. This division, not an accident, furthers our shared oppression and makes us agents in maintaining a social order that does not serve us and that is anti-self-determination.

Beyond periods and breastfeeding, American patriarchy also plays a role in the way we describe other biological processes, like conception. A fascinating 2020 study, "Chemical Signals from Eggs Facilitate Cryptic Female Choice in Humans," showed how even our understandings of fertilization were taught to us from the perspective of male domination and control instead of women's choice and agency. For many years it has been accepted that conception happens when sperm enters the fallopian tube and races to find an egg to take over. Successful fertilization was described as beginning when the strongest and fastest sperm "won" by dominating the passive egg. So when this particular study found that the egg actually plays a role in "choosing" the "winner," that the egg sends signals to attract the sperm it wants, therefore determining the winner, even the scientists conducting the research were surprised. A senior author of the study said, "The idea that eggs are choosing sperm is really novel in human fertility." Beyond what this means for our understanding of conception, it reveals how influential the narrative of men being in control is, how it skews our view of natural processes and dictates every single story we tell. Furthermore, it reminds us that we often describe natural processes through the lens of American patriarchy and therefore cast women's bodies as less capable in every way.

Anthropologist Emily Martin called attention to this in her 1991 article "The Egg and the Sperm: How Science Has Constructed a Romance Based on Stereotypical Male-Female Roles," where she wrote, "The picture of egg and sperm drawn in popular as well as scientific accounts of reproductive biology relies on stereotypes central to our cultural definitions of male and female. The stereotypes imply not only that female biological processes are less worthy than their male counterparts but also that women are less worthy than men." We have continued to witness authorities in science and medicine replicate patriarchal stereotypes in their work that often go unquestioned because of their positions as researchers, doctors, and scientists. These titles come with power that is unfortunately routinely used to represent women as incapable.

Along with an inaccurate description of the process of conception comes an unbalanced understanding of infertility. While the stigma associated with infertility in general is painful and unfair, things are worsened by the fact that women are more often than not blamed when they and their partners are unable to conceive. In the 1940s, doctors even believed that infertility could be caused by women's hatred of their husbands. Medical writer Randi Hutter Epstein states, "An infertile woman treated with psychoanalysis was not an oddity at all. . . . Repressed fear and hostility were thought to foil normal female biochemistry, that in turn triggered physical changes in the body, ultimately clobbering the reproductive system." To this day, women still feel the burden of infertility and they often internalize the blame. For example, many women who choose to delay or feel they have to delay trying to have children in order to reach their career goals feel judged if they have difficulty conceiving. Even though research has proven that older sperm contributes to infertility, birth defects, and increased risks of childhood illness, men are not told that their biological clocks are ticking. In their article "Infertility and Moral Luck: The Politics of Women Blaming Themselves for Infertility," Carolyn McLeod and Julie Ponesse write, "Women have internalized the view that their social role as women is to reproduce. And if that is their role, then as women, they *should* be able to reproduce. If they cannot do it, then there must be something wrong with them. . . . Thus, they attribute the cause of the unexplained infertility to themselves and also blame themselves for it." The authors argue that this happens as a result of women living in a society that encourages women to see having children as their natural duty and also keeps them from assuming other duties, wants, and passions.

While we are discussing the disproportionate burden women feel when they face infertility, we can also comment on the language used when describing the loss of a pregnancy. The term "miscarriage," with the prefix *mis-*, which signifies "incorrectly," "mistakenly," "badly," seems to imply that a woman has done something wrong, or that her body doesn't work the way it is "supposed" to, rather than properly describing a spontaneous end to a pregnancy that can happen for any number of reasons. In fact, many women throughout American history up until today have been criminalized after they suffered pregnancy loss or stillbirths. Every year there are dozens of women who are prosecuted, convicted, and jailed for manslaughter after losing an unborn baby. Some of these women fell down while pregnant, others were blamed for giving birth at home even though such instances happen in hospitals as well, many have done drugs while pregnant, and even if it is unclear what the cause of the loss was, women are not only blamed but also punished when things go wrong.

Despite American patriarchy telling us that women are weak and in need of control, patriarchs are fully aware that the human race cannot continue without women. Therefore different strategies have been employed to make women feel defective, broken, powerless, and dependent, especially when it comes to anything concerning them doing the ultimate thing that men cannot: bringing children into the world. In other chapters I have discussed the founding fathers, presidents, officers, the Supreme Court, and more; the authorities in this arena have largely been scientists and doctors throughout American history who have used their titles to advance their biases, by making their opinions seem like fact, and by excluding women from their research so that we are still facing mysteries in women's reproductive health today. The control over our bodily powers has taken several strategies that can be difficult to keep track of, but I will summarize them here: We are taught to hide our abilities and any reminder of them, these abilities are policed and controlled, they are spoken about as if they are weaknesses while also being represented as our only abilities. These are then used to blame us if anything goes "wrong," as well as to judge and divide us no matter what we choose to do.

With all this in mind, in part 3 I ask the following: How has American patriarchy controlled and policed reproduction in order to keep us from accessing our power and maintain the social order that American patriarchy requires to survive? The levels of manipulation surrounding even the potential to reproduce are overwhelming, but they only grow when reproduction does actually take place. Therefore the study of the relationship between American patriarchy and pregnancy, labor, delivery, and experiences of motherhood requires its own deep dive.

12

TURNED IT INTO WEAKNESS

✴

The word "midwife" derives from Old English, where *mid-* signifies "with" and *wife* signifies "woman." "With women" is the basic definition of midwifery, one of the oldest professions. While we have sadly lost much of the wisdom of midwifery in our nation, largely because many midwives were women of color who have been erased, we know it was the respected practice for pregnancy and childbirth in the United States until the beginning of the twentieth century. Apprentices learned their skills from elders who were experienced midwives in their communities, they traveled to the women they cared for, and they offered individualized support whether it was physical, mental, emotional, or spiritual. Black, Indigenous, and immigrant women in particular passed down traditional healing practices surrounding pregnancy and the ceremony of childbirth, as well as ways to care for mothers in the postpartum period. However, as we have learned, American patriarchs are intent on controlling the powers of women, especially in areas that highlight the incapability of men. In this vein, in the 1800s, white male physicians began to explore how they could insert themselves in pregnancy and childbirth, believing they had a rightful place in these experiences.

It should be stated that doctors before the 1900s were largely experimenting without much formal training in their fields, and sadly much of the earliest medical interventions in women's reproductive health were just this, experiments. Even worse, our contemporary understandings of health stem from such experiments as well as from the biases of those who performed them. One example is J. Marion Sims, a physician who practiced several kinds of medicine from pediatrics to surgery to dentistry, and who also thought he could aid with childbirth complications. He experimented on Black girls and women who were enslaved to test out his theories, cutting into these human beings without the use of anesthesia, and even inviting other doctors to watch while the girls and women were chained so that they wouldn't interfere with his procedures. Sims subjected one girl, named Anarcha, to at least thirteen surgeries without any medicine for the pain. From this torture he gained the title of "Father of Gynecology." In fact, all the "fathers" of medicine impacting women's reproductive health have had detrimental effects on birthing people to this day.

Another man who heavily influenced the experience of pregnancy and birth in the United States was Abraham Flexner, a nonmedical American educator who in 1910 published a book-length report of medical education in the US and Canada that transformed the nature of our entire medical system and earned him the title of "Father of Modern Medical Education." The primary conclusion of Flexner's report was that too many different medical schools were operating across the nation with their own standards, that many of these needed to be closed, and that there needed to be more uniformity in approaches to medicine. He argued that the standard of care that all medical education should be based on was the biomedical model, which argues that a state of health is defined purely by the absence of illness. The model relies on viewing human bodies as being similar to machines that can glitch at times and can be fixed only by medical doctors; it also presents white male bodies as the standard of health. In a sense, this already presents everyone else as defective in one way or another and makes aspiring to be as close as possible to a white male body equivalent to achieving "health."

While the report standardized medical education in some beneficial ways, such as increasing prerequisites for entering the medical field and pushing physicians to gain more training and knowledge in science, when we look more closely at what the conclusions meant for pregnancy and labor, especially as it relates to women of color, the problems reveal themselves. Flexner called for the closure of numerous schools, many of which educated Black as well as female physicians, forcing them to walk away from their desired careers, and he solidified the standing of white men as the primary medical practitioners in our nation. Flexner also believed Black doctors should be subservient to white doctors and that they should serve only Black patients, writing, "The practice of the Negro physician will be limited to his own race." He also wrote that Black doctors should be trained in "hygiene rather than surgery." Regarding female physicians, the Flexner report greatly limited their opportunities to receive training and practice. By 1930, only one women's medical college remained open. The authors of the article "Unintended Consequences of the Flexner Report" write, "The proportion of women who graduated from medical school decreased to an all-time low shortly after the Flexner report was issued (2.9% in 1915), and the proportion remained below 5% until the 1970s." Furthermore, Flexner encouraged poor people to seek treatment at charity hospitals that served as places where doctors in training could practice on them.

The report also recommended the abolishment of midwifery by categorizing midwives as being below the standard of medical professionals. Even though these women were willing to share their knowledge with doctors, Flexner, rather than accepting midwives as experts in their field, deemed them subpar to white male physicians who were still relying on experimentation when it came to pregnancy and childbirth. One of these experiments was the twilight sleep method, originally employed in Germany. Women were put into a semiconscious state with morphine and scopolamine so that they could give birth without remembering anything. Although women could not remember what happened to them, the twilight method was filled with torment. The drugs caused the women to thrash around, bang their heads on walls, and scream as they clawed at themselves and medical staff. Their faces would be covered with towels, and they were often restrained in straitjackets as they lay in their own vomit or feces for as long as the labor lasted. The drugs also had a horrible effect on babies. Born drugged, many of them experienced difficulty breathing and arrived in a comatose state. With mothers and their children essentially poisoned, doctors forcefully pulled the babies out using forceps. Twilight sleep continued to be used on women well into the middle of the century. Despite how awful these experiences were, women who were terrified of labor sought to give birth this way because it was only the medical staff who knew what really transpired.

Women had learned from doctors that childbirth was something to fear. Joseph DeLee, an American physician who practiced through the early 1900s and became known as the "Father of Modern Obstetrics," viewed childbirth as a pathological process that damaged both mothers and babies and proposed methods of intervention to save women from the "evils natural to labor." Unsurprisingly, DeLee was also antimidwives, claiming they were untrained and unable to handle the dangerous condition of pregnancy and the treacherous event of birth. He once stated:

> The midwife is a relic of barbarism. In civilized countries the midwife is wrong, has always been wrong. . . . The midwife has been a drag on the progress of the science and art of obstetrics. Her existence stunts the one and degrades the

other. For many centuries she perverted obstetrics from ob-
taining any standing at all among the science of medicine.

The primary result of DeLee's hatred for midwives was the eventual male monopolization of women's reproductive health, as well
as the introduction of a host of new potential issues for mothers and
children through unnecessary intervention.

Inspired by Sims, Flexner, and DeLee, the foundation of gynecology and obstetrics as we know it today was built by white men
who were guided by the control they could exert over a process
that did not previously include them. Midwifery started to be seen
as unhygienic, unprofessional, and dangerous despite the fact that
midwives, especially those working with Black women, had and
continue to have more success in keeping mothers alive. One midwife, Margaret Charles Smith, who lived from 1906 to 2004, delivered more than three thousand babies over her career in Alabama,
including twins, children who were breech, and even premature
babies, without once losing the mother. She primarily worked in
rural areas with women who were often underresourced and in
poor health. Despite numerous examples of success rates like this,
however, midwifery was eventually outlawed in Alabama and several other states. In states where it didn't become illegal, training
programs did not exist to give midwives the licenses they needed to
practice legally, or midwives were asked to take literacy tests even
though many of them were Black women who had been kept from
learning to read or write. The goal was to eliminate midwifery in
its entirety.

By 1940, out-of-hospital births had fallen from 100 to 44 percent. This trend was fueled largely by general medical practitioners
who were not experts in labor and delivery. Although many people argue that bringing pregnancy into hospitals helped save more
mothers and children, the data shows it actually contributed to

high maternal mortality and infant mortality rates at the beginning of this switch. Births that were attended by midwives had fewer complications than those attended by early obstetricians, who were uneducated in caring for women and infants. The surge in preventable deaths was so high that it caused the federal government to intervene, which subjected both doctors and midwives to necessary regulations. However, these regulations were used to exert control over midwives, as doctors continued to shift blame to them even though data proved that deaths were more likely to occur in hospitals. One study found that "26% to 31% of maternal deaths from puerperal sepsis were attended by midwives; 59% to 71% were attended by physicians." Furthermore, the same study showed that "the number of infant deaths from birth injuries had actually increased by 40 to 50 percent from 1915 to 1929," correlating with an increase in hospital-based and physician-attended births. Despite these numbers, state regulations made it nearly impossible for midwives to gain the licenses they now needed to practice their profession.

Better hygiene practices and the use of antibiotics allowed the maternal and infant mortality rates to decrease by 1948, but the growing stories of women and children dying contributed to a shifting view of birth as something that was natural to being seen as a dangerous illness. Medical professionals began to heavily employ intervention methods such as inductions, forceps (a metal tool clamped onto a baby's head in order to pull them out), episiotomies (cutting a woman's vaginal wall to speed the process), vacuum extraction (suctioning a baby out of the birth canal), and cesareans, believing that birth was not an act women could or should perform without medical help. Indeed, the most influential people on the way pregnancy and childbirth are viewed in the United States to this day have been white men who attempted to master the process of childbirth and wanted women to rely on them to bring children into the world. Although men could not give birth, they believed they knew how to do it better, and they wanted women to see them as the experts.

The switch from birth being something that was natural and at times in need of medical intervention to being overmedicalized and connected to expensive procedures, combined with the switch from seeing other women who were experts in pregnancy and delivery as the best guides to seeking help from men, who had higher degrees and found pregnancy and birth to be damaging, has resulted in a despicable state of maternal health in America. The maternal mortality rate in the United States is far higher than in any other industrialized nation, and Black mothers face the deadliest odds. Black women are three times more likely to die in pregnancy and childbirth than white women. Even worse, the maternal mortality rate only continues to increase in America even though the CDC estimates that four out of every five pregnancy-related deaths are preventable. In 2020, the Commonwealth Fund's article "Maternal Mortality and Maternity Care in the United States Compared to 10 Other Developed Countries" summarized the primary issues contributing to poor maternal health outcomes in the United States:

> Obstetrician-gynecologists (ob-gyns) are overrepresented in [the United States'] maternity care workforce relative to midwives, and there is an overall shortage of maternity care providers (both ob-gyns and midwives) relative to births. In most other countries, midwives outnumber ob-gyns by severalfold, and primary care plays a central role in the health system. Although a large share of its maternal deaths occur postbirth, the US is the only country not to guarantee access to provider home visits or paid parental leave in the postpartum period.

In addition to midwife usage being far lower in the US, interventions in birth are used far more often here than in other wealthy nations. C-sections, for example, account for one in three births in the US even though the World Health Organization states that C-sections should be necessary for only 10 to 15 percent of deliveries. C-sections typically come with greater risks than vaginal births, including more blood loss, more chance of infection and blood clots, more complications in future pregnancies, and a higher risk of death, and recovery is much harder. Inductions, which normally require longer hospital stays and therefore are more expensive, have more than tripled in the United States since 1989. While very few births take place outside hospitals in the US, in other industrialized nations, like the UK, France, and Australia, midwifery is at least as common as care by obstetricians. Many have drawn attention to the fact that the various interventions used in labor in the United States today also correlate to the amount of money that can be made off a laboring person. Several studies have found that there are financial incentives that encourage private, for-profit hospitals to perform more inductions and C-sections, for example.

Although more women and people of color work in medicine than ever before in the United States, the obstetric system is still based on a patriarchal standard of care where even many female physicians see pregnancy and labor in the same way Joseph DeLee did in the early 1900s. For women of color, especially for Black women, entering hospitals that continue to operate from the perspective that white men are the standard and women do not know what they are talking about when it comes to their own bodies and what they are going through in pregnancy and labor, the stakes are even worse. Black women often report feeling ignored and unheard in hospital settings as they cry out in pain or express feeling like something is going wrong whether their providers are female or not, Black or not. One of the most recent examples of this took place in Inglewood, California, on January 9, 2023, when thirty-one-year-old April Valentine died in childbirth after saying for hours that she was in pain and that she couldn't feel her legs. Her pleas for help were ignored and she died before she could meet her newborn daughter. Stories like April Valentine's are tragically common, yet the field of obstetrics continues to operate the same way, and women still grow up believing that they should not trust their own instincts and that doctors know better.

Women have strategically been taught to fear pregnancy and childbirth rather than feel empowered by it because in this fear they relinquish their control. I believe that any way that children are brought into this world is remarkable and commendable, and I am also grateful for medical intervention when it is necessary. However, I am heartbroken each time I hear friends regurgitate messages they have heard over the years that are intent on robbing them of knowing how powerful they are. These range from women who state immense fear of labor and who hang on every word their doctor speaks without question to women who tell their partners they don't want them to see what's happening "down there," fearing they will seem less attractive, to women who think the process of giving birth is negative or grotesque. My heart breaks when I hear of a mother losing her life to something that was avoidable, or a mother feeling she did not fully understand the treatments being recommended to her and regretting making a decision she felt coerced into. Many mothers report feeling confused about the directions they are given during childbirth, feeling scared and vulnerable, and in retrospect they wish something had gone differently had they simply been given more knowledge and control over their labor experience. What many mothers do not know, however, is why they feel this way, and they often blame themselves for their decisions when they have simply experienced yet another product of decades of patriarchal rule.

When a woman doubts herself so much that she agrees to something that goes against her intuition in pregnancy and childbirth; when she is nervous to ask questions about advice she's being given; when she doubts that a midwife knows as much as a male practitioner who will never be able to give birth; when she blames herself for anything that might go wrong; when she is convinced that a doctor has authority over her, rather than being a partner in her pregnancy and birthing experience meant to offer advice, intervene only when necessary, and engage in dialogue with her, American patriarchy has accomplished one of its goals.

Midwifery has started to make a return in the United States as more women have sought better experiences of pregnancy, labor, and delivery separate from hospitals. However, women find themselves having to pay for these experiences out of pocket. According to *Time* magazine, "Even though the average home birth in the US costs much less than the average hospital birth using employee-sponsored insurance—$4,650 in total payments from insurers plus individuals, compared to $13,811, respectively, the sum of what is paid by insurers and families—major insurers often deny claims to fully cover home births, as well as the prenatal and postnatal care that accompany them." In effect, this maintains the status quo. Families with means can make choices that better serve them, while those with less resources must remain under control despite what we know about the danger and deadliness of institutions that operate with patriarchal mentalities.

Trying to survive pregnancy and labor is only the beginning of the struggles mothers face in the United States, because when our children arrive, we become even more aware of how the system of American patriarchy was never built to serve us and, by extension, was never built to serve them either.

13

SO WE CANNOT WIN

◾

L et me tell you something, Elvin," the stunning, thin, and eloquent woman says as she points her left index finger. She's wearing a light purple jumpsuit with a silver belt that matches her earrings. Standing in her and her husband's beautiful home, filled with elegant furniture, she continues:

> You see, I am not serving Dr. Huxtable, okay? That's the kind of thing that goes on in a restaurant. Now I am going to bring him a cup of coffee just like he brought me a cup of coffee this morning and that, young man, is what marriage is made of. It is give and take, fifty-fifty, and if you don't get it together and drop these macho attitudes you are never going to have anybody bringing you anything, anywhere, anyplace, anytime, ever.

The studio audience erupts with applause. They have become familiar with the feminist teachings of Clair Huxtable, the fictional character played by Phylicia Rashad, who is not only a devoted wife and a mother of five children but also a successful lawyer. Her husband is a doctor. There is virtually no presence of a nanny in her home to help with raising her kids, or a cleaning person to help keep her house immaculate; there is simply the illusion of a woman who somehow does it all. She even has time to offer guests coffee and educate them on their sexist attitudes.

Clair Huxtable debuted in 1984, and she is still widely regarded as one of the best TV moms of all time, as well as a feminist icon who provided an example of a mother who was also dedicated to her career and who challenged anyone who questioned that. She was a woman in charge of her choices; she symbolized our ability to have it all. However, in the same way that the *Cosby Show*'s lead actor has now been revealed in all his insidiousness, upon further examination of Rashad's defining role, the perfect image begins to disintegrate. We realize it was only ever a mirage, especially when it is compared to the experiences of real women, specifically women with children, even more specifically mothers of color, and the impossibilities they faced and continue to face when trying to emulate such an example of perfection. It is difficult to believe in the existence of Clair Huxtable, in the notion that she and her husband truly achieved equality, in the possibility that they both earned degrees, found success in their careers, and had five children without her burning out in our American patriarchy.

In part 3 we have discussed how our reproductive abilities serve as a foil to American patriarchy because of the reminders they carry of what cisgender men cannot do. We've explored the various tactics used to control these abilities or even the potential of these abilities. We have seen how it plays a role in our interpretations and treatment of menstruation, conception, pregnancy, labor, delivery, and breastfeeding, and now we have arrived at the ways in which American patriarchy controls and manipulates experiences of motherhood. In this chapter I will discuss not only the experiences of mothers who work outside the home, such as Clair Huxtable, and mothers who work inside their homes without getting paid (usually referred to as "stay-at-home moms"), I will also briefly discuss divisions of labor for mothers in heteronormative relationships, as well as the unique challenges single mothers face as a result of American patriarchal norms.

The manipulation of motherhood in American patriarchy stems from initially telling women that motherhood should be our only focus, again taking something powerful and making it the thing that is enforced and controlled. When mothers do indeed dedicate their time to motherhood, they are often told by their partners and by society that they are simply doing what they are "supposed" to do. They are not compensated or celebrated for their labor day in and day out and, as a result, their impact on their children and households is taken for granted. Furthermore, they often report feeling unappreciated, depressed, and unfulfilled. This form of manipulation consists of representing motherhood and caretaking tasks as natural and easy for women, making support and appreciation for them unnecessary. Then the manipulation evolves if motherhood is not our only focus. Mothers who work outside the home find that they are not supported in having other pursuits, and they find themselves under pressure to balance everything. They are still put in charge of caretaking tasks no matter how much money they make. Furthermore, they will be shown examples of women who pull it all off so that if they struggle to do the same thing, they are the ones to blame. If women can hold and care for children while also doing everything men do, it makes matters even worse for American patriarchy by further displaying deficiencies in men. Therefore, challenges are laid out for mothers at every turn on private, public, corporate, civic, and institutional levels. Single mothers are further punished because it is viewed as an act against American patriarchy for a woman to lead her home without a man. Regardless of the circumstances, she will be the one punished for the offense.

I focus on experiences of motherhood in the last half of the twentieth century, in comparison to what we see today, because this is the time period when second- and third-wave feminism most influenced our current relationship to motherhood. Put simply, first-wave feminism is used to describe attitudes from around 1900 up until the 1960s that were concerned with achieving political equality largely between white women and white men. Second-wave feminism, in the 1960s to the 1980s, was more concerned with challenging the notion that women should be relegated to the domestic sphere. The 1980s to the first decade of the 2000s is when popular feminist thought began to consider the differences between women depending more on various layers of our identity. Second-wave feminism encouraged women to move out of the domestic sphere, but American patriarchy still made it hard for them to do so, and even harder for women of color and women living in poverty. A product of American patriarchy combined with second-wave feminism was the division of women from one another by sending the message that working outside the home was better, therefore minimizing the role of mothers at home and also erasing the labor of other women who helped to care for children and/or maintain homes, by pretending they did not exist.

A US Census Bureau study published in 1984, the same year Clair Huxtable appeared on TV, documented that "the number of families maintained by women increased by more than 84 percent between 1970 and 1984. The number of children living with a divorced mother more than doubled between 1970 and 1982, while the number of children living with a never-married mother increased more than fourfold." In other words, mothers were leading homes more than ever before, not only in the ways they were traditionally allowed to lead through caretaking tasks, for example, but also financially. The US State Department reported in 1985 that the most significant development in the employment of women over that decade was the rise in the number of working mothers to nearly 20 million.

However, our nation did not respond to this shift in labor by providing more support for mothers. Instead, working mothers were often met with accusations of disintegrating their families, and elected officials focused on keeping women at home. Women were not guaranteed any leave to be with their children when they birthed them or when they were sick. There was not any access to affordable childcare. Most women formula-fed their children in the 1980s partially because there would not be a space or time available for them to pump at work. The expectations of and pressures on mothers came alongside continued societal enforcement of gender norms that attempted to dictate the composition of families and reified the division of labor within the home, even when a mother also earned money. President Richard Nixon vetoed federally funded childcare centers nationwide in 1971, stating they worked against "the family-centered approach," making it so that mothers would have to stay at home or spend most of their salaries on childcare.

These strategies made mothering difficult no matter what. Women's labor of child-rearing and home-managing became more invisible as mothers' work inside the home wasn't viewed as providing money for her family, yet if a mother tried to work outside the home she was forced to deny her own needs in order to assimilate, and she would have a very difficult time climbing up the career ladder.

Take the inspirational story of Anna Lee Fisher, one of America's first female astronauts. In 1983, Fisher was called into her boss's office and told that she was being considered for a mission to space. This had been her dream, so she was elated, but she was also pregnant with her first child, eight and a half months pregnant, to be exact. Fisher, knowing she couldn't pass up the opportunity of her career that she had worked so hard for, decided to accept, telling herself she could figure it out. A month later she gave birth to her daughter on a Friday, then went back to work the following Monday to show her male colleagues that she might have a baby but she was still committed to her job. For the next fourteen months, Fisher continued her work while also caring for her daughter. One day during communications training, Fisher waited until mission control lost contact with another flight in orbit in order to run into the bathroom and pump breast milk. Her own 3.3-million-mile, seven-day-and-twenty-three-hour journey was successful, and she made history as the first mother to travel to space.

Fisher's story is absolutely remarkable, and it also poignantly illustrates the pressures mothers felt to do it all and to not complain while doing so, to appear as though they didn't need support, to show up to work days after giving birth, to hide their motherhood at times, to hold it all together, to be grateful for the opportunities to enter spaces they were previously barred from, and to therefore extend themselves beyond what was healthy to fit almost seamlessly into male-dominated careers. The message was that the only women who would attain any success in choosing to go against the dictates of American patriarchy would have to be absolutely exceptional, without any mistakes, to have even the smallest chance of living a happy and healthy life, while working and also caring for their homes and kids. This goal, virtually unattainable, was presented in the media as easy so that real women would blame themselves when they could not achieve it.

The challenges were worse for single mothers who were judged for not adhering to the traditional rules, told they had made immoral decisions, and burdened with low wages and jobs that did not provide any benefits. The 1980s also saw the presidency of Ronald Reagan, whom many have called the most antiwoman president of the twentieth century. Among other actions that attempted to rob women of their rights, Reagan popularized the term "welfare queen" in his attacks against single mothers, specifically single mothers of color, to limit resources being spent on families that were exclusively led by women. Reagan also opposed raising the minimum wage, believing that paying lower-income workers more would cost jobs. In 1984, the US poverty level was 15.2 percent, and women comprised 57 percent of the poor. While the poverty rate declined for both white and Black people between 1983 and 1984, for Black children under six years old, the poverty rate rose to 51.1 percent. Closely linked to poverty among children were the 70.9 percent of single female heads of households.

These statistics are the results of national and systematic attempts to maintain the order of American patriarchy. We know that American patriarchy tells us that white women should not have the same rights as men, that they should be relegated to the domestic sphere, that women of color should support white women in their domestic roles without aspiring to higher-paying jobs and without caring about their own families, and that we should all happily remain in these cycles of inequity and poverty.

Mothers today face much of the same rhetoric and challenges that mothers faced in the 1980s. They are reporting burnout and depression at higher levels than ever before. A Pew Research Center study published in 2023 found:

> Even as financial contributions have become more equal in marriages, the way couples divide their time between paid work and home life remains unbalanced. Women pick up a heavier load when it comes to household chores and caregiving responsibilities, while men spend more time on work and leisure. This is true in egalitarian marriages—where both spouses earn roughly the same amount of money—and in marriages where the wife is the primary earner. The only marriage type where husbands devote more time to caregiving than their wives is one in which the wife is the sole breadwinner. In those marriages, wives and husbands spend roughly the same amount of time per week on household chores.

In other words, mothers still take on the brunt of work within the home, whether they work outside the home or not.

In addition to household tasks, they are also in charge of the mental labor of thinking of everything for their families and keeping track of everyone's schedules and tasks. The study "Gendered Mental Labor" states, "Mental labor related to unpaid work in the household and childcare is cognitive work that consists of managerial activities aimed at achieving communal goals (e.g., goals related not only to the individual, but also to the family, partner, children), which are directed toward a future outcome and goes undetected and unseen as a component of unpaid work." The article concludes that in order to achieve gender equality in relationships, we must not only focus on changes on the behavioral level but also consider different expectations of our cognitive responsibilities. Lawyer and writer Eve Rodsky also calls attention to this in her book *Fair Play*, where she shows the importance of finding a solution to the current labor imbalances in our homes that are both mental and physical.

Furthermore, our country still does not have national paid family leave or universal access to childcare. The strategy is to exhaust mothers, to make us appear weak and unable to perform tasks. We see this in the way mothers are often described, especially when others make light of our exhausted brains by referring to "mom brain," for example, when we experience forgetfulness or brain fog. This is another example not only of people making light of the burdens mothers carry but also of something powerful being described as something weak. The reality is that women do not become dumber in motherhood; instead, our neurological development kicks into a higher gear. In fact, research suggests that caretaking roles in general allow our brains to change and grow.

Single mothers are still caught in an oppressive cycle where they are up to five times more likely to experience poverty than two-parent households. What is now called the "benefits cliff" summarizes the predicament many poor and usually single mothers find themselves trapped in. The benefits cliff refers to the experience of people living in poverty who are receiving assistance and are doing their best to earn more money, but who fall behind when they make just enough to lose their benefits. They are forced to pay out of pocket for resources they cannot afford, making life more expensive than it was when they were eligible for governmental assistance. Although welfare recipients, especially single mothers, are often portrayed as freeloaders looking for handouts, they are, by the current system in place, bound to stay put or are reproached for trying to claw their way out of the depths of poverty.

When women express frustration with systems outside their homes that do not support their motherhood, they are often told that they should not have chosen to work. When women feel unseen and unsupported inside their homes, they are often scolded for not choosing to work and made to feel like second-class citizens. And when women have anything negative to report about their difficulties raising children, they are asked why they had children to begin with.

In 1986, the *Newsweek* cover story "A Mother's Choice"—illustrated with a baby next to a briefcase under the words "America's Mothers: Making It Work: How Women Balance the Demands of Jobs and Children"—framed the dilemmas and challenges of motherhood we've discussed as a result of mothers' decisions and not as the lack of support for them. But the truth is that this isn't a result of mothers' choices, but of societal choices that are not mistakes but strategies to keep women in "their place" according to the dictates of American patriarchy. Despite forced motherhood, mothers in the United States were and continue to be put in a position where, by design, they cannot win either way. Furthermore, what we also know is that for women who choose not to have children, as well as for nontraditional families with children, their deviation from the patriarchal dictate leaves them vulnerable to other forms of criticism and lack of support as well.

14

TOLD TO NEVER QUESTION THEM, AND ALWAYS DOUBT

◢

E arth is the center of the universe" is a statement we now know to be false, yet it was believed by most people for 1,400 years. Aristotle, the famous Greek philosopher, is credited with first asserting that Earth's rightful place was at the very center of everything, and Roman mathematician Claudius Ptolemy built on Aristotle's geocentric theory. Ptolemy came up with his own mathematical and scientific formulas to prove that Earth stayed fixed at the center of the entire universe while everything else rotated around it. In 1543, Nicolaus Copernicus, known as the "Father of Modern Astronomy," proposed that Earth and other planets actually revolved around the sun, a theory referred to as the heliocentric model. His findings were seen as controversial, heretic, and contrary to the Catholic Church. The famous astronomer Galileo Galilei was even instructed to abandon the heliocentric model, and in 1616, the Catholic Church went so far as to prohibit Copernican theory. The idea of Earth being at the center of the universe became a religious belief when the church started teaching that God made Earth special and powerful, and that naturally it was the planet everything else revolved around. It wasn't until 1822 that the ban on Copernicus's model was lifted. In 1992, the Vatican finally admitted that Earth rotated around the sun like other planets, and that the Church had been wrong to vilify thinkers who declared as much.

Although Westerners were fond of the geocentric model for centuries, scientists in other cultures around the world proposed heliocentric theories. For example, in the Aitareya Brahmana, an ancient Indian collection of sacred hymns that were written somewhere between 1000 and 500 BCE, there is the following: "The Sun causes day and night on the earth, because of revolution, when there is night here, it is day on the other side, the sun does not really rise or sink." Many consider this one of the earliest examples of heliocentric observations.

Our evolved understanding regarding the behaviors of Earth and other planets is just one of many times when something that was called a law of nature, or a law of physics, or a religious and divine dictate was in fact found to be merely a human opinion. As we have discussed, American patriarchy also relies on such "laws," including but not limited to: first, the gender binary, which states that there are only two genders, man and woman; second, white supremacy, which says that white people are more special and powerful, and naturally the group that everything else revolves around; and third, heteronormativity, which says heterosexuality is more natural and superior. I like to think of all these laws as being just like the disproved geocentric model, merely opinions based on white men's ego. In part 3 we have been exploring how we are organized in the United States based on these "laws," particularly because these laws define our roles in reproduction and justify strategies used to control women's power. In this chapter we examine another law of American patriarchy that is based on reproduction and stems from the aforementioned three. Relying on the gender binary, white supremacy, heteronormativity, and views of our differing roles around reproduction comes the law of the all-American nuclear family.

Similar to the concept of Earth being the center of the universe, the concept of the nuclear family takes inspiration from the nucleus at the center of an atom, and is heralded as the center of our nation. The nuclear family in the United States is a social construct that is seen as the basis of our country because it romanticizes a white family unit that consists of a husband and a wife and their children. This family makeup has been held up as an ideal for all Americans to aspire to because it replicates American patriarchy's ideal organization of our nation as a whole where men provide, women reproduce, and children continue our legacy. Despite the rise of nontraditional families, most Americans still aspire to eventually fulfill their role in creating their own nuclear family, not only because of messages we receive from politicians, researchers, and the media, but also because of how our policies are designed to reward our fulfillment of the nuclear family model. This kind of organization prioritizes our individual units over our connection to our extended families and communities; it gives husbands and wives rigid guidelines, and encourages everyone to assimilate to heteronormativity and whiteness.

Many scholars and politicians have argued that protecting the nuclear family is essential to the survival of our nation, and we have seen both historically and today how American patriarchy upholds the nuclear family while rejecting those who do not aspire to it, or pushes away those who are not seen as fitting into it, leaving them unprotected and vulnerable to judgment, interference, and punishment. The nuclear family is still the basis for our rights as well as for our social and economic benefits. We have already discussed in the previous chapter the mistreatment single mothers face in our nation, and here I add more groups that have historically been seen as interfering with the nuclear family or who have been seen as being separate from the all-American nuclear family. These include people who do not have children but especially women, nonheteronormative families, and, at times, immigrant families and families of color, even if they consist of a husband and wife and their kids.

Women who do not have children, perhaps because they do not want kids or because there are obstacles in their way to parenthood, are often seen and treated as outsiders in our society. While we have progressed from the witch hunts that we discussed in part 2, women without children are still critiqued for trying to "be like men." On a variety of online platforms, women without children have called attention to the ostracism they experience when they are called abnormal, stupid, immoral, selfish, cold, and even psychopathic. In a country that was built with the assumption that women are born to have children, the decision not to is sometimes viewed as resulting from an adverse, mind-altering experience. In their article "Women Without Children: A Contradiction in Terms?," published in 2000, Myra J. Hird and Kimberly Abshoff write, "Precisely because of the indelible association between women and parenthood, those women who do not view parenthood as a central life-goal are considered to suffer 'psychopathological disturbance.' . . . This 'psychopathology' has been variously explained to be the result of childhood trauma, poor parental role models, oppressive child-rearing, too much sibling childcare responsibility or negative identification with their mothers." While these negative experiences might have an influence on some women who do not desire children, they do not apply to all women without children. The belief that something is psychologically wrong with women who do not have kids becomes even more present when they are married to men, and women report feeling judged more for their decision than their husbands are.

A recent study shows that single and child-free/childless women also face stigma, stereotyping, and discrimination at work when they are seen as lacking leadership skills. As the *Washington Post* summarizes it, "These women were often seen as too 'masculine' for leadership when the same traits benefited single men. They also lacked the 'communal, relational' leadership traits expected of women who were coupled and raising children." While mothers experience a larger wage gap at work compared to men than women without children do, women without children are still subject to others' scrutiny and mistreatment, solely based on their going against the grain of gendered societal expectations. According to a Pew Research Center report, "The Enduring Grip of the Gender Gap,"

> Among employed men and women, the impact of parenting is felt most among those ages 25 to 54, when they are most likely to have children under 18 at home. In 2022, mothers ages 25 to 34 earned 85% as much as fathers that age, but women without children at home earned 97% as much as fathers. In contrast, employed women ages 35 to 44—with or without children—both earned about 80% as much as fathers. The table turns for women ages 45 to 54, with mothers earning more than women with no children at home. Among those ages 35 to 44 or 45 to 54, men without children earned only 84% as much as fathers.

This research calls attention to the fact that men without children also experience a slight penalty at work, as well as the fact that the prioritization of the traditional nuclear family benefits fathers while hurting mothers.

During the pandemic, people without children but especially women reported feeling like they were being forced to fill the gaps that working parents could no longer cover with their children out of school and without other childcare. Employers who tried to alleviate the workloads of parents often did so by piling more on workers without children. This dynamic caused division and anger between employees with children and those without, making it seem like they were on different teams, when in fact the most important issue was the need for employers to allow flexible schedules for all and support a healthy work-life balance regardless of someone's parental status. As is often the case with all our discontent when we lack national and company-wide policies to protect us, we take our frustration out on one another rather than turning our attention toward the system at play.

Nonheteronormative families are also seen as breaking the laws of American patriarchy even when they desire to and do have children. A case in February 2023 displays ongoing discrimination against same-sex couples and a continued lack of protection for their families. Kris Williams, a lesbian mother in Oklahoma, lost her parental rights to her son when a judge ruled that the rightful parents of the child were Williams's ex-wife, Rebekah Wilson, and their sperm donor, Harlan Vaughn. In an unexpected twist, Wilson and Vaughn are now dating, but this does not change the facts that Williams was originally on her son's birth certificate and that she has been his parent since he was conceived. The judge stated that Williams failed to adopt her son and therefore gave up her rights to him when she and the woman who held their child in her womb parted ways. He declared that the sperm donor, who did not originally intend to parent the child, was the rightful father. This is a unique example, but it poignantly demonstrates how our rights are intertwined with the social construct of a heterosexual nuclear family.

Another example of how nonheteronormative families are disrespected in our American patriarchy can be seen in the hurdles some couples face when trying to adopt. For example, even though it has been legal for gay couples to adopt children since gay marriage was finally protected by law in 2015, according to FindLaw, "only 28 states and Washington, DC, have laws preventing bias against same-sex couples during adoption. Other state laws allow some discriminatory practices. Or they are silent about discrimination. Several states allow adoption agencies to discriminate because of religious preferences." Furthermore, private adoption and foster care agencies can continue receiving taxpayer funds even if they exclude LGBTQ+ prospective parents and others who do not meet the agency's religious criteria.

Lawyer Diana Adams has made it their mission to serve nonnuclear families and provide them access to resources that are not built into the current operations of our country. They state, "Our laws should move away from the idea that there's one ideal family form and value all families as they exist." Adams has witnessed time and again how people who fall outside the husband-wife-and-children nuclear model are punished, seen as deviant, and denied protections, including single people and same-sex couples as well as platonic partners raising children together, grandparents who are raising their grandchildren, lesbian couples coparenting with a male friend, and polyamorous partners in a committed relationship of three or four. Through legal advocacy, Adams helps all people design family agreements and pushes to change laws as they currently stand, hoping that eventually the United States will switch from our safety nets relying on our membership in a nuclear family to existing between every citizen and the state regardless of family composition.

While at times discrimination against families that are not seen as nuclear is more explicit, like in the examples I have mentioned concerning nonheteronormative couples, other times the mistreatment requires careful observation to realize the forces at play. These forms of discrimination are not necessarily written in law or a company's policy but instead appear in troubling trends around the separation of families of color. Because, as we know, the "nuclear family" that is protected in our nation is not only heteronormative, in American patriarchy it is also meant to be white. Take, for example, the disproportionate number of Black children who are removed from their homes and placed into foster care in the United States. According to

Dorothy Roberts, a professor of law, sociology, and civil rights at the University of Pennsylvania, "more than half of all Black children will experience a child-welfare investigation by the time they reach age 18—53%." Furthermore, the American Bar Association estimates that nearly 10 percent of Black children will be removed from their parents and placed into foster care, double the rate of white children. As Shereen White and Stephanie Marie Persson write in their article "Racial Discrimination in Child Welfare Is a Human Rights Violation—Let's Talk About It That Way,"

> That the state can intrude into the private lives of families and separate children from their mothers and fathers hits at some of the most fundamental aspects of our humanity. It touches on the right to family integrity and on a child's right to his or her identity, and, when compounded by the racial discrimination our child welfare system is structured to impose, it becomes a question of basic equality and human dignity.

The data shows that these trends represent biases against Black families rather than being a result of poor parenting by Black parents. These separations often lead to the termination of parental rights for Black parents. Today, a shocking 1 out of every 41 Black children in the US will have their legal relationship with their parent or parents terminated (compared with 1 out of 100 children in the US).

Furthermore, scholars and storytellers like the author of *Relinquished: The Politics of Adoption and the Privilege of American Motherhood*, Gretchen Sisson, and filmmaker Lisa Elaine Scott have brought attention to the way this plays out in adoptions across the United States, where there is currently a supply-and-demand problem. There are many families seeking to adopt infants and not enough infants to adopt. This sadly leads to many poor mothers of all races reporting being influenced to relinquish their parental rights without them fully understanding what they are signing away. Thousands of stories have recently emerged of poor mothers stating that they were coerced into giving their babies to adoption agencies without being able to change their minds, many of whom are still fighting for their children to be returned to them. Adoption can indeed be a wonderful thing, but not when power imbalances come into play and agencies are more concerned with making money than with whatever is best for all parents and children involved.

Family separation is also prevalent and devastating in the cases of immigrants. In 2018, images of children in cages on the floor of detention centers with aluminum-foil-looking "blankets" appeared in the news, shocking viewers. Stories surfaced of the poor conditions children were being forced to endure in addition to being separated from their parents. They would go weeks without access to showers, beds, toothbrushes, or clean clothes. Most of them became very sick. That year it was estimated that more than five thousand families crossing the US-Mexico border were separated with no plans for their reunification, and many of these families remain separated to this day. The youngest child separated from their family at the time was only six months old. These families were torn apart even though it was not required by United States law or regulation and even though it would take an obvious mental, physical, and emotional toll on them.

There is nothing wrong with being a member of a more traditional nuclear family, but the idea that we should all aspire to achieve a white nuclear family is a trap of American patriarchy. It seeks to reproduce cycles of oppression and exclusion by replicating the status quo of our nation in our family units and making false promises of protections if we fall in line. Furthermore, the celebration of the all-American nuclear family also celebrates the exclusion, discrimination, and abuse of those who are not included in its original definition. Moreover, many who do adhere to the dictates find that they are still excluded from being treated humanely not only because of sexism and genderism but also because of factors including but not limited to racism, homophobia, xenophobia, and classism.

The United States currently operates with an antiquated notion of what makes people worthy of recognition and rights. Our entire nation is based on fabricated "laws of nature," laws that have been "backed" by "science" and "math," represented as sacred and divine: The nuclear family consists of a father, a mother, and their children, in that order. Anyone who does not follow these laws or laud them as their primary motivation is unnatural, wrong, and iconoclastic, in need of punishment and correction. These laws appear to communicate the message that people who do not want children are defective; families that do not consist of a husband, wife, and their children are not families at all; families of those who are from communities that have historically been marginalized do not always deserve to be recognized; and families that were not formed in the United States may not be recognized either. But here is the thing about the terms "laws of nature" and "laws of physics": Like the geocentric model, they simply mean, "This is how we *think* things work." So when something defies that "law," it is high time we do some rethinking and ask who and what the original law is trying to protect.

15

WHAT WE KNOW TO BE
TRUE FOR OURSELVES

◼

I am thirty-two years old. I am married to my college sweetheart. Together we have three kids. In many ways it seems I live more of a traditional life in terms of what is expected and celebrated for women. Still, I stand firmly against a system that tells people that this is their only choice, or that makes assumptions about our unique identities to fit us into existing, accepted categories. I do not think that we must eradicate marriage and move away from having children in order to find liberation, as other scholars and activists have suggested. Instead I operate with the belief that we can value the many different paths and choices individuals should be allowed to make with equal support and opportunities. Furthermore, if we do make the choice to marry and have children, we do not have to be limited by problematic dictates meant to make these experiences inequitable and unjust. I have been able to make decisions that were best for me while pushing back against oppressive guidelines and still advocate for others to choose differently if they would like to, primarily because I am a Black woman who specializes in subjects that are constantly playing out in real time.

The through line between my degrees in anthropology, gender studies, and sociology has been the study of the imbalance of power in the United States, specifically concerning gender and race, from my lens of growing up largely outside this country. While we are all confronting the power struggle that is American patriarchy in every single one of our interactions and day-to-day experiences, I walk through life always keenly aware of it, and I am deeply grateful that my work has coincided with my major life transitions. Case in point: Not only did my husband and I start dating while we were both in college and I was writing a thesis on the antifeminist socialization of American youth, we also got engaged while I studied Black feminism and counterhegemonic pedagogy for my master's. We got married while I pursued my PhD, focused on fighting the erasure of Black women, and we were expecting our first child while I was writing a book about the power and influence of Black motherhood. The awareness that stems from my personal experiences paired with my studies has taught me that making my own choices, pushing against limitations, and opening doors for others to do the same means that I must trust in my own intuition, power, and wisdom above all else, and expose the ways American patriarchy tries to rob me of them and deny my self-determination whenever it can.

In my life thus far, this theft and denial have been most flagrant in my roles as a wife and a mother. Discussions with friends and audience members where people feel most confused, scared, and controlled happen around these identities as well, even outside these being part of their experience. In other words, even when people are not wives or mothers they feel pressured to get married, or they experience a fear of losing their identities in motherhood, for example, but they cannot always explain why. Hence part 3 has focused on reproduction and assigning us all roles as a means to uphold the story of American patriarchy that we discussed in part 1 and builds on our understanding of the limits and punishments we discussed in part 2. Part 3 has also been concerned with revealing other patriarchal authorities in addition to the founding fathers, archetypal presidents, Supreme Court justices, and more that we have studied thus far. Researchers and scientists, as well as some doctors, as we've seen, have also attempted to make American patriarchy and its laws seem natural and scientifically backed, even going so far as to describe our bodily processes as following American patriarchal law.

In the years between meeting my husband and becoming a mother, I had my own confrontations with American patriarchy and its authorities. Sometimes the examples in my life point to microaggressions—those routine insults, put-downs, and offensive statements that happen so often they are difficult to keep track of— while other examples that are more blatant, carrying the potential for life-threatening physical harm, stick out in my mind. Usually the moments come as a result of someone's subconscious alignment with American patriarchy, and other times they are a result of someone purposefully trying to uphold the status quo. In each of these, I chose to take my frustrations paired with my intuition, knowledge, and power to forge my own path and hopefully make a difference beyond myself. Experiencing dating, marriage, and early motherhood in the United States has made me more aware than ever of our country's need for change.

After completing my master's, I spent a few years teaching eighth- through twelfth-graders in Stockton, California. I moved there from England because my fiancé at the time was on Stockton's city council and was planning to run for mayor of his hometown. He would be Stockton's very first Black mayor, as well as the youngest mayor of a major city in American history. His drive to do whatever he could for the city he grew up in was inspiring, not only to me but to people around the world who were watching the beginning of his historic political career.

Although I knew that female partners of male stars were usually erased and that partners of politicians, especially, were often viewed more as accessories than as their own persons, it didn't keep me from feeling frustrated by people's attempts to reduce my story, my dreams, and my accomplishments in the shadow of his. In speaking about me people conveniently left out the fact that we met because we attended the same elite school, and most assumed the only thing I had going for me was dating him. When we got engaged, someone excitedly said to me, "Now you'll have something to do! You'll be busy planning the wedding!" It seemed impossible in their minds that I could be just as driven and talented as he was, less concerned about my wedding day and more concerned about starting my PhD or about the lesson plans I was organizing for my students. What made me more uncomfortable, however, were the constant comments I received about my looks. I was called a "trophy girlfriend" to my face more than once; people said I was the beauty and Michael was the brains; older men looked me up and down and congratulated Michael on finding such a "looker," while I was expected to stand there, smile, and be grateful for the "compliments." If I spoke up for myself I was advised to calm down, play my part, and accept that this was simply how things were.

Although it disappointed me, I knew I had to trust my power and wisdom and do something more with these growing moments of frustration, something larger than myself. I knew it was no individual's fault but instead a result of the ways in which we socialize people to learn that women's purpose in life is to marry and have children, to stand there and be pretty while remaining largely silent. I channeled my anger into publishing the first-ever report on "The Status of Women in Stockton." As a researcher I knew that my feelings were likely not only mine but instead reflective of a collective frustration of women throughout the city who might be feeling ignored or unseen, women with less privileges than mine whose roles in their families and larger communities were likely being taken for granted, women who were being made to feel uncomfortable or unsafe. I collaborated with the local data co-op and my copublisher, Sukhi Samra, to run focus groups, interviews, and surveys and collect data on how women in Stockton were doing compared to the rest of the county, state, and country. I knew it was within my power to help shift conversations surrounding women and girls, and to do my part in creating a tool that might alleviate our concerns and showcase the need to center the stories of those who have been relegated to the margins.

Later on, when Michael and I got married and were expecting our firstborn, I was well into my PhD, still working as a college counselor, and I had recently sold my first book. We pooled our resources together to buy and move into our new home. A neighbor, an older white man, walked up to me one day as I was on my way out the door; he was curious about something. As he often did, he launched into his reflections without any concern about what I was doing or where I was going, expecting me to pause everything and listen. He said, "You two have a really nice home; Michael must have to work two jobs to afford it." I replied, "That's interesting; instead of considering the fact that I might make money, you think Michael, the mayor of the city, somehow works two jobs?" I shrugged and said I needed to go. As I drove away, I shook my head thinking about the constant erasure of my contributions even when it didn't make logical sense. That same day, as I walked into a doctor's appointment to check on the baby, a man behind me whistled and said, "Okay, hot mama!" I had experienced catcalling before, but the fact that I was visibly pregnant made me feel more vulnerable and afraid. My heart began racing and I walked toward the entrance as fast as I could.

This frequent erasure of women, Black women in particular, as well as everyone's constant disregard for our safety and our time became one of my primary motivations in writing *The Three Mothers*, in reconstructing the lives of Alberta King, Berdis Baldwin, and Louise Little and putting them in the spotlight. Because I was fighting not only for them, I was also fighting for myself to be seen and respected. I was fighting for the women who raised my husband to be acknowledged and no longer overlooked as well, for their struggles and perseverance to be acknowledged. I realized early that when journalists told my husband's story they largely highlighted his father and the men in his life. Sadly, my husband's father has been unable to be present but his mother, aunt, and grandmother have proudly raised him, his brother, and two cousins in a beautifully close-knit nontraditional family. Despite the fact that Michael always credits his "three mothers" for his perseverance and success, his father continues to receive more coverage and visibility. In documentaries and short videos that have been made about Michael's career, this denial of the women in his life has been equally problematic. For example, I have been asked to be filmed alongside him, but I am usually not miked because what I have to say appears not to matter. I once was asked to be filmed while making him dinner; another time I was filmed being asked to talk about our wedding and future children, and nothing else. In the films, Michael's father receives more attention than his mother and me combined. I carried these frustrations with me as I examined the treatment of motherhood in the United States through my research for my dissertation and my book.

I became painfully aware of how disrespected, controlled, and limiting mothering is in our nation, how at almost every turn women are told they should want to become mothers and then mothers are told they should not trust themselves, that they are unworthy of support, that they shouldn't complain, and they are made to feel small and alone. In many ways, mothers are being forced to relinquish their power and wisdom to doctors, to their partners, to policymakers, even to their children, and these messages in their various forms are not accidental but instead very strategic and ingrained.

Another time I was working with a contractor, a man who often stated that I loved "spending my husband's money" on house projects. We were quickly approaching our son's due date when for no reason at all, other than to tell me his opinions of childbirth, he launched into sharing the story of his own daughter's birth. He said, "It was gross; I almost had to leave the room. I didn't want to see all that going on down there," as he laughed. I shook my head; his comment was emblematic of a much larger problem.

Again, I found myself wanting to do something that was largely expected of me, to have a child, but wanting to do it differently, wanting to show that it could be empowering, that I didn't have to lose myself, that I could return to the practices of my ancestors, that I could seek support in other women of color, that I could mother from a position of awareness about my incredible abilities and my state of deserving love, respect, care, and admiration. I was not going to be reduced, or made to feel like bringing life into the world and nurturing that life with everything in me could be described as anything short of astounding. How dare anyone call it gross?

In studying Black mothers and becoming more aware of all the ways our personhood and relationship to our children have been attacked and denied in American history, I came to find that these two words, "Black" and "mother" combined, were resistance in and of themselves; together they made a statement in the face of American patriarchy that said, "Everything can be done differently." Because one of the primary tenets of American patriarchy is the belief that Black people do not deserve to be treated as people, and therefore that Black women and children do not deserve the same love and protection as everyone else. I experienced this in some of the statements people made online when we announced that we were expecting. While most Stocktonians were supporters of my husband, there were also many who were incredibly racist and who often made threats to our safety via online platforms. They called him racial slurs, accused me of getting paid to be with him, and even published our home address online. But I thought my unborn child would be exempt from their hatred, so I was shocked when I read comments like "I hope your baby dies of SIDS." Again, I was grateful for my work, grateful for my knowledge of the ways the decisions of Black mothers have always flown in the face of the fallacy of our inhumanity and the belief that we do not deserve to be treated with dignity and respect.

The crux of Black mothering is the statement that freedom, transformation, and self-definition are possible regardless of the forces that might tell us differently. It is not an act of assimilation, or about fitting the system as it currently stands, but instead a message of all that can change. In her essay "m/other ourselves: a Black queer feminist genealogy for radical mothering," Alexis Pauline Gumbs writes about mothering as a queer and revolutionary act,

> in the global context of "population control," a story that says poor women and women of color should not give birth. A story with a happy ending for capitalism: we do not exist. The queer thing is that we *were* born; our young and/or deviant and/or brown and/or broke and/or single mamas did the wrong thing. Therefore we exist: a population out of control, a story interrupted. We are the guerrilla poems written on walls, purveyors of a billion dangerous meanings of life.

Writers like Gumbs ignited more power within me, but I still had a ways to go.

As soon as I came across the stories of "granny midwives" in my research, I decided I wanted to deliver my child with other women of color by my side. I was either going to have a home birth or I was going have doulas with me; I refused to enter a hospital that was built on fearing my ability without advocates whom I deeply trusted. I was given the incredible gift of witnessing my sister give birth to one of her children at home, I had seen how beautiful and empowering an experience a home birth could be. This beauty and empowerment stood in contrast to moments of bias I observed with my OB and nurses that made me feel unsafe and judged. For example, when I first met our doctor, she assumed I was unmarried and made a comment about how young I was to be having a child. On the first visit she was already curious what my plan for birth control was to keep myself from getting pregnant again. Although I couldn't find a midwife of color who lived close enough, I did find three doulas who upon our very first meeting showed me both how wise I was and how much I still had left to learn. They asked why I wanted to work with them, and I responded by telling them that I knew I had little control over what would happen on the day I went into labor, that I wanted people beside me who would make decisions I was comfortable with and help me understand my options. They listened to me and when I was finished one of them said, "We understand your concerns but you are wrong about one thing: *You* are the one in control, *you* are the one who makes the decisions, and we are here to support you each step of the way." I smiled with relief; I knew already I had made the right choice.

My doulas told me to trust myself through my labor, one that I know would have gone completely differently without their presence. The nurses who assisted my labor at the hospital told me that they had never seen someone come in who was voluntarily opting to give birth without any medication, so they had never witnessed an unassisted birth. Throughout the hours that I spent laboring they repeatedly tried to get me to lie down, something that felt entirely unnatural to me and something my doulas told me I didn't have to do. The nurses told me my son was in distress and that my movement was making it difficult for them to track his heartbeat, something my doulas said was normal for all babies in labor as they held the monitor on me so I could move as much as I wanted to. The nurses were entertained by how much "noise" I was making and told my husband I was being loud. They also pointed at my hemorrhoids and made fun of them. On the other hand, my doulas massaged my body and encouraged me to grunt. I had to write in my birth plan that I did not want to be "coached" through my pushing, but instead wanted to push when it felt right to me, to avoid being instructed to push harder or move faster than what felt natural to me. This message to trust myself carried forward in the newborn phase when it felt best to me to nurse my son and to sleep with him in my arms, rather than wrap him and place him in a bassinet away from me like mothers are advised to do in the US. I again had to call on my instincts and my study of the history of controlling women, as well as my knowledge of other countries, to make choices that felt right for me and my family without carrying judgment for anyone who might do all this differently.

I tell you these stories because in my life I have come up against American patriarchy at every turn, just like we all have, but the difference is that I am well aware of the enemy I am facing. With this awareness I rely on my intuition because I know how powerful it is, and how it threatens instances of American patriarchy as well as the system of American patriarchy in its entirety. I do not want everyone to feel that they must make the same decisions that I have with my knowledge, and it's important to reiterate that our ability to act on our intuition has purposefully been limited. However, I do want everyone, especially girls and women, to be aware of how they are currently being made to feel like they are not authorities in their own lives or over their own bodies because their potential and power is so deeply feared. American patriarchy relies on our fear of ourselves, our lack of confidence in ourselves, our willingness to make ourselves smaller and quieter and follow the rules. These truths simply become most obvious around actions that are directly related to our reproductive "roles." We learn these roles from the moment we are born, so I ask myself: How can I make sure my children are aware of their power while raising them in a country that doesn't want them to know they have any?

Part 4

OUR
CREATIVITY
AND JOY

16

WITH DEAFENING VOLUME
AND REPETITION

◼

S he's social and he is shy," a stranger said to us regarding our
son and daughter. This person was referring to the fact that
our daughter had smiled at her while our son looked away
when she stopped to say hello as we pushed our kids in the stroller.
I held myself back from correcting her, and waited until she passed
to tell them both that they could agree or disagree with her opinion
and that smiling didn't necessarily mean you were social, nor did
looking away necessarily mean you were shy. My son was only two
and a half at the time, and our daughter was even younger, so I am
not sure they processed anything I was saying, let alone anything
she had said. However, it has always been important to me that my
kids not be labeled by others, and that they are not spoken about as
opposites of one another, especially before our third child was born.

I have often noticed that when there are only two factors in
any study, people have a tendency to compare them to try to find
the differences between them. But when you introduce even one
more factor, we are suddenly able to see a spectrum of other possibilities. In the case of having a son and a daughter, people often
commented not only on their supposed differences in personality
but also on their capabilities: "He is the walker, she is the talker,"
for example. But what most people are unaware of is the influence

of the messages they are sending to children with each observation and label that they assign them. What's worrisome is that if these messages are repeated, they might become what children believe to be true about themselves. But I believe that we are not supposed to tell children who they are, and instead that they will show us who they are as they grow into their own self-discovery.

I use this simple story to illustrate the need for each of us to be thoughtful about the conclusions we reach and the messages we share and, perhaps more important, to be cautious of the messages we hear and have heard since we were children ourselves. In part 1 I focused on the narrative of American patriarchy: white people are recognized as human beings with rights, white men are superior to white women, everyone else is unworthy of humane treatment but they can try to access it through playing their part to uphold the power structure and by assimilating to the dominant group. I spoke about the ways in which our founding fathers crafted American patriarchy through the laws that dictate our nation. In part 2 I focused on methods of keeping people in the place that American patriarchy has assigned to them, and the consequences that are employed to implicitly and explicitly punish people seen as diverging from "their place." I presented these consequences as part of the master plan to constantly remind us of our subordination and scare us from challenging the powers that be, like those in the highest courts of our nation. In part 3 I showed how external control of our reproductive abilities is the ultimate means of reproducing American patriarchy. I spoke about how all of it—the narrative, the laws, the punishments—revolve around taking the reproductive abilities of those who are not considered the rightful power holders in our country, and using or controlling these to solidify everyone's place in the social order.

I have tried to make the many tentacles of American patriarchy obvious and as plain to see to you as they are to me, and to make it clear how strategic the creators and maintainers of American patriarchy have been. All this has been in preparation for us to now study how something so evident that is crafted and formulated, even written out explicitly in the documents our nation is built upon, starts to feel inevitable. Part 4 is concerned with understanding the presentation of American patriarchy as natural by first ensuring our familiarity with it from the moment we are born through the messages we receive, and then reifying it with rules on how we perform our parts, through the ways we dress to the activities we can or cannot participate in. In each part I have presented certain "authorities" who contribute to the maintenance of American patriarchy and, in this part, I focus largely on media specialists such as in broadcasting and journalism. I also pay attention to experiencing American patriarchy through the eyes of young people who have yet to become aware of the strategy behind it all, but who will quickly become familiar with its dictates and consequences that are presented as undeniable truths.

There are many ideas we believe to be true simply because we have heard them before. Some of these beliefs are not completely inaccurate; they can be semitruths. Take, for example, the belief that human beings operate with five senses. Many of us were taught from a young age that the five senses were sight, smell, touch, hearing, and taste. Scientists now estimate that we have many more senses; some say there are dozens, including our sense of movement, our sense of time, and our sense of temperature. It isn't necessarily harmful to still teach the five senses; it is simply incomplete information.

Other beliefs presented as facts can carry consequences. For example, a notion that became popular toward the end of the twentieth century was the belief that human beings could be divided into two groups who approached everything they did differently based on which part of their brain was more active than the other, left-brain thinkers and right-brain thinkers. "Left-brain thinkers" were seen as more logical and analytical, better at technical skills, but lacking in their ability to interact well with others, while "right-brain thinkers" were more intuitive and creative, better in the arts, and better with people but worse with organization and planning. Books were written about the two supposed groups of humans, and online tests were created so people could see which group they fit into and what careers they should pursue.

Researchers have since found that the human brain does not operate by favoring one side or the other and in fact is always using both sides, dispelling the myth that humans can be divided by dominant brain-side function. But you might still hear people say that they are left- or right-brain thinkers. Beyond people taking a quiz to see which group they fall into and then acting accordingly, this myth also has serious repercussions when biases come into play. As showcased in the 2012 article "Neuromyths in Education: Prevalence and Predictors of Misconceptions Among Teachers," at the time of its study, many educators still subscribed to the idea of these two groups long after it was labeled a myth and divided their students by supposed brain functioning. These divisions also led to students limiting themselves, some believing they were either creative and unable to succeed at math or other analytical tasks, while others believed they lacked and would never be able to improve their artistic skills. I hope you are starting to notice the similarities between this kind of semitruth and our treatment of a construct like the gender binary, where someone proposed an idea concerning human difference; others took up the charge and backed the idea; still others took the idea a step further and divided people accordingly, keeping everyone from being able to become their full selves; and individuals then began to believe they were destined to these designations and would never be able to disprove them, and therefore perhaps they might never try.

One of the reasons we can continue to believe semitruths or even myths and, at times, feel very strongly about our belief in them is due to what researchers call "illusory truths" or the "illusory truth effect." This refers to our tendency, as human beings, to believe false or incomplete information so long as it has been repeated to us, sometimes only once and sometimes over and over again. The term was coined in the 1970s, when researchers at Villanova University and Temple University found that even when people knew something was false to begin with, if they heard it enough times, it became familiar and eventually accepted. In the study, subjects were given a list of true or false statements that ranged from politics and sports to the arts. These participants were asked to decide which category the statements fell into. Then they were asked to return two weeks later. They were given another list of true and false statements and asked to repeat the exercise; some of the statements were new, and others were the same as the ones they saw before. Researchers found that people were more likely to say something was true if they'd seen the statement more than once. As they put it, "Frequency of occurrence is apparently a criterion used to establish the referential validity of plausible statements." In other words, familiarity is confused with fact.

Knowing this about ourselves, as human beings, should serve as a warning and an invitation to become more aware and prepared for challenging what we hear, and training ourselves to know what and whom we can and cannot trust. We should ask ourselves why we are being told something, what purpose it serves for us to know the information, who the storyteller is, what they have to gain from us believing their argument, and what other credible sources have to say about the same thing. These are the basic premises of research that everyone should employ in their processing of information, especially regarding media literacy and the way we navigate all the messages we are exposed to on a daily basis, because illusory truths can be incredibly dangerous. The scarier fact is that those who are in fields that control information we are exposed to are very aware of the effect of repetition and the power of saying something over and over again.

Take the onset of the coronavirus pandemic. Myths circulated about herd immunity, conspiracy theories abounded stating that the problem never was and was never going to be as bad as scientists warned, President Trump suggested that people could inject themselves with disinfectant as a treatment, but perhaps most notable of all were our differing beliefs concerning masks. Mask-wearing or lack thereof made it apparent that what we believe to be true is dictated by whom we are listening to on repeat, who the authorities are in our lives that make us experience that feeling of familiarity that can easily be confused for fact. This phenomenon, especially as it relates to newscasters and journalists such as those employed by Fox News, is also called disinformation. While "misinformation" refers to the inadvertent spread of false information without intent to harm, "disinformation" is false information designed to mislead others and is deliberately spread with the intent to confuse fact and fiction. We cannot understand the power of disinformation without comprehending the illusory truth effect and the extent to which we can attach ourselves and our entire identities to mere repeated opinions.

People started to believe masks were unnecessary because they had heard it enough times. People hung their worldview on mask-wearing, making it a decision not only about protecting themselves and others against illness but about their political leanings, their patriotism, and, of course, because our nation is most influenced by these parts of our identity, it became about their gender and race. Antimasking protesters around the United States, who likely support abortion bans, held signs saying MY BODY, MY CHOICE! with a mask crossed out in red ink as they swung American flags. They saw their disdain for masks as a fight for their American freedoms. Other signs read REAL MEN DON'T MASK, implying that the choice to wear a mask stood in opposition to manhood because it showed weakness. Even though Covid-19 hit men harder than women, and in New York City alone men were dying at twice the rate of women, men were less likely to mask across the US. "Real men don't mask" became another illusory truth that cost people their lives. White people were also less likely to wear masks than other

racial groups, and as we could see from images of antimasking protests around the nation, most of the people opposed to the mandates
were white men who believed that they were all-knowing and
all-powerful and that no one had a right to challenge that. There
were a few others sprinkled throughout these protests who thought
they could benefit from aligning themselves with such "real men"
and, therefore, also took up the banner. Although communities of
color, especially Black people, were disproportionately affected by
the pandemic at its onset, by 2022, it was white people who were
more likely to die from the virus. Researchers believe this switch
happened because white men, who often identified as members of
the Grand Old Party, were the least likely to get vaccinated and
wear masks on a regular basis.

This group was also most likely to guide their decisions based
on advice from their trusted source for "news." According to the
Pew Research Center, "Around two-thirds of Republicans and
Republican-leaning independents (65%) say they trust Fox News
for political and election news." Furthermore, in November 2020,
Americans ages sixty-five and older accounted for around two-fifths
of those who said their main news source was Fox News (37 percent),
compared with 21 percent of all adults. And around nine in ten who
turned to Fox News (87 percent) identified their race and ethnicity
as non-Hispanic white, compared with 65 percent of all adults. Fox
News has consistently been the top cable news network for years
in the United States. According to Statista, in November 2023, Fox
News boasted "1.72 million primetime viewers. Fox News viewers
in the 25–54 demographic amounted to 199,000, while MSNBC had
just 109,000. When looking at Fox News viewers compared to CNN,
the overall average number of prime-time viewers was notably different. CNN has been losing viewers in recent years." According to
their own data, in 2024 Fox News made history as the "first network
to mark 22 consecutive years at number one."

Regarding American patriarchy, Fox News is dedicated to

ensuring that it continues. This is evident in its unabashed commitment to sexist, racist, xenophobic, and transphobic reporting.
Fox News anchors have been obsessed with conspiracies like "the
great replacement" theory that says white people are in danger of
becoming a minority in the United States as a result of immigration
policies and movements aimed at achieving equity in our nation.
Furthermore, they added to conspiracy theories suggesting that the
2020 presidential election was rigged with statements like "Yes,
the election was stolen from Trump." They have made irrelevant
comments such as "Jesus was a white man. . . . That's a verifi-
able fact. . . . I want you kids watching to know that." They have
blamed immigrants for making America "poorer" and "dirtier."
Another host suggested that crime was up because more women
were in office, and that women should take "a ladies week off"
because our policies have become too "soft." Guests invited on air
have said things like "We don't need a military that is woman-
friendly or gay-friendly." Another guest suggested that women are
"less ambitious" and "happier at home." Headlines such as "Trans-
genderism Is the Most Dangerous Extremist Movement in the
United States" run regularly on their site. Yet another guest said
that gender-affirming healthcare for trans youth allowed providers
to "basically molest and abuse children."

Research has also found that Fox News and its viewers are part
of a negative feedback loop where not only is Fox News influencing how its viewers think, the platform is worried about losing
its viewers, so its content is tailored to continue feeding their per-
ception of how our country is and how it should continue to be
organized. For example, a recent lawsuit revealed that Fox News
faced a ratings slide when they accurately reported that Joe Biden
was going to win the election. With this knowledge and fear they
started reporting false claims of a stolen election instead. When
such a large portion of the population watches Fox News, we have
to consider its effect on our understanding of identity.

Fox News is not the only one to blame. The crafting and survival of American patriarchy relies heavily on television, movies, and magazines as well, and the people primarily in charge of these messages across the board are overwhelmingly white men. About 80 percent of film directors are white men, followed by minority men, white women, and then minority women splitting the rest of the pie. When it comes to book publishing, in 2020 the *New York Times* reported that the leaders of the Big Five publishers were all white, and that only one was a woman. The *Times* report also found the following: The people who edited the ten most-read magazines were all white and only three were women; out of the fourteen people who influence most of the music people hear, twelve were white and only one was a woman; out of ninety-nine people who owned professional baseball, basketball, and football teams, ninety-three were white. A Women's Media Center report found that men occupied two-thirds of guest spots on major TV news programs, and that white people comprised three-fourths of all guests and commentators on the most popular Sunday news programs. The following are statistics from a report by the Institute for Diversity and Ethics in Sport: 79.2 percent of the sports editors were white and 83.3 percent were men; 72 percent of the assistant sports editors were white and 75.8 percent were men; 77.1 percent of the columnists were white and 82.2 percent were men; 77.1 percent of the reporters were white and 85.6 percent were men; 77 percent of the copy editors/designers were white and 75.3 percent were men; and 72.4 percent of web specialists were white and 78.1 percent were men.

The way we think about identity in the United States is a list of illusory truths that American patriarchy relies on to survive. Another way to describe these is by the cultural meanings we assign to our performance of our assigned roles and how these meanings appear in the messages we consume. Take gender, for example, and the meanings we are taught from the moment we are born without any explanation for how they came to be. A statement like "sex and gender are the same thing" is not factual, but many people believe it to be true because they have heard it before. "Girls like pink and boys like blue," "women wear makeup and dresses while men do not," and "men don't cry" are other examples.

Again, at times illusory truths are relatively harmless. It doesn't necessarily hurt anyone if they're unaware of the many other senses humans employ beyond the primary five. But illusory truths and the overreporting of them in relation to gender, as a result of American patriarchy and power displacement, have become detrimental. These falsehoods have torn families apart, kept individuals from achieving their full potential, even killed people. In a country organized upon sexism that is intertwined with all other forms of discrimination, what the majority believes to be true about our sex and gender, especially when it is backed by their trusted and familiar sources, carries the highest stakes in each of our lives. We are forced to live by myths or are shunned; strangers take it upon themselves to enforce their beliefs on anyone who walks by them showing the glitch in what they've accepted to be true; even parents start to believe that if their children do not fit an illusory truth about identity, their children must be threatened, kicked out of their home, and/or disowned.

With this in mind, in part 4 I ask: How has the crafted and carefully maintained system of American patriarchy relied on its messages and messengers to appear as something inevitable and naturally occurring? It has always astounded me that the simplest of things become divisive and threatening if they do not align with the illusory truths of American patriarchy. I cannot wrap my mind around the lengths people will go to maintain an order that is harmful, unjust, twisted, isolating, and limited. How is it possible that a little girl can be forced to wear a dress or a skirt to school when she states she is more comfortable in pants? How are female athletes still being forced to wear uniforms that they do not agree with? How is it possible that a parent could beat their son because he wants to try on heels, a simple pair of shoes, or he wants to try on makeup, or paint his nails, or play with dolls? How could these actions turn a parent against their most precious, dependent loved one, leaving them without protection or an understanding of what they've supposedly done wrong? How is it possible that a parent would kick their child out of their home and into the streets because they are attracted to someone of the same sex? How does someone's sexual orientation condemn them to being disowned by their family? Why is a person who is nonbinary or transgender put in harm's way when they walk down the street wearing whatever it is they want to wear? Why would any person care so much about what another person chooses to do when it has no effect on them other than showing them that what they are familiar with, what they believe to be true, may in fact simply be a repeated fallacy or incomplete information?

All these tragic instances continue because of recycled illusory truths that many of us are trapped by when we are born into American patriarchy and are faced with misinformation and disinformation that is presented as the undeniable whole picture. We then seek this familiarity that we have with the story in the sources we have available to inform us. But there is hope, because the effect of illusory truths and the loop can be interrupted once we are aware of it, and once we realize that, we can be the trusted sources of information for others around us, including our children. We can also encourage each individual's discovery of themselves rather than telling them who they must be. We can liberate ourselves from thinking we must tell other people how to dress, how to act, and how to exist. We can transfer energy used to control others into energy used to allow all of us to live freely. The semitruths can become the harmless kind; for example, "girls like pink" could be true for some, but still wouldn't negate the fact that some girls don't and some boys do, and that some people don't identify with being girls or boys at all.

17

CRITIQUE AND SILENCING

✖

I n the spring of 2013, I took a class called Sex and Love in Modern US Society. It was my junior year, and I was excited to be enrolled in something that felt radical simply because of its title. I couldn't wait to dive into the readings and discussions with my peers, who were mostly seniors. If I'm being honest, now that more than ten years have passed, I don't particularly remember what we read in that class and, no offense to the lecturer, who I thought was great, I don't really remember what she told us. The experience that remains crystal clear in my memory, however, was being in the presence of one of the most powerful individuals I have ever met, one of my fellow classmates, Alok V. Menon.

I thought Alok was incredible, always dressed in such a chic way, treating others with the ultimate kindness, and possessing a balance of elegance and force each and every time they opened their mouth to speak. When Alok added to the discussion, I perked up, ready to hear whatever wisdom they were about to share. I could tell I was in the presence of greatness, of someone who would change the world; they were already changing the minds and hearts of everyone listening in our class. For me, Alok expanded my thinking that was committed to gender and race equity but that I didn't realize, up until that point, was still operating in the confines of American patriarchy, particularly the confines of the gender binary. I so deeply admired Alok that it made me nervous to introduce myself and tell them that; I was just happy to glean from their presence. I carry the wisdom Alok passed on to me in my work and in my parenting because of the vision they offer to liberate ourselves from the teachings of American patriarchy, so that those coming after us can avoid ever learning them to begin with.

Alok has now become a famous poet, comedian, speaker, and author with over a million followers on Instagram for spreading the insight they shared in class all those years ago with the world. The insight is both plain and profound because it flies in the face of so much of what we have been taught is true and is based on Alok's own experience and their human desire to live freely. Why might this basic desire that we all share become something world-changing? Well, as we have come to understand through the progression of this book, only some people are allowed the right to live freely according to American patriarchy, and a person who is a gender-nonconforming South Asian American who identifies as transfeminine and proudly wears makeup, nail polish, and stunning outfits that showcase their figure, while also putting their body hair on full display, is seen as a foil to the foundation the United States is built upon. American patriarchy tells us that Alok, and others as wonderful as they are, are simply not supposed to exist and, if they somehow do, they will certainly not be treated as human beings but instead will be judged and punished. Even worse, those making the judgment and doing the punishing will often be applauded and will avoid any consequences.

One of the primary ways we are taught that people like Alok are unworthy of being treated as human beings is through the strategic lack of respectful representation of trans and gender-diverse people in the media. In the United States especially, where we rely heavily on films and TV as our means for understanding our world around us, it is important to know that for most of our country's entertainment business history, trans and gender-diverse people have often gone unrepresented. When they have been written into our narratives, it is as comedic characters for audiences to make fun of, or solely as sex workers or victims of violence. These limited presentations of identities that exist outside cisgender men and women have sent the message that such people are less important, a joke, or doomed to mistreatment. Furthermore, trans and gender-nonconforming people are often reported about inaccurately where they are misgendered or called names that they no longer go by in news stories.

Representations of nonbinary people in the media have grown from a history of criminalizing and punishing such identities in our nation. During the nineteenth century and well into the twentieth, portraying yourself as someone of the "opposite sex" was considered a crime. Across the United States cities wrote laws to prevent nonbinary gender expression both as part of someone's core identity and to prevent nonbinary performance as well as costuming. In 1845, New York declared it a crime to present yourself in public with a disguise or a painted face that concealed your identity. In the 1850s, it was illegal in Chicago for someone to appear in public in clothes that did not pertain to their sex. In the 1860s, San Francisco also enacted a masquerade ban that prohibited wearing clothing in public that did not pertain to one's legal sex. If you were to break these laws you could not only be arrested and subjected to abuse, your name would also appear in newspapers to further vilify and endanger you. Other laws were also used to target transgender people and drag performers, even when the law did not specifically state anything about clothing. One of these was written in New York in 1976, and has been referred to over the years as the "walking while trans" law, supposedly to prohibit loitering for the purpose of prostitution. LGBTQ+ community members and advocates have said for decades, however, that the law was used to stop and frisk any trans person, particularly trans women of color, arrest them, and accuse them of prostitution and sexual deviancy. This law was repealed only in 2021.

In recent years representations of nonbinary and trans communities have started to change, with more diverse characters being written into the shows and movies we consume as well as more accurate reporting in journalism. However, this progress has been met with a growth in hurtful rhetoric fueled by those who fear that they will lose something if gender-expansive people are treated with dignity and are allowed to live without fear of persecution or harassment. These unnecessarily alarmed people spew lies about how policies that are aimed at creating inclusion for everyone who does not fit the gender binary pose danger to the safety of those who do, even though it is the people who identify as gender minorities who face the most safety hazards.

As a *New England Journal of Medicine* article, "Persons of Nonbinary Gender: Awareness, Visibility, and Health Disparities," based on surveys that included trans people and gender-nonconforming people, states:

As compared with the general public in other studies, gender-minority persons are more likely to live in poverty (29% vs. 12%), be unemployed (15% vs. 5%), be uninsured (14% vs. 11%), be the victim of intimate-partner violence (24% vs. 18%), have attempted suicide (40% vs. 4.6%), have experienced severe psychological stress in the past month (39% vs. 5%), and have HIV (1.4% vs. 0.3%). Thirty percent have been homeless at some time, and 9% report having been physically assaulted in the previous year because of their gender identity. Gender-nonconforming persons are more likely than transgender persons to have experienced mistreatment in school (70% vs. 59%) or by the police (29% vs. 22%) and are less likely to be "out" in the workplace (33% vs. 44%) or with family (35% vs. 64%).

The outcomes are worse for people who are gender minorities and who also experience other forms of marginalization such
as being people of color. These devastating numbers highlight yet
again how American patriarchy makes it so that if we do not fit
the narrow confines of identity it offers us, we will confront disadvantages in employment, as well as in our access to resources and
protection, and our mental, physical, and emotional states will be
inevitably impacted. The statistic concerning the mistreatment of
gender-nonconforming people in comparison to transgender people
also highlights the slight benefit that comes with adhering to the
gender binary, again showing how attempts at assimilation will
be rewarded and encouraged.

It is one thing to not understand identities outside cisgender
people due to lack of exposure and lack of visibility, but it is another
for this confusion or unawareness to turn into hatred and violence
without laws in place to protect individuals from such hostility. In
a recent tragedy, a nonbinary sixteen-year-old student named Nex
Benedict died after they and a friend who identifies as trans were
beaten up by some of their peers in a school bathroom. The three
older students reportedly banged Nex's head against the floor. The
day after the beating, Nex passed away. At first it was believed that
Nex died due to complications from brain trauma, but it was later
concluded that Nex committed suicide. This heartbreaking loss
feels even heavier because of how young Nex was and how early
in life we are taught to uphold the status quo from what we might
hear at home, to what we see and don't see on TV, to what articles
tell us to believe about the danger of people living freely as themselves, and the permission that gives us to do something about it.

The organization of our nation remains as strong as it is today
not only because of the institutional, legal, and media powers that
be, but also because many individuals take it upon themselves to
be enforcers of the "rules" and feel personally offended by anyone
whom they see as breaking them. In following Alok's epic jour-

ney, it is distressing to witness how many people harass and tear Alok down. In one interview Alok says, regarding the public harassment, "It is so constant and terrifying I'm constantly in pain because of it." Comments on social media are one thing, but Alok faces even more danger as they walk down the street and people yell slurs and statements like "You are disgusting!" and might try to get physical.

It is in the face of such violence, where the need for Alok's world-changing work becomes obvious, that you realize that their fight to live freely as themselves is a fight on behalf of all of us. Alok's stance is that we are told from the moment we are born that to survive our world we must kill the more feminine parts of ourselves, the parts that are vulnerable, tender, concerned with others, which has led everyone to be sad, lonely, and angry, unable to fully be or express our true selves. In an interview for *Scapi Magazine*, Alok says, "The reason I am punished so ruthlessly is not just because I am gender-nonconforming, but because I am unfettered by social beauty norms, because I am externalizing my creativity and joy in a world that polices it." In referencing that the only places where different expressions are allowed are in the form of entertainment in a show or in an art piece, they continue, "In this country, we cordon off and privatize creative expression: restrict it to the screen, to the gallery. It's not allowed to spill out into the public because doing so makes people imagine an alternative to the status quo." Alok uses their art, which they also see as taking form in the way they dress and show up each and every day, as a way to transform hearts and minds and bring joy and liberation to more people.

Alok focuses much of their work on reclaiming the feminine and pushing their audience, whether in arenas or on the street, to think about why the feminine has been put under attack and suppressed in all of us. I am also fascinated by Jack Halberstam's work on female masculinity and the way it can be put in conversation with Alok's revolutionary perspective by showcasing that any disruption of the binary, including the seeming dichotomy of female masculinity, becomes policed. Halberstam teaches in the Department of English and Comparative Literature and is director of the Institute for Research on Women, Gender, and Sexuality at Columbia University, and says he, she, or they are "loosey goosey about pronouns." Halberstam once wrote, "The back and forth between he and she sort of captures the form that my gender takes nowadays. Not that I am often an unambiguous 'she' but nor am I often an unambiguous 'he.' . . . My floating gender pronouns capture well the refusal to resolve my gender ambiguity."

In 2015, Halberstam delivered a visiting professorship lecture at the University of Cambridge while I was there pursuing my MPhil in multidisciplinary gender studies. My cohort and I read Halberstam's 1998 book *Female Masculinity* in preparation for our time with such a highly esteemed visiting professor, especially for our field. In the book, Halberstam uses their personal experience as a starting point to explain how society tells "girls in all kinds of ways that they must accept and take on femininity," especially beginning in their adolescent years. But in Halberstam's opinion, such femininity should be avoided to save girls and young women from pain. Halberstam writes, "Femininity tends to be associated with passivity and inactivity, with various forms of unhealthy body manipulations from anorexia to high-heeled shoes. It seems to me that at least early on in life, girls should avoid femininity." They argue instead in favor of different forms of masculinity that are separate from the belief that white manhood is the only acceptable form because this accepted form of manhood isn't working for anyone. Halberstam writes:

> The question, then, might be not what do female masculinities borrow from male masculinities, but rather what do

men borrow from butches? If we shift the flow of power and influence, we can easily imagine a plethora of new masculinities that do not simply feed back into the static loop that makes maleness plus power into the formula for abuse but that re-create masculinity on the model of female masculinity. . . . Cut off from the most obvious rewards of masculinity—political power and representation—many masculine women have had to create elaborate rationales for their ways of lovings [*sic*], their desire to provide for and protect a loved one, their decisions to live explicitly masculine lives.

These words reminded me of Black feminist commentary concerning what those in power could gain in learning from what those outside of power have created while being cast away from American patriarchy, rather than us always falling for the trap of trying to gain something from assimilating to those with power.

Halberstam's work also broadened my perspective. I hadn't realized before how much of feminist scholarship and politics relied on living comfortably within the two categories of the gender binary, and how limited a feminist revolution would be if it didn't always also consider women who were being punished for not being "womanly enough," women who were not identified as women at birth, people who were feminist but who did not identify as men or women, and even women of color who had been villainized and objectified when they were represented as not feminine enough. I hadn't considered how powerful an embrace of different forms of masculinity could be. I realized that it wasn't necessarily masculine characteristics that were always wrong, but more so the meaning they took on in a nation that promoted a masculinity that was fully available only to white men and relied on the domination of others.

Bringing Alok's stance into the conversation, I started to see that they were saying almost the same thing was true for femininity: femininity did not have to be weakness; it didn't have to be less than; it could mean strength, power, love for oneself and for others; it could encompass more stereotypical representations but it didn't have to. Masculinity and femininity had more to do with our being rather than our appearance, and they both could be strong and gentle, protective and vulnerable, available to all of us regardless of the sex we were assigned at birth, regardless of the position American patriarchy tried to push us into.

I became much more aware of the intricacies of the American patriarchal trap even for those of us who think we are radical; we can easily fall back into reproducing the system because it can feel more comfortable to do so. For example, we may say we are accepting of trans identities but mean this only when a trans person can pass and perform their part in the gender binary; we may say we are allies and then still keep our son from wearing a skirt, or our daughter from cutting off all her hair, or our child from saying they want to be referred to as "they" because we fear that these things signify something larger that might keep them from being treated humanely. I pushed myself to ask just how far my belief in equity extended and where I still needed to grow, because it became obvious to me that until people who see themselves in Alok V. Menon, Jack Halberstam, and others like them can walk down the street safely, unafraid of what others might do to hurt them, the work would not be complete. Until they could see themselves represented in the media not as entertainment for others but as human beings like everyone else, our efforts would be all for naught. Until I could let go of my own attachments to the meaning of clothing, hair, and pronouns, I was perhaps no better than what I wanted to change.

I am not saying that we need to reject every single one of the stereotypical qualities we have come to associate with the illusion of the binary but that we must accept the fact that most people, if not all people, do not fit neatly into these boxes. That the spectrum of our identities is beautifully vast and this acceptance is liberating for each and every one of us. While we may be against American patriarchy, we are often afraid of what it means to leave it behind, yet the bravest among us are those who do not fit it at all and who have come to the conclusion that they will choose to live freely in a country that tells them they cannot. If we're being truthful and pay attention to the hierarchy as it currently exists, the majority of us are more like Alok and Jack than we were previously aware of; they have simply been more courageous.

In their courage we find guidance. On one of Alok's posts a stranger commented: "I don't know who needs to tell you this so I'll just do it. You are not a woman, bro. Man up." Alok reposted the comment but blocked the name of the person to protect their identity, still invested in their well-being despite their disregard for Alok's, with a caring response:

My friend! I don't know who needs to tell you this, so I'll just do it. You are hurting. You mistake your armor as an identity & your pain as a personality. You are climbing a tree that bears no fruit. Ascending a ladder that goes nowhere. What you seek isn't here with me, it's within you. This isn't about my freedom, it's about your repression. You resent me because I live what you fear. I love you because I have no fear. I'm sorry you've been told you can't express yourself. You can. I promise. Have a great day!

Alok invited the person harassing them online to try to recognize their own repression, to discover what their own self-expression might look like, to realize that the road we have all been traveling only leads us to continue driving in circles of the same cycle, to open their eyes to why we have been taught such rigidity and how, perhaps, in answering this, we might instead find freedom.

One of the first steps toward experiencing the revelation that is detaching ourselves from American patriarchy is to identify the ways it manipulates everything we do and how this manipulation is intent on maintaining a social order. Things like our clothing and activities are decided for us, the way we should walk and talk are instructed, and we practice it all so much that it becomes muscle memory. But the thing about muscle memory, that neurological process that allows us to remember motor skills and perform them without conscious effort, is that it can be changed.

18

THEY EXCLUDE, DIVIDE,
AND LIMIT US

◼

O n April 19, 1967, the seventieth annual Boston Marathon took place. The marathon was part of an official celebra- tion of Patriots' Day, and hundreds of runners, which to- day has turned into thousands, eagerly participated. This year's marathon would go down in history and produce one of the most famous images of American patriarchy. A woman with the num- ber 261 across her chest is being heckled by an older man who is attempting to pull her out of the race by her clothes. The man is clearly enraged. The pair is surrounded by other male runners who mostly look on at the scene but one man is pushing the older, angry man in an attempt to free the woman from his grasp. The story behind the image is that of Kathrine Switzer, who at the time was a nineteen-year-old journalism student at the University of Syracuse. She had convinced her coach, Arnie Briggs, that she could run the entirety of the Boston Marathon. He was reluctant at first; running long distances was said to be dangerous for the delicate white fe- male body, but he eventually gave in when Kathrine told him that women had done it unofficially before and that she could run the distance in practice ahead of traveling to the race. She signed up as K. V. Switzer, and was pleased when she didn't see any language on the form that limited women from participating. Her boyfriend at the time decided to sign up too, saying, "If a girl can run a marathon, I can run a marathon."

When race day finally arrived, Kathrine put on her lipstick like she always did. Her boyfriend scolded her, saying it would make her gender more obvious and she should take it off. But she didn't want to appear less girly in order to participate; she wanted to show that women could run regardless. She was given her official race number, 261, and ran with joy and confidence. The men around her did double takes, some of them confused by her presence, but several were excited to see a woman running alongside them. Kathrine waved at them proudly and continued. Everything was fine, even though it was a cold and wet day, until Kathrine felt someone's hands on her and heard, "Get the hell out of my race and give me those numbers!" He was pulling her back and insisting she stop running, but Kathrine kept moving forward as best she could. Her boyfriend tackled the man—who they later learned was Jock Semple, the race manager—giving Kathrine the room to keep running. But she didn't feel relieved at that moment; she felt terrified. She was mortified by the feeling of being manhandled by an angry stranger, scared that her boyfriend had responded with aggression, and worried that she was going to be in trouble as a result of it all, simply for having a desire to run in a race. She transferred these feelings into movement and continued to put one foot in front of the other to complete the marathon.

In chapter 16 we discussed how illusory truths, semitruths, and misinformation contribute to the viability of American patriarchy by making it the thing we are most familiar with, the thing that is so ingrained in our experiences that we do not question how it came to be. In chapter 17 we examined how those who can see and try to live beyond the seeming comfort and familiarity of American patriarchy are hidden, cast away, disowned, and punished so that they are unable to disrupt our collective conscious and subconscious states of performance. I ended with a metaphor of seeing

American patriarchy and its specific dictates about how we should act, how we should talk, how we should sit, and how we should dress our bodies as a form of muscle memory that can appear "natural" and unrehearsed but is actually taught and practiced. As a result, it is much more malleable than we have been led to believe. So malleable are the dictates of American patriarchy that those in power have often bent the rules when it benefited them. Other times, those outside of such power have braved the consequences of attempting to break the rules entirely, believing that the outcomes would be worth the risk. In this chapter we explore how such malleability has been used both by those who want to maintain American patriarchy as well as by those who stand against it. The former can appear like progress, but it often still serves inequitable structures, while the latter is more concerned with lasting liberation from the rigidity and an embrace of personal choice. One of the most obvious spaces to discuss the changing of rules and the reshaping of illusory truths is through the study of sports in the United States, specifically an analysis of women's involvement.

Jock Semple was so angered by Kathrine Switzer's presence in the marathon because he was taught that women could not and should not exert such physical effort. It was believed for many years that if women participated in sports they would harm their reproductive organs, men would find them less attractive, and because their bodies "possessed much less energy" than those of men, they would produce weak offspring if they wasted their energy on pursuits like sports and higher education. Edward H. Clarke's 1870s book *Sex Education; or, A Fair Chance for Girls* displays some of the dogma used to control women's activities that holds power to this day.

Clarke was a doctor with degrees from Harvard and the University of Pennsylvania who specialized in otology, the anatomy and physiology of the ear. This ear doctor somehow became seen as an expert on how women and men should be trained differently. In *Sex*

Education he writes, "Educate a man for manhood, a woman for womanhood, both for humanity. In this lies the hope of the race." His book cites examples of women whose ovaries stopped working or who developed hysteria because they moved their energy away from their reproductive organs and more toward learning and/or physical activity. Clarke argued that men and women could not be given the same opportunities, nor the same training, saying, "Identical education of the two sexes is a crime before God and humanity, that physiology protests against, and that experience weeps over." He continues later in the book to explain that women can try to do what men do but, suffering as a result, they would be better off in their naturally weaker state. He quotes another male doctor, Henry Maudsley:

> While woman preserves her sex, she will necessarily be feebler than man, and, having her special bodily and mental characters, will have, to a certain extent, her own sphere of activity; where she has become thoroughly masculine in nature, or hermaphrodite in mind, when, in fact, she has pretty well divested herself of her sex, then she may take his ground, and do his work; but she will have lost her feminine attractions, and probably also her chief feminine functions.

These leading voices of their time represented their opinions as facts and argued that if women tried to do what men did, they would sacrifice what they were "meant" to do as women. We continue to see this logic appear for female athletes today when they declare they can continue their careers while also starting families if they desire to, and are met with disbelief, critiques, and even being dropped by companies that previously endorsed them. As we discussed in our chapters on reproduction, American patriarchy and its authors, journalists, and media experts spew the narrative that women cannot do what men do without losing something because if they do, it signals a lack and a weakness in those who claim to be more powerful.

Of course Clarke and Maudsley were considering the delicacy only of white women and the need for them to protect their reproductive organs above all else. Women of color have been forced to labor and exert themselves under harsh conditions in the United States since before its founding, forced to trek thousands of miles with children on their back, forced to pick tobacco and cotton under the pounding sun, forced to wait on white people hand and foot without anyone caring about sustaining their energy. As is typical of American patriarchy, white women were kept from fully pursuing opportunities and told what to do under the guise of protection, while women of color were excluded from protection and from being seen as human altogether.

American patriarchy's dictates concerning physical activity are another space where the desired hierarchy of our nation is reproduced, where men have been represented as more able than women, where women have been divided from one another, and where the themes of muscle memory and malleability are on full display. Over time some recreational activities became available and encouraged for white women so long as they were seen as gentle enough to protect women's primary function of reproduction, such as leisurely engagement with croquet, archery, tennis, and synchronized swimming, once also known as bathing-beauty swimming. Tennis courts, lakes, and swimming pools were segregated, barring women of color from entering. Furthermore, women who participated in these activities were instructed to wear overly feminized outfits to send the message that they were not trying to compete aggressively like men but instead were solely interested in healthful, relaxed, and unimportant play.

It wasn't until World War II that women were encouraged to take on a new form of femininity that rallied them to take jobs that were typically held by the men who had been drafted to fight

overseas. Because women were needed in factories to help produce bombs, tanks, airplanes, and ships, our American patriarchy
was willing to bend previous rules. These women also operated
drill presses and machine tools, and became welders and riveters.
A riveter is a person whose job is to fasten metal pins, hence the
creation of Rosie the Riveter. As a result of pure necessity women
were suddenly told they could do all the things that men could do
in the absence of their husbands, fathers, brothers, and sons. The
song "Rosie the Riveter" had lyrics that said, "All the day long,
whether rain or shine, / She's a part of the assembly line. / She's
making history, working for victory, / Rosie, the Riveter. / Keeps a
sharp lookout for sabotage / Sitting up there on the fuselage. / That
little frail can do more than a male can do." Despite the fact that
women of color were continuing to support the nation with their
backbreaking labor in addition to joining war production factories, Rosie the Riveter celebrated white women's efforts exclusively
while still emphasizing their beauty and femininity, going so far as
to say that they could do "more than a male can do."

In addition to factory work, women were also encouraged to
participate in sports, particularly softball and baseball, to keep fans
engaged and excited while men were away. During World War
II the All-American Girls Professional Baseball League was born.
Two hundred eighty women were invited to try out in 1943, and
sixty became the first women to play professional baseball. While
this was a previously unimaginable opportunity for the women,
the malleability of the rules under the command of those in power
stretched only so far. The women had not escaped the ever-
persisting guidelines that they were required to follow to "maintain" their femininity. They were each handed a manual to guide
them in their personal appearance and behavior. The players were
required to carry a beauty kit that contained lipstick, rouge, hair
remover, and face powder. They were to have an "after the game
beauty routine" where, following their shower, they were to reap-

ply lipstick, powder, and eye makeup. The president of the league, Ken Sells, said, "Femininity is the keynote of our league. . . . No pants-wearing, tough-talking female softballer will play on any of our teams." The AAGPBL was successful for twelve seasons until support started dwindling after the war ended, with the return of messages that encouraged women back into the domestic sphere now that they were no longer needed.

Not only is the AAGPBL an example of the way American patriarchs take advantage of the changeable nature of their supposed rules and social norms, as well as the limits placed on such changes, it also showcases continued adherence to the hierarchy and status quo that excluded people of color from the same experiences. The AAGPBL was an opportunity available only for white women. Seventeen-year-old Mamie Johnson realized this when she tried playing for a team and was turned away because she was Black.

However, Mamie found a home in the Negro Leagues, where Black women played alongside Black men and stood against the forced rules of femininity that the AAGPBL held dear. The Negro Leagues brought a glimpse of what it might look like to break a rule entirely and find more freedom in such a departure from the norms. The first woman to sign with the Negro Leagues was Toni Stone, a self-taught thirty-two-year-old from St. Paul, Minnesota, who had grown up playing ball with the boys in her neighborhood. When Syd Pollack, the owner of the Indianapolis Clowns, signed her in 1953, he wanted her to wear a skirt like the women in the AAGPBL, but Stone would not oblige. Even as a little girl she preferred to wear pants, and she felt more comfortable when playing her sport in the same uniform her teammates wore. She played fifty games in her season with the Clowns, and attendance at the games reached a record high when she started playing. According to the National Baseball Hall of Fame, "at one point in the 1953 season she was batting .364, fourth in the league, right behind Ernie Banks." Stone paved the way for other Black women to play baseball professionally, like Mamie Johnson, who became the first female pitcher in professional baseball, and nineteen-year-old Connie Morgan, who blew fans away with her athleticism. Both women chose to play in the same uniform as Stone.

The stories of Toni Stone, Mamie Johnson, and Connie Morgan highlight the possibilities that come with breaking the rules and making new ones that allow people to decide for themselves what they wear and what activities they participate in. Sadly, though, they also remind us of the punishment people confront when they are some of the first to courageously challenge the dictates of American patriarchy. On the less severe end, the women dealt with journalists whose reports highlighted their continued domesticity, femininity, and sexuality despite their participation in a male sport. On the more severe end, all three women encountered harassment both physical and verbal from teammates and fans alike that ran the gamut of being sexist, racist, and homophobic. Stone left professional baseball after only two years, tired of being objectified and exoticized. At the same time, however, she had already made her crack in the glass structure of American patriarchy.

Telling women what activities they can and cannot participate in, dictating what clothes they should wear, and instructing them on how they should carry themselves while tailoring these rules to apply differently across race all highlight the creation of American patriarchy as well as the weakness of the argument. If it requires so much policing, enforcement, and reminders, how can it be natural rather than fabricated? Even more surprising is the fact that these dictates concerning sports, as well as the role our media plays in reifying them, continue to be some of the most effective protectors of the same status quo the founding fathers envisioned. To this day, sports are a reflection of the hierarchy that is our American patriarchy in countless ways. White men are the ones in charge who make most of the money; Black athletes are often treated like property rather than as human beings; Black women confront sexism and racism as well as policing of their reactions, often described or drawn as problematic tropes; trans athletes face continued exclusion; the list goes on. But again, these should not be read as unavoidable or as the way things will always be. Instead they should be seen as part of the many tactics to maintain the status quo fueled by those in power who want to remain in power. When we look at it this way and speak about it this way, we can continue the chiseling that those before us have begun.

As a result of what Kathrine Switzer accomplished, Jock Semple later changed his stance on women participating in the marathon. He went on to become one of their staunchest supporters, even publicly reconciling with Switzer and, according to her, they became the best of friends. When Semple was diagnosed with liver and pancreatic cancer, Switzer would visit him at the hospital where he was being treated until he passed. Their initial interaction produced one of the most memorable images of American patriarchy, but their relationship symbolizes the simplicity of the shift we can make in our mindsets that allows people to participate in their desired activities and look the way they want to look while doing so. If the rabid sixty-four-year-old white man, with his teeth bared as he tried to take down a nineteen-year-old woman, can come to that conclusion, perhaps we all can.

As we move to the next chapter I want us to keep that famous image of Jock Semple in mind: the anger on his face, the determination with which he tried to impede Switzer. I want us to think about the desperation that appeared to fuel him, and I want us to reflect on what was going on in his mind and body that told him he had something to lose if she were to keep running, I want us to picture the shock he experienced when his fellow white men pushed him away. When I look at his expression and stare at the scene, it reminds me of the images of white mobs yelling at Black children as schools were integrated, as well as the images of rioters at the Capitol, the lunacy of it all, their rage, their clear sense of wretchedness yet continued desperation to keep things as they are, their fear. I wonder what keeps them all from making the shift in their minds that would bring them peace. It cannot be a happy way to live.

19

THEY PUT US IN DANGER,
THEY DO NOT SPARE

■

When wealthy white men hoard power among themselves, they also need a cost-efficient way to keep the masses from threatening the status quo. How do you keep the average white male American invested in a system that disadvantages him? You give them whiteness. You give them maleness. You give them an identity that will provide a sense of victory in good times and bad. All you need to be successful as a white man is to be better off than women and people of color. And all you need to do to distract white men from how they are actually faring is to task them with the responsibility of ensuring that people of color and women don't take what little might be theirs.

These poignant words are from Ijeoma Oluo's book *Mediocre: The Dangerous Legacy of White Male America*, and if I had room to quote even more of her work I would because she so beautifully captures the heart of the issue that we are all facing and shows that even white men, the benefactors of American patriarchy, are trapped by it. In fact, white men and their reactions to American patriarchy pose the most danger for all of us. Therefore it is crucial that we each understand the crisis white male America believes it is facing.

As Oluo puts it, white men have all been told they are the rightful power holders in our nation, that they are meant to live above women and people of color, that they should have everything they could ever want in life without even having to work very hard for it, that they should be in control of other people's actions and decisions, and that they are the prototype that everyone else should aspire to be. So when they do not live up to these promises—maybe they do not make a lot of money, maybe they experienced something in childhood that robbed them of their sense of security, maybe a woman turned down their advances, maybe they weren't accepted into the best schools, maybe they simply have low self-esteem, maybe they are hiding a part of themselves that doesn't fit the patriarchal ideal, or maybe they experienced tragedy—whatever it may be, the only way they can make sense of their lacks and any misfortune is by blaming those who are supposed to be below them. Sometimes this blame is subconscious and even they are unaware of why they hold these feelings. Other times they know exactly who they want to target as they turn their feeling of inadequacy into action. They believe they will feel better, even vindicated, if they take their pain out on others. They also know that if/when they do, they likely won't have to face any consequences for their actions, that they might actually receive praise, acceptance, and fame.

As a reminder, part 4 is concerned with exposing how American patriarchy, a system that is carefully crafted and maintained, has been communicated to all of us as something natural and unavoidable. We have examined how it is based on illusory truths that we become familiar with, that we learn and practice until they become second nature, and that we begin to believe are the natural order of things even though we have been presented with plenty of evidence of the malleability of the social order. Such malleability has not only presented itself in times when groups other than white men have been given access to opportunities, usually only temporarily; it has also allowed for groups who were initially considered to be another race entirely to be deemed white enough. We see this in the cases of Jewish, Irish, and Italian people, for example, who are now included in whiteness, even if they do not always fully identify as white.

We have also examined how things can change for the better and break away from American patriarchy entirely, sometimes quickly, with a simple shift in our mindsets. Other times, breaking away from what we have always been taught takes more time and requires the courageous acts of those who are willing to risk their safety and comfort to expose the system for what it is. These courageous acts signal to the rest of us that things are not as natural as the messengers of American patriarchy would have everyone believe. For some, that signal resonates with us; we feel freedom, we feel empowered too, and we become aware of the policies and people pulling the strings we have just come to realize were attached to us. We try to cut those strings for ourselves and others around us. For other people, however, the signal is alarming, and they worry they will lose something if what they were told was undeniable all along was actually only ever just an opinion reified in the messages that surround us and infused into the laws and policies that govern us. They panic over what might happen if they are not owed any more than anyone else, if the resources they have been told were rightfully theirs might belong in the hands of everyone.

At the end of the last chapter I asked you to reflect on the experiences of those who perceive themselves as being in power. I asked you to think about what it must feel like to believe that if someone else even attempts to climb the ladder of the hierarchy of American patriarchy, you will lose what makes you "better" than them and perhaps lose your own access to protections and being treated as a human. I asked you to think about the fear and desperation that must come with not fully understanding why you are filled with such hatred of everyone else. In this chapter we explore how the invisibility of American patriarchy is dangerous not only for those excluded from power, such as women, gender-nonconforming people, and people of color, but also extremely dangerous for the majority of white men. These white men are fed messages that fuel their fears and encourage them to act upon them. While those relegated outside of holding power in our nation are told that they should blame themselves for the struggles they might face when trying to live freely and with dignity, those attached to power, i.e., white men and often white women, are instead empowered to blame others to keep the superiority they perceive themselves as having.

I recently started reading *The Body Keeps the Score* by the famous psychiatrist Bessel van der Kolk. The bestselling and acclaimed book explores how trauma reshapes people's bodies and brains, compromising their ability to find trust, feel pleasure, be engaged, and practice self-control. It is a striking book that has brought healing and understanding to thousands of people, but what stood out to me was that many of the conclusions were based on the writer's experiences of working particularly with white people, many of them men, and largely veterans who had experienced trauma. In one of the first chapters van der Kolk talks about a veteran named Tom, who experienced an ambush while serving in Vietnam, where he witnessed the men around him getting shot and killed one by one. He especially mourned the loss of his "only real friend," a fellow soldier who died from a gunshot wound. What van der Kolk described next shocked me. In the aftermath of losing his platoon members, Tom responded with revenge: "The day after the ambush Tom went into a frenzy to a neighboring village, killing children, shooting an innocent farmer, and raping a Vietnamese woman. After that it became truly impossible for him to go home again in any meaningful way." What stunned me more was that this was described as a common response to such trauma.

Of course war is already inhumane and brings out the worst in people. But I couldn't help but question how privilege and power changes how people react when they become victims, or when they perceive themselves as victims in less extreme examples. When I think about the Vietnamese woman whom Tom raped and who witnessed the death of the innocent farmer and children around her, do I believe she then took that trauma and inflicted it in such a monstrous way on someone else? Absolutely not. Do refugees from war-torn nations who have seen their neighbors and loved ones tortured and dismembered typically go and kill innocent children? No, they usually run for their lives, seek shelter, find community again; they may eventually lead healing workshops or help families reunite with one another. Power, privilege, and victimhood—whether very real like in the case of Tom or simply perceived, like in the case of the average white man—are a dangerous combination. If you have been told that the world belongs to you, you see yourself as above the law, above the rules; you grant yourself permission to follow your own orders, to act on even your most detrimental desires.

In times of war, propaganda is filled with hateful rhetoric in order to justify such brutality. Historically, posters often used problematic caricatures to represent the supposed enemy as being more akin to animals than to human beings who were brutally attacking white American ways of life. For example, a 1942 poster titled "This Is the Enemy" circulated around the United States following the Japanese attack on Pearl Harbor. The image depicts a figure that looks more like a monkey than a man. In it, the "enemy" is shown holding a knife in one hand while trying to grab a white woman with his other. He is wearing a hat that symbolizes he is a Japanese soldier. Other posters often displayed strong white men rescuing women and children as flames roared all around them. In one poster for the film *A Yank in Viet-Nam*, a white soldier is holding a Vietnamese woman in his arms, his gun hanging on his shoulder. Helicopters, fires, and bodies are behind them, the words "A fighting US Marine, a jungle beauty, and a handful of guerrillas" printed beside them. Beyond times of war, some media outlets expose white men to these same kinds of messages emphasizing the need for them to protect themselves and their families from such threats as "rapists," "terrorists," "murderers," and "robbers," and they encourage them to do so with guns. These sources feed white men messages that represent them as saviors, and other people as wrongdoers intent on destroying the social order.

This is apparent in the many devastating examples of mass shootings in the United States. According to the Violence Project, 98 percent of such crimes were performed by men. The majority of the shooters are also white men. In an article titled "US Mass Public Shootings Since Columbine: Victims per Incident by Race and Ethnicity of the Perpetrator," researchers reported finding that mass shootings by white men resulted in more deaths. They concluded, "White shooters were overrepresented in mass public shootings with the most victims, typically involving legally owned assault rifles."

Founders of the Violence Project Jillian Peterson and James Densley, whose research on mass shootings has received global attention, say that we can prevent more of them from happening by understanding the predictable factors linking many of the shooters, one of the primary ones being young boys and men with suicidal thoughts. Peterson and Densley say that mass shooters almost always commit their crimes with the hope that this will be their final act in life; they expect to die too and want to leave their mark by ending the lives of others as part of a personal vendetta and/or to contribute to the goals of a larger group. The manifestos many of them leave are in effect suicide notes. Men across all groups are more likely to commit suicide, and according to the American Foundation for Suicide Prevention, "the rate of suicide is highest in middle-aged white men. . . . White males [also] accounted for 69.68% of suicide deaths in 2020." Furthermore, white men are the most likely to use a firearm to commit suicide. Data also shows that another overrepresented group when it comes to suicides are American Indian and Alaska Native people, yet we do not see this group represented anywhere close to as much when it comes to hurting others with guns. Something unique is happening with white men where many of them are not only trying to take their own lives, they also want to kill/injure other people along the way. The data on perpetrators of all this violence, especially when it comes to the large overlap between those who are likely to injure themselves and those who are likely to injure others, points to a group that believes they are entitled to something that they are being denied.

In relation to this, Oluo describes messages she has received from white men in response to her work, emails or tweets where white men degrade and threaten her and also threaten to hurt themselves, usually with guns, as a result of her publications against violent misogyny and white supremacy. These men also detailed the hardships they'd experienced, like poverty or perceived discrimination. Oluo writes,

> These men wanted me to know that they were miserable, they felt screwed over, and they felt demonized. They wanted me to know that the only option available to address white male patriarchy was either to maintain the status quo that was making us all miserable, or death. They wanted me to know that they were not capable of growth or change and that any attempt to bring about that growth or change would end them.

Oluo ends this paragraph asserting that "nobody is more pessimistic about white men than white men."

I believe this pessimism comes as a result of white men thinking they are failing at something they were told should come naturally to them. My hunch is further backed by other scholars like writer Edward Lempinen, who in a 2022 article states, "Though white men as a whole remain dominant across society . . . their wide-spread feelings of loss and insecurity are linked to deep psychological reactions—a sort of bitter nostalgia, a sense they are being cheated and left behind, a growing conviction that they must take justice into their own hands." Clearly the promise of success and stability for all white men, if they are simply to keep the social order, is failing and causing severe turmoil for everyone, not least of all white boys and men themselves. They do not see other ways out of American patriarchy beyond hurting others and/or ending their own lives, and they believe these actions can, at the very least, make them valiant protectors of the social order. White boys and men often do not realize they are pawns whose insecurities and fears are being used to maintain a system that doesn't serve them either. So what is keeping our nation from protecting us, or at least these said members of the chosen group, from guns, the preferred tool of choice in many instances of violence? The answer is also white men.

The National Rifle Association (NRA) has grown into one of the most powerful political organizations in the United States and has made it its mission to lobby against all forms of gun control while promoting the message that having access to guns makes our country safer. The NRA relies heavily on its media strategy to convince its members of their rightful superiority while stoking their fears of groups that are meant to exist below them. According to *Forbes*, the NRA is a $3.5 billion organization, and the NRA's CEO alone is worth $10 million. The NRA's power comes from its ability to spend as much money as it wants to on political campaigns, and the fact that it boasts over five million members. These members are mostly made up of Republican white men who fund Republican white men in office and who believe that owning a gun is essential to their personal freedom. Even if perpetrators of gun violence are not all members of the NRA, the NRA is what allows for such easy access to firearms across the board.

In Carol Anderson's recent book *The Second: Race and Guns in a*

Fatally Unequal America, she presents the undeniable case that the right to bear arms is not about everyone's freedom to protect themselves but instead has always been about controlling other groups, specifically Black people. Guns were needed to keep slaves in place and their revolts from succeeding. Pair that with gun sellers' obsession of telling buyers and potential buyers to "man up" and we arrive back at the primary components of American patriarchy. As the *New York Times* puts it, "The sales pitch—rooted in self-defense, machismo, and an overarching sense of fear—has been remarkably successful." In a stunning example, after Kyle Rittenhouse was acquitted of murdering two other white men during antiracism protests in Kenosha, Wisconsin, in 2020, a Florida gun dealer featured an image of him holding an assault rifle with the words BE A MAN AMONG MEN written across the picture.

Much healing is needed for white men that helps them to see that even many of them would not be considered by the founding fathers as worthy of reaping their same benefits. This is where the classism of American patriarchy becomes much more obvious: It is built to advantage elite white men, who also suffer from their actions and feelings of dissatisfaction, guilt, and unhappiness but who might inflict/deal with their pain in systemic ways that are more easily hidden. The average white man needs to know that it is not women's fault they are not satisfied; it is not trans people's fault, either; it is also not the fault of people of color, nor the fault of immigrants. It is the fault of a system founded and led by rich white men, one that hides itself from them, one that communicates with them through ranting talking heads and ads and billboards encouraging them to both hate others and arm themselves, one that relies on them to do much of its dirty work, one that leeches on their pain, worry, and pessimism and charges them with a responsibility to act if they feel they are being robbed, to maintain an order—even if that order hurts them–at all costs, even to kill and die in service to it.

20

OUR CHILDREN

■

Are you a boy or a girl?" my son's pediatrician asked him as he looked back at her with the silence he employed with all adults except for my husband and me. We were there to check on a concern I had about him snoring; he hadn't yet turned three. She then looked to me to explain, "I just thought I'd try it out, sometimes by this age they're able to tell us." She said this with a sense of excitement, her eyes widened, as if speaking about any other milestone in a child's development that I could look forward to. I hadn't even considered this before that second, the moment when a child knows that in their given society they are considered a boy or a girl. Two and a half years old seemed so early. I spaced out temporarily, thinking about what this question really meant and what my son might have already come to associate with the answer I knew he was likely reserving for when we exited her office. Even upon leaving the appointment, memories rushed through my brain filled with the information he had already received in his short life about the two supposed options for gender that his pediatrician and larger society offered to him, and how these differed from each other. Furthermore, I wondered what else he had already come to learn about his own identity and about the organization of the nation he was born in.

There was the time when we took him and his sister on a play-date to meet some of the classmates he'd be going to preschool with in the fall. One of the dads approached me to comment on how cute our daughter was and to say how much he wanted his second child to be a girl. I doubted I would agree with his reasoning for saying that and didn't really want to know what it was, so I simply smiled. We were new to this group of people and I wanted to avoid getting into a heated conversation in front of our kids. Neverthe-less, the dad continued, "I want a child who will take care of me when I'm older." I could almost feel my husband sigh; he knew this wasn't something I could just agree with and move on from. I could not keep myself from responding. I asked him why he thought his son wasn't capable of providing the care he thought that his future daughter would, to which he replied, "That's just not what boys do." I took a deep breath and said, "But boys could if we socialized them differently; don't you think that's up to us as their parents?" He laughed and the conversation ended there. As I often experience when trying to push my parental peers to think differently about their long-held beliefs that they are passing on to their own children without question, this parent seemed a little bothered and confused as to why I was turning something he thought was a given into a deeper discussion on "socialization." I suppose he expected me to say "thank you" for the compliment that my daughter was cute and to nod along with his declaration that girls were caretakers and boys were not.

In accordance with what we have explored in part 4 regarding American patriarchy and all the strategies that go into creating and maintaining it becoming unnoticeable, we further our discussion here regarding its relevance in parenting. We have discussed the reproduction of illusory truths, especially through the messages we receive from the media "experts" we are exposed to that instruct us all on how to dress, how to carry ourselves, what activities we should participate in, and so on, and in this chapter I speak to my experience as a mother of young children and the ways in which I have already noticed how American patriarchy is communicated to them on a consistent basis.

As a sociologist, I often say that our families are our first societies, the first places we learn how we fit into the world, the first example we see of how individuals are treated in an organized group. These groups are led by parents, and therefore parents become the leaders who, in relation to what we have discussed in part 4, curate the messages our children are exposed to and give children the basis for interpreting other messages they will encounter separate from their parents. We cannot take this responsibility lightly and we must reflect on what we are passing on to them, not only about their identities and their place within our family units, but also about their place in society outside our home. We are the first ones to tell them how they deserve to be treated, as well as how they should treat others, and the first to instruct them on how we think the entire nation and world should work. In our analysis of how American patriarchy comes to be seen and felt as natural and unavoidable, it is critical that we reflect on the role parents, grandparents, aunties, and uncles play in that presentation as well as the role we can play in communicating differently about the system we find ourselves in. We must be thoughtful about what we say about their identities, about how we guide them to process what strangers may say to them or even what family members who hold on to and share problematic views might say. We must even be thoughtful about how the messages they receive from songs, books, and movies will inform them about their place and ultimately play a role in determining just how long our American patriarchy will be allowed to persist. What our children are led to believe, especially in their earliest stages, will be what makes or breaks things as they are.

Children pick up on much more than they are usually given credit for, they process the world around them speedily and sort all the data they are gathering into the formation of their identity almost immediately. In my kids' lives there have been several times beyond the playdate mentioned above when strangers would add to my children's bank of knowledge, even in the quickest of interactions. Sometimes these are relatively harmless reproductions of the guidelines of American patriarchy, while other times they carry the potential to be much more damaging. For example, recently my three kids and I were on an elevator after their dentist appointments when a woman entered right behind us. She looked at the kids and said "Girl, girl, boy?" as she pointed at each of them. My eldest son said, "I'm a boy," to which the woman replied with surprise, "But your hair is so long." My son does indeed have beautiful long locs and I guess this woman believed boys should always have short hair. I smiled and said, "The world is full of possibilities now," before we exited. In these moments I try to make sure my kids know that while the random stranger might believe there are certain dictates for boys and girls like how they should wear their hair, I see things differently and that they don't have to even ascribe to being a boy or a girl. I make sure to tell them they will be loved and accepted by me no matter what.

There have also been times when family members tried their hardest to enforce the "traditional" ways of doing things on our children. Just as annoying as a stranger inserting their unsolicited reactions into our lives, so too are comments like "big boys don't cry," or "girls need more protection than boys," from our children's older family members and other caretakers who unknowingly try to stunt our son's emotions and who show our daughter that they don't think she is capable of trying things on her own by hovering around her in ways they never did with our son. Additionally, within our family we have faced conflict surrounding our approach to disciplining our children. Because we do not use time-outs or corporal punishment, we have been met with opinions that Black children must be taught to behave before they experience the consequences of acting freely, just like other children, outside our home. In moments like these I try to make sure my children know that it is good to feel a range of emotions and that I am here to help them navigate any and all of their feelings; I also try to demonstrate to them what treating them with respect and dignity looks like, even when they are not listening or are "misbehaving" and I am being more firm. I want them to know that they deserve respectful treatment no matter what. I acknowledge the worry that comes with raising Black children in a country that will see them differently than other children, but I cannot bring myself to be another source that makes them feel like they must be defined by that.

I think about the simplest of moments, like listening to a list of classic kid songs that I thought were harmless enough to not fully pay attention to, until I realized we had heard the words "the farmer takes the wife, the wife takes the child, the child takes the nurse, the nurse takes the cow, the cow takes the dog," a clear explanation of the status quo as well as a gendered and economic hierarchy that I'm not at all in agreement with. I remembered the first time I heard all the lyrics to "The Wheels on the Bus" when we had taken our son to a Parent and Me class. The kids knew most of the gestures to each verse and they were taught that the mothers on the bus say, "shhh, shhh, shhh" while holding their index finger to their lips in response to the baby crying, while the daddies on the bus get to say, "I love you, I love you, I love you." This communicates the message that moms are the ones who nag and control while dads are the fun and loving ones. And of course, these "classics" also reiterate heteronormativity. Now I change the lyrics to "the parents on the bus say I love you, I love you, I love you" and the kids on the bus say "I love you too, I love you too, I love you too." These examples only highlight the nursery rhymes that I find to be sexist; the number of racist nursery rhymes is another long list.

The American patriarchal organization of our society appears in our classic and long-loved movies as well, movies my husband and I looked forward to sharing with our kids even before we had them. Take *The Lion King*, a story that I grew up adoring but that is actually an inaccurate representation of lion behaviors. Following the 2019 release of the *Lion King* remake, with the advanced use of highly realistic computer-generated images that created a beautiful virtual reality experience, experts in lion behavior commented that although the images looked like real animals, the narrative did not follow the behaviors of real lions. Rather, the story is a patriarchal human one that has been cast on animals. Craig Saffoe, the Smithsonian National Zoo's great cats curator, says that lions are actually matriarchal and the female lions are the ones who lead their tribes. The males in the tribe happily coexist and are unlikely to show aggression toward one another. The type of aggression that exists between the characters of Mufasa and Scar, the driving narrative that everything else follows, is representative of human male experiences and normalizes male competition, domination, violence, and anger. The story is largely modeled on Shakespeare's *Hamlet* and was, unsurprisingly, directed by two white men.

I also think of the activities our kids participate in, like soccer, swimming, art, and music, and the different odd comments some people in positions of leadership make around them. When my son was only eight months old, we signed him up for infant swim lessons. One day his instructor told us that he had "angry" kicks that she did not like. I was shocked that such microaggressions began so early. In another example, with our eldest son, people often emphasize his strength and athleticism; with our daughter people have been more likely to emphasize her beauty. One of my son's coaches called the little girls his "girlfriends" and told the boys that he didn't hold boys' hands. Another coach was clearly meaner to the boys than the girls in the class, always using a firmer tone with them and far less patience. He also confused Black children with one another on more than one occasion. In these situations, I observe the other adults in my children's lives closely, and when the environment seems damaging, I first try to provide feedback and hope for change before we seek another space for them to explore their interests if need be.

I also reflect on what my husband and I are teaching our children regarding their identities when it comes to things like the division of labor in our home as well as the books we read together every day. I wonder, based on the examples we have shown our kids, what they would say were the attributes and possibilities of all people: girls, boys, and others. Yes, we have chosen a diverse set of books that we expose them to; we question the messages of songs and movies that reiterate harmful stereotypes and have conversations with our kids; we buy them toys that encourage them to love building blocks, puzzles, cars just as much as caring for their baby dolls, cleaning with their set of supplies, and prepping food in their play kitchen, and we overemphasize a love of themselves with constant affirmations. But I still wonder if it is enough: Are my husband and I both showing the gender equity we believe in by example? Are we speaking to our children equally, reacting to them equally, encouraging them and protecting them equally? Are we leading our home with fairness at the center? Are our words and examples enough to equip them beyond our home?

You may find dramatic all this analysis of the interactions between my children and strangers, comments they've heard from family members, silly songs, animated movies, and leaders in their extracurricular activities. But it is this combination of sources that affects the identity of small children, especially those who are not yet of the age of attending school, who do not have access to their own phones nor social media, and who certainly do not yet know how law and policy might affect their lives. They are simply taking in all the cues and rules around them, learning when they are encouraged and celebrated as well as the opposite. They are seeing how they are treated differently from others and what might contribute to that different treatment. These are the years where parents have the most influence and control over the messages their children receive than they ever will again in their kids' lives. These are the years that most impact a child's future brain development, as well as their cognitive, emotional, and physical health. They are the years where we should think deeply about every single message the children in our lives are receiving from us, their immediate relationships, and the materials they engage with.

Existing data supports this. An article published in *Science* magazine in 2017 stated that "by the age of 6, girls are less likely than boys to believe that members of their gender are 'really, really smart'—a child-friendly way of referring to brilliance. Also at age 6, the girls in these studies begin to shy away from novel activities said to be for children who are 'really, really smart.'" Another study, published by the University of Washington, showed that children's self-esteem was established by the young age of five, and that students enter school with their self-esteem already formed rather than school being the place where they establish it. Of course, interactions in school with teachers and peers impact that sense of self-esteem, but the foundation that children have going into school is highly predictive of their ability to maintain it, regardless of experiences at school. Children who feel encouraged to explore various interests regardless of their gender and who receive messages that are affirming of their identity are more likely to live healthier and happier lives and promote that health and happiness among their peers. Around the world, studies have shown that exposure to gender bias, prejudices, and stereotypes at young ages limits opportunities for all children and is linked to poor mental and physical health; some direct links include higher rates of suicide among boys who have been told to limit their emotions, and more eating disorders among girls who have been told their looks are their most valuable quality.

When we got back to the house from that doctor's visit, we went to the playroom and I observed my kids in one of their happy places. I thought about their brilliance, strength, kindness, their unique interests and talents, and wondered how much their parents' love and acceptance could protect them in a country that seems intent on maintaining the status quo. I wondered about their futures, about how much harder it might all become as they grow more connected to their peers and other sources of information beyond our house. I thought about how technology might replicate the status quo as well, how social media, other apps, and artificial intelligence that carry potential to be world-changing might instead make matters worse. If those creating these advances aren't questioning the ills that we have been told are natural, might they, knowingly or un-knowingly, rewrite them in their code? I have always known that it is not enough to simply teach my children differently or to go against the grain in our own household, but that we must also par-ticipate in changing as much beyond our homes as we can while our children are still young. This way, they might actually stand a chance.

Part 5

OUR SENSE
OF SAFETY
AND
COMMUNITY

21

NONE OF US ARE PROTECTED

◼

When I was a little girl, I often dreamed about moving to California, and I couldn't tell you exactly why. I didn't even visit California until my college Admit weekend when I was seventeen, but even as a middle schooler I was aware of California's appeal. I knew it was sunny; I knew Californians were the creators of TV shows and movies; Californians seemed happier than everyone else, and they definitely appeared to be in better shape. I have lived in this great state since I decided to go to college in the Bay Area in 2010, and my husband and I moved to Southern California in 2021. The things I observed from a distance, likely in magazines and TV shows, as a preteen were accurate: The weather is amazing; storytelling makes things go around here, which is inspiring for writers like myself; people smile and engage more; and everyone is hyperconscious about their appearance. However, this obsession with looks in a place that is the apex of content creation, combined with people's general unknowing of what truly influences it, is perilous. It is a clear example of the danger that arises and only continues to grow when we think we're formulating our own thoughts and decisions about ourselves, but in reality we are just fulfilling what the messengers of American patriarchy want.

Don't get me wrong, it is not bad to be healthy and in shape. But I have never met more people, especially women and girls, in my entire life and in my travels all over the world, who want to alter themselves than I have in California, especially Los Angeles. I worry about raising children, specifically my daughter, in a place where everyone wants to be skinnier or curvier, to look older if they are teens, younger if they are grown women, to Botox every wrinkle and get surgery to tuck any sagging skin. All these desired changes are fed to us by the media so we can be "sexier" or "prettier," which puts us in danger from a young age.

In her review of the docuseries *Pretty Baby*, Rhonda Garelick writes: "She was a living contradiction, conveying both doll-like innocence and premature, sexualized knowingness." The series follows actress and model Brooke Shields as she reclaims her power in adulthood after being sexualized as a young girl. Shields recounts the many disturbing moments she experienced throughout her career of being deemed the archetype of American beauty from the young age of eleven. As a fifteen-year-old in her famous Calvin Klein ads, she twisted on the floor in skintight jeans and was told to recite suggestive lines she didn't fully understand, such as "I've put away childish things and I'm ready for Calvins," before she stuck her thumb in her mouth. Looking back on her career, Shields realizes the things that happened to her were wrong; she sees clearly that she was objectified and represented as a commodity, and she uses her film to caution against the dangers young girls and women face in our society even if, and perhaps especially if, they represent the ideals of American femininity. While one would hope things have improved for girls and women today, sadly this commodification is still present and even more widespread as a result of advances in digital technology such as social media.

To review, in part 1 we discussed the origins of American patriarchy, the men who not only saw themselves as the natural leaders of humanity and who put themselves above the women in their

lives, but who also saw everyone else as being unworthy of humane treatment altogether. With these views they formed their
idea of a perfect nation with a clear hierarchy in place, and rules
that would keep this hierarchy intact. In part 2 we explored how
this intactness relies on reminders of the social order and punishments of varying degrees for offenders who challenge the social
order (knowingly and unknowingly). We made the connections
between our founding fathers and the current Supreme Court of
the United States clear. In part 3 we paid special attention to reproduction and examined how our relationships and reproductive
abilities are manipulated to maintain American patriarchy. We also
saw how certain doctors and scientific experts contributed to those
manipulative strategies. In part 4 we dove into an exploration of
the persistence of American patriarchy as a result of the messages
we are exposed to through traditional forms of media; we saw how
the desired social order that the authorities we discussed up until
that point were invested in maintaining became so familiar that we
accept it as our norm. American patriarchy employs talking heads,
infiltrates news sources, and even seeps into the songs we listen
to and the movies we watch to appear so natural that it becomes
undetectable by design. Now we have arrived at part 5, as we look
toward our future and examine the ways in which all the strategies
we have discussed up until this point to keep American patriarchy
alive will only multiply if they continue to go unnoticed, unquestioned, and uninterrupted. Here the authorities are those who are
in charge of the technologies, codes, and algorithms we interact
with on a daily basis.

In this chapter we segue from a discussion of traditional media outlets into social media platforms, and examine how all of
the above has persisted but in new ways. As disturbing as it may
be, I want us to consider the effect of the continued objectification
of young girls and women who are representative of the ideals of
American femininity, to showcase the dangers of the images we

uplift as the standard for all girls and women to aspire to. Additionally, I want to explore how a study of this specific group offers a window into analyzing all the other ways social media reifies the status quo. I discuss social media first because for many people in the United States, social media platforms are seen as spaces where they can find their news; they have even taken the place of trusted news sources for countless people. Disinformation and illusory truths abound on these platforms, with very little in terms of requirements concerning accuracy and decency. With all this in mind, I ask us to think about what women of the future, those who are young girls right now like my own daughter, might say when they reflect on their experiences growing up in the United States with the kinds of messages they receive and are exposed to in a landscape different from the one my mom grew up in, and different from the one I grew up in. I wonder, will they feel the same as Shields, or will we finally be able to stop the cycle from repeating itself?

While certain forms of journalism, movies, TV shows, and magazines have been key in reproducing American patriarchy by romanticizing unrealistic beauty standards for all, promoting the sexuality and supposed controllability of young women, excluding older women, radicalizing men, and more, social media has taken these themes to new heights. Platforms like Facebook, Instagram, X (Twitter), YouTube, Snapchat, and TikTok carried the potential to be freeing at first, as they allow for more self-definition, empowerment, and access to information. But in reality they have become spaces that allow American patriarchy to thrive and multiply.

According to a 2022 study by the Pew Research Center, 92 percent of teen girls report using YouTube. Another 73 percent say they use TikTok, 69 percent say they use Instagram, and 64 percent say they use Snapchat. Girls are more likely than boys to say they spend too much time on social media—41 percent to 31 percent—and also are more likely than boys to say that it would be hard for them to give up social media, 58 percent compared to 49 percent, the survey found. These statistics are concerning when we know how dangerous social media is for all young people, but especially for young girls.

Let's begin with a discussion of how sexualized images of girls and women have become normalized on social media, and how these have caused a myriad of issues beyond those that already existed with traditional means of communicating information. The American Psychological Association Task Force on the Sexualization of Girls has detailed a number of negative effects that occur when girls are exposed to images that sexualize and objectify them. These include "decreased cognitive functioning (e.g., impaired ability to concentrate), worsened physical and mental health (e.g., eating disorders, low self-esteem, depression), unrealistic expectations about sexuality, and reductionist beliefs of women as sexual objects." Because social media not only includes celebrities but also appears to feature "normal" people and peers, the overwhelming message of the need for girls and women to look and act a certain way, one that is backed by more likes and higher-performing posts, increases. As a result, young girls have reported feeling ashamed of their bodies and experiencing lower self-esteem ever since the invention of social media platforms. This low self-esteem translates into devastating effects on their mental health, including higher instances of depression, anxiety, and self-harm.

A disturbing example recently emerged that showed how dangerous social media is for little girls even before they are the ones using it. In "A Marketplace of Girl Influencers Managed by Moms and Stalked by Men," the *New York Times* detailed how mothers who are trying to make their daughters famous on Instagram post images of their children online and are followed by men who have openly expressed being sexually attracted to children. The article explores how social media is not only reshaping the world of young girls in dangerous ways, but how it does so with engagement and permission from their parents. As the writers state, "The accounts range from dancers whose mothers diligently cull men from the ranks of followers, to girls in skimpy bikinis whose parents actively encourage male admirers and sell them special photo sets. . . . Some girls on Instagram use their social media clout to get little more than clothing discounts; others receive gifts from Amazon wish lists, or money through Cash App; and still others earn thousands of dollars a month by selling subscriptions with exclusive content."

What's even worse is that the founders of such social media platforms are well aware of the devastating effects of their products on users, but especially on young girls, because algorithms are known to target people's vulnerabilities. When it comes to young girls, their suggestion pages are filled with content that gives the impression that they are not good enough as they are, that they need makeup, they need to get work done on their bodies, or they need to go on an extreme diet. Research has proven that teenage girls are shown this kind of content twelve times more than other users on TikTok, for example. In the case of the availability of sexualized images of young girls online, the racier the images are, and the more of a following (largely made up of grown men) the accounts garner, the more visibility Instagram's algorithm afforded them.

In its own research, Meta found that five hundred thousand child Instagram accounts had inappropriate interactions every day, but its stance is that it is the fault of the parents who posted the problematic images to begin with. Furthermore, when Frances Haugen leaked Meta's research and became a whistleblower, she exposed the fact that Meta was well aware of the following: "Thirty-two percent of teen girls said that when they felt bad about their bodies, Instagram made them feel worse," and that the more depressed young girls became, the more likely they were to use the apps that fed them hurtful content.

Beyond making matters worse for young girls than they already were in our American patriarchy, social media also plays a role in recruiting more American patriarchs as well as spreading such ideals across the world. While social media platforms have emerged outside the United States, such as TikTok, most of them began here, all of them are used here, and are therefore heavily influenced by American ideals. For young men, social media platforms have become a space where they are vulnerable to being indoctrinated into becoming more violent and taught to hate, discredit, and objectify women. A study by University College London found that the algorithms of social media present harmful content as entertainment. As stated in the *Guardian*, "Toxic, hateful or misogynistic material is 'pushed' to young people, with boys who are suffering from anxiety and poor mental health at increased risk." The research showed that young boys who were vulnerable to being radicalized were shown content that normalized sexual harassment as well as the discrediting and objectification of women and girls. With this, misogynistic ideologies become ingrained in the mainstream of youth culture. With social media, something that is old-fashioned and even archaic reemerges in fresh ways.

Young men are also targeted by hate groups with an agenda to maintain the most extreme parts of American patriarchy. As documented by the Associated Press in "White Supremacists Are Riling Up Thousands on Social Media," white supremacists are using social media platforms to build "macho communities" on Instagram, Telegram, and TikTok. Through social media they can find people and rile them up on issues like restricting abortion, protecting their access to guns, and spreading hateful rhetoric about people of color, LGBTQ+ people, and immigrants. In several of the mass shooting attacks over recent years that we discussed in an earlier chapter, the shooter was exposed to hateful messages on social media that empowered them to take action. Sexist, anti-Semitic, racist, and homophobic comments were found in coded hashtags and memes aimed at amplifying American patriarchy on sites largely used by young people.

Here too, it is not only users who make hateful content possible; those in charge of the platforms who do not feel obligated to do more about the rise of hatred on social media are also to blame. American patriarchy is further allowed to thrive in instances where censorship is applied disproportionately and unfairly. We have seen that grown men asking for explicit images of young girls on Instagram is allowed, but women have found that content they post that promotes female empowerment is often censored and removed. Women's bodies as they naturally are, especially when featured in images and messages that promote awareness, pleasure, ownership of our own bodies, and self-confidence, such as posts about female orgasms, cellulite, or periods, are often deemed "inappropriate." Words that have been censored on social media include "period," "uterus," "nipples," "puberty," "vulva," "vagina," "miscarriage," "menopause," "infertility," and "boobs." In 2022, the Center for Intimacy Justice studied sixty women's health companies and found all their ads were rejected on both Facebook and Instagram over the previous three years, with almost half of those companies having their accounts suspended during the period. But in several instances, the ad policies only penalized content related to women and nonbinary people's sexual health, while men's sexual wellness brands were approved. LGBTQ+ content creators also report facing censorship at higher levels on social media in what Alexander Monea, a professor of cultural studies, has coined as "the digital closet." Furthermore, social media users of color who are vocal about the ills of white supremacy face heightened censorship and shadow-banning, the practice of blocking someone's content without them knowing it.

When questioned about these discriminatory censorship practices, creators of such platforms state that they are in place to keep people safe from harm, but somehow harassment on social media continues to be rampant. According to the Pew Research Center, "Nearly half of US teens have been bullied or harassed online, with physical appearance being seen as a relatively common reason why. Older teen girls are especially likely to report being targeted by online abuse overall and because of their appearance." People of color and LGBTQ+ people report high rates of online abuse as well.

In part 5 I ask the following: How is American patriarchy reproduced by the technologies and platforms that promise to usher us into the future? It is evident that those in charge of social media platforms are playing their role in maintaining American patriarchy, whether they are fully aware of that or not. The more that girls and women are objectified; the more that men and boys are indoctrinated; the more girls and women hate themselves; the more men and boys hate women; the more neo-Nazi groups grow; the more women, LGBTQ+ people, and people of color are censored while American patriarchs are allowed to thrive and organize, the more money social media companies make. Even scarier is the fact that the leaders of American patriarchy today who have become the new faces of maintaining the social order use all this to their advantage.

22

FROM ITS GROWING REACH

■

On August 24, 2023, Donald Trump tweeted a picture of his mug shot with the words "ELECTION INTERFER-ENCE. NEVER SURRENDER!" written below it. It was viewed by 284 million people. With a following of 87 million people on Twitter alone, Trump has shown the world just how powerful and dangerous social media can be when it comes to the endurance of American patriarchy. Trump may very well be the best personification of American patriarchy to have ever existed; therefore it is crucial that when we think about the future of our nation, we understand how Trump, his team members, and others like him have used and will continue to use digital advances to uphold the status quo that serves them. While it is true that technological advances always have the potential to disrupt the hierarchy of our nation, they can do so only when we are well aware of their ability to do the opposite. Only with this awareness can we interrupt such patterns. In upcoming chapters we will explore other advances beyond social media, but because it is estimated that 90 percent of Americans use social media actively, I continue my analysis of this particular digital sphere here.

In chapter 21 we explored how social media builds on traditional forms of media that reify the status quo, but we primarily analyzed the harm it can do in terms of online harassment and the growth of objectification, hatred, and exclusion. Now we'll look one step further and consider how advancement in the digital sphere through online platforms renders into consequences far beyond the Internet, even further beyond hurting our individual self-esteem. Here we examine how something that begins online can influence our nation as a whole through swaying our elections and public policy; we see how online chat groups and social media can empower people to turn their violent and exclusionary theories into action; we learn how they can not only reproduce American patriarchy but can, in very tangible ways, make it that much stronger and that much deadlier. As we examine the narrative of American patriarchy in modern times, we can see that social media reminds us of our place in the hierarchy and punishes those who are seen as transgressing.

Trump began his social media presence and campaign long before the 2016 elections when he joined Twitter in 2009, and has used the platform, in addition to Facebook, to grow his loyal following all the way through to his reelection. Fully aware that such sites provide the opportunity for him to speak directly to voters, incite fears, and capitalize with unchecked claims and falsehoods on vulnerabilities, Trump and his team masterfully employ social media to espouse problematic rhetoric in service of American patriarchy. While some initially believed Trump was making a mistake by spending less money on traditional ad services like those on television in his first presidential campaign, they quickly realized what Trump knew all along: targeting people through social media would have higher returns. He tweeted approximately 8,000 times during the 2016 election campaign and over 25,000 times while he was in office; that's an average of 17 tweets per day over four years. In an interview with CBS News's *60 Minutes*, Trump stated, "I wouldn't be here if I didn't have social media." Elon Musk, one of Trump's greatest allies and another terrifying modern American patriarch, who shows that you do not have to be born here to become one, used his ownership of X to prime voters and bolster Trump's reelection.

A man named Brad Parscale has been described as "the genius who won Trump's campaign." He figured out how to use platforms like Facebook to do more than any other campaign had been able to do before. Facebook enabled Trump to raise $280 million that he could use to spend on advertisements on the same platform. This fact, Parscale says, led to tech companies wanting to get a piece of the pie. In an interview after the election, Parscale stated, "If you're going to spend $100 million on social media, a lot of people show up at your office wanting to help you spend that money on their platforms, so Facebook, Twitter, Snapchat, Google—they were all wanting to have that money." This use of ads on social media was especially effective as a result of the widespread personal data misuse by Facebook and Cambridge Analytica. Leaked information of millions of Facebook users without their permission aided Donald Trump's campaign by influencing these users to support him. All these elements combined to secure his first presidency. As Parscale put it, Twitter was for "Mr. Trump. And Facebook [was] for fundraising."

Beyond his first election, for most of his presidency, Trump's social media pages were unmonitored in the name of "free speech," which allowed him to knowingly post and retweet statements that were false and that fed right-wing conspiracy theories. He was also unafraid to post blatantly sexist and racist comments across his pages, aware that these allowed for his following only to grow. It was not until the attack on the United States Capitol that Trump's Twitter and Facebook accounts were suspended, but the damage had been done. The conspiracy theories that might have fizzled out had someone with his overwhelming number of followers not become involved had already gained momentum and inspired deadly events.

Take, for example, the QAnon belief that the world is controlled by the "Deep State," and that Donald Trump is the only person who can defeat it. For QAnon followers, the "Deep State" is a "cabal of Satan-worshiping pedophiles who control the world and run a global child sex trafficking ring, murdering children in ritual Satanic sacrifices in order to harvest a supposedly life-extending chemical from their blood known as adrenochrome." QAnon theories, popular among far-right extremists and Trump supporters, all carry undertones of anti-Semitism, anti-LGBTQ+ hate, and anti-immigrant bias. While the sexism embedded in QAnon is more hidden, as Lorna Bracewell points out in her article "Gender, Populism, and the QAnon Conspiracy Movement," there are clear gendered roles that are encouraged for QAnon believers and right-wing voters who might not subscribe fully to QAnon. Bracewell writes, "Depending on the nature of their gendered investments, supporters can participate in the QAnon movement as either masculine protectors of the republic who swear an oath to defend the Constitution and become 'digital soldiers' in Q's army or as feminine guardians of hearth and home who organize rallies and social media campaigns to protect children from sexual and moral contamination." In other words, online pages become a new battleground for the male followers of such alt-right theories where they must assert their dominance online as well as offline, while women see their contributions as part of playing their traditional roles of being the protectors of the home, children, and virtue.

Here again, online platforms have allowed for problematic and crazy theories to spread and come to be seen as truth. In other words, advances in social media have been used to make everything we have discussed throughout this book that much more effective. Illusory truths, misinformation, disinformation, and downright lunacy have been able to gain large followings of people who feel called to traditional American gender roles. These followers take from what they've discovered online to fulfill what they see as their callings offline. Brian Friedberg, a Harvard researcher who has studied QAnon for years, states, "I really do not think that QAnon as we know it today would have been able to happen without the affordances of Facebook."

Other conspiracy theories that have prompted violence and have gained traction as a result of the unlimited reach they are afforded through social media include the "white replacement" and "white genocide" theories. Both of these refer to fears of white people being replaced and even killed by nonwhite people. They also place much of this blame on women who are either failing at reproducing white babies, or are reproducing too many nonwhite ones. Hence why groups like the Proud Boys not only espouse racist rhetoric, they also emphasize the need for women to stay at home and raise the next generation. In fact, members of any far-right movement that is based on white power will also inevitably be based on controlling gender and reproduction. So powerful has the online presence of white supremacist, and by design sexist, fringe groups become that believers feel empowered to run for office, and politicians who may not have originally been associated with the fringe theories now cater to ridiculous messages to gain the support of such a large following.

A recent report found that approximately one in five Republican state legislators joined at least one far-right Facebook group during the 2021–2022 legislative period. According to Odette Yousef, a national security correspondent focusing on extremism, "these legislators have been involved in sponsoring nearly a thousand bills across a number of areas, including limiting access to voting, limiting discussion of race in schools, restricting women's access to abortion, anti-LGBTQ+ legislation, putting restrictions on protests and more." Knowing this, Yousef warns that we must pay attention to how our elected officials are getting their information online, and how these groups are informing legislation that affects all our lives.

Above state legislators are the governors, senators, and congresspeople representing each of our states. At these levels too the growing influence of far-right opinions, combined with the power of online platforms, becomes dangerous for all American citizens. Liberal media group Media Matters tracks QAnon's political clout and found nineteen congressional candidates, eighteen of whom are Republicans, who it says showed support for QAnon conspiracy theories and who ran for office in the 2022 election cycle. The faces of the extreme-right agenda can be found all over the United States, reminding us that Donald Trump is not the only threat to our antipatriarchal gains. In fact, there are many who can and would like to do just as much damage as he has already done to our national progress, showcasing the strong state of American patriarchy today.

One such example is Marjorie Taylor Greene, often referred to as MTG, who won her seat in Congress in 2020 and was re-elected in 2024, representing Georgia's fourteenth district. The self-described Christian nationalist has voiced her belief in QAnon theories that ranged from suggesting that Jewish space lasers were responsible for wildfires to stating that 9/11 was a hoax. She has also called Democrats pedophiles for supporting gender-affirming care for trans youth, has said that calling someone a white supremacist is a slur that is just as dangerous as the N-word, has advocated for the "divorce" of red and blue states from the Union, and has declared that some Democratic leaders should be assassinated. As the *New York Times* describes her,

> Her daily litany of often-vicious taunts, factual contortions, and outright falsehoods on social media and behind any available lectern depicted a great nation undone by Biden's Democrats, with allusions to undocumented immigrants as rapists, transgender individuals as predators, Black Lives Matter protesters as terrorists, abortion providers as murderers, and her political opponents as godless pedophilia-coddling Communists.

This quote provides a summary of the groups that are seen as separate from American ideals in the eyes of an American patriarch. To these far-right followers, immigrants, trans people, Black people, and those who believe in women's bodily autonomy are all threats to their way of life, and are therefore described as possessing inaccurate and dehumanizing characteristics. MTG also reminds us once again that you do not have to be a white male to be an American patriarch. White women have long aligned with white supremacy and, in turn, kept themselves from actively dismantling the hierarchy of American patriarchy. We briefly discussed this in part 2 regarding white women's participation in upholding slavery as well as donning their own Ku Klux Klan uniforms.

MTG's rise to fame, in addition to the rise and return of Donald Trump, shows how something that was already in existence became more powerful and dangerous with the allowances of social media. For example, a hundred years ago in the 1920s, KKK members served in all levels of American government. As Tara McAndrew writes in "The History of the KKK in American Politics," "This second-wave Klan emerged as a morality police to fight immigration, minorities, and the loose morals of speakeasies, bootlegging, and political corruption. . . . While men made up the majority of Klan members, women 'poured into' the group, which valued home, hearth, and the sanctity of womanhood. . . . Doing so turned some of the Klanswomen into leaders and activists." Furthermore, one "Klan newspaper, *Dawn: A Journal for True American Patriots*, encouraged members to recommend and become candidates for office to accomplish their aims." The biggest difference between the "Invisible Empire" of the 1920s and those elected today is that digital media has emboldened them to more openly state their views, encourage violence, and grow their followings by doing so at a rate faster than anything we have previously witnessed.

White women like Marjorie Taylor Greene are not the only members of alt-right groups who through their membership only hurt themselves. While the overwhelming majority of those who are active online members of alt-right groups are white men and women, sadly, some members are people of color. There is a particularly disturbing trend of Latino men who identify with white supremacist content and find community with such groups online. When the 2024 election results returned, many were surprised to see that it was not only white men and women who voted in high numbers for Donald Trump, but that he had gained ground with another group who helped him secure victory: Latino men. It should be noted that Latino is a term that lumps several different heritage groups together and it requires deeper analysis, yet the growing right-wing support from this diverse group is still very concerning. In their desire to assert their manhood and allegiance to the American patriarchal social order, some men of color might also be willing to take their activism offline to prove just how far they will go to make their desired community proud. On May 6, 2019, Mauricio Garcia killed eight people in Allen, Texas, after leaving behind social media posts professing his "self-loathing" and belief in white supremacy, saying things like, "We're going to make America white again."

Another example is Enrique Tarrio, one of the leaders of the Proud Boys, who allegedly claimed credit for the January 6 attack on social media in an encrypted chat room. Just to become a Proud Boy requires passing tiers that include: declaring allegiance to the group at any opportunity whether online or in one's personal life; stating "I am a Western chauvinist and I refuse to apologize for creating the modern world" repeatedly; being able to recite the name of five cereals while getting beaten up; getting a tattoo or brand showing the permanency of their dedication to the Proud Boys; and getting arrested or getting in a violent fight in service to the larger mission to restore their desired order for our nation. The Proud Boys are active online and are becoming more active offline every day.

Social media and online chat groups are just the beginning when it comes to digital advances. They show the potential dangers not only of what people might experience online regarding harassment and manipulation, but also the extent to which online hatred and violence translate into the real world and impact our politics as well as our safety. They demonstrate how those who declare allegiance to the dictates that American patriarchy offers us, telling us we must aspire to holding power over others in order to be accepted, find that acceptance in the darkest corners of the Internet, as well as on pages that are becoming more mainstream. But social media is not the scariest advancement in the digital sphere. What we have discussed so far in part 5 is reliant on humans writing their own opinions and turning their own thoughts into action, but where we move next explores what happens when it is no longer only human intelligence but artificial intelligence that takes human input and magnifies it. We also see how American patriarchy is replicated and fed by the blurring between the artificial and real through augmented and virtual reality.

23

NOR ITS SEEDS OF DIVISION

◆

Toward the end of 2022 a new trend started taking over online. Everywhere you looked you saw images of your friends that resembled them but weren't really of them, exactly; they each had a fantastical quality. Friends were suddenly in robot form, in some kind of fairy tale or a made-up future world, and you wondered how you could have similar pictures of your own. The leading artificial intelligence app that was used to create such images is called Lensa, and users flocked to it in November and December 2022 as they became more curious about what might be produced when they uploaded ten to twenty selfies onto the platform. Lensa quickly became the number-one app, ahead of Instagram and YouTube during this time, amassing 22 million worldwide downloads by the beginning of that December. As with any other picture trend on social media, such as the one where people posted photos of themselves from ten years ago alongside a more current photo, messages of warning and caution followed the wave of people impulsively continuing what everyone else seemed to be doing.

The first concern surrounded the general strengthening of AI algorithms, making it more likely to replace real digital artists, for example, and endangering their work as well as their ability to make money. Another problem was the privacy of users who sub-mitted their photos to the app. There were questions surround-ing how these images and data would be used beyond creating the avatars—were they now the property of Lensa since they had been given freely by users? This wasn't clear. What did become obvi-ous, however, was the replication of American patriarchy complete with various elements of sexism and racism. Lensa is a product of Prisma Labs, which was founded by Russian developers but is based in Sunnyvale, California. Therefore, again, although it tech-nically was not American men who created the company to begin with, we see how American patriarchy is still reproduced, as well as how influential American patriarchy has been worldwide.

In the images, people, mostly women, quickly noticed that the app generated oversexualized images of them, sometimes even producing nude shots, despite the fact that they had uploaded only headshots. The app was more likely to add sexualized features when users selected the "female" option, such as portraying peo-ple in more sultry poses and enlarging breasts. Women of Asian descent reported an additional layer of hypersexualization where they felt like their images were modeled from anime characters, which is known to be highly sexualized and even pornographic at times. Muslim women were also especially concerned about the reproduction of their faces without their hijabs even when all their submissions were of them wearing their head coverings. People of color reported that their images were whitewashed, their skin lighter and their features presented as more Eurocentric, with thin-ner noses and lips, for example. Women of all different body types also reported that the images they received showed them as much thinner than they were, which was particularly triggering for those who dealt with disordered body images in the past or present. Male images were more likely to result in pictures of the users as astro-nauts, warriors, or scientists, while female images were more likely to result in nudes, fairies, and fantasy images. Clearly the app was presenting people as the status quo wanted them to be, and not as they actually were in all their wonderful variability. This signaled a larger issue, the reproduction of oppressive hierarchies through artificial intelligence, and it emphasized the fact that American patriarchy is not only embedded in the founding of our country but is already written in code that will continue dictating our future.

In part 5 so far we have discussed how social media plays a role online and offline in strengthening American patriarchy by allowing misinformation and disinformation to grow, replacing verified news sources, presenting an opportunity for harassment and misconduct that goes largely unrestricted and unchecked, reifying the notion that people are not good enough as they are and that they must aspire to the hegemony, emboldening hate groups to take their theories and turn them into action offline, becoming a place where the most problematic among us can find one another and plot how they will hurt others, giving room for dangerous candidates to raise money from users and take their data in order to sway them to vote while igniting fears and spreading lies. All this is incredibly concerning, but it feels easier to address how humans are using social media by implementing better checks and balances. It is much more daunting to address how computers and machines simulate problematic human behavior.

The reasons why such images have been generated are many, and they relate to technologies far beyond an app that produces interesting portraits. Lensa pulls images from a massive open-source dataset that's composed of images across the Internet, and since the Internet is overflowing with sexism, genderism, and racism, the app simply follows the trends that already exist. Equal visibility of all different kinds of bodies and people across platforms and media has long been a problem in need of correction. Limiting what we can see is a strategy to tell anyone who differs from the "norm" that something is wrong with them, rather than something being wrong with a system that aims to limit our identities. The hope is that if people cannot see themselves represented, perhaps they will be more likely to fall in line with what they can easily find everywhere, that they will change themselves to fit what is acceptable and feel overwhelmed by the prospect of trying to fix the world around them to be more inclusive. Even if Lensa's creators did not intend for this to be the message, the fact that AI is based on what is already available only makes it multiply such harm.

Before we move further into our understanding of the new frontier of technological advancement that is artificial intelligence and augmented realities, we must understand how we have arrived where we are today. While technological advances should be used to transform current systems of power, unfortunately they will continue to reproduce them if the people behind their creation are those who benefit from keeping things as they are: Again, these people are largely privileged straight white men. The tech industry as a whole has tried and successfully kept women from participating in it. Women currently hold only 26.7 percent of tech-related jobs in our nation and receive only 18 percent of new computer science degrees. In addition to many of the issues we have discussed thus far, including sources that tell boys to pursue STEM fields while telling young girls to pursue different subjects, the tech industry has also proven to be unwelcoming to women who still persist and continue down the path. Women in tech are underpaid in comparison to their male counterparts; over 50 percent report feeling discriminated against at work because of their gender; they are often passed over for promotions, left in junior-level positions for years, and many report experiencing unwanted sexual attention. As we discussed in part 2, all of the above are reminders to women of their place in our American patriarchy.

The problems only worsen for women of color. Out of the 27 percent of computing roles held by women as a whole, only 3 percent are held by Black women, and 2 percent by Hispanic women. These women also experience a larger pay gap, and they report

higher levels of discrimination and unwanted attention. In summary, young girls are dissuaded from entering the science, engineering, and technology pipeline largely because of the story and
illusory truths American patriarchy relies on that say these fields
are meant for boys and men, and even if they can push beyond the
limiting messages and continue pursuing their passions through
adulthood, they are further punished in ways that endanger their
emotional, mental, physical, and fiscal security.

These factors lead many women to leave their jobs in the tech
industry. It's estimated that women leave tech at a 45 percent
higher rate than men. Studies show that several of the women who
made this decision said they were forced because their companies
did not have a sufficient maternity leave policy. This point highlights how many of the proposed fixes to the current culture of tech
have largely been placed on women, telling them that they would
succeed if only they acted more like men. Not only have women
been told they should simply be more confident and assertive to
be taken seriously, but they have also received the message that
they should not pursue having children, or they should delay having children, because they won't receive the support they need to
make both work. It should be noted that tech companies are seen
as leaders when it comes to parental leave because they offer it at
higher rates than companies from other private industries. However, this is because our bar in the US is extremely low; only 30 percent of tech workers have paid family leave benefits. Furthermore,
in 2022 many tech companies significantly reduced their parental
leave policies or dropped them entirely. As we discussed in part 3
around reproduction, when a company does not support mothers
in their desires to have children while continuing to work, it is
clear that said company does not believe that women should be able
to do both. Rather than addressing toxic work environments that
are not inclusive to anyone who isn't considered white and male,
the onus has unsurprisingly been placed on those being hurt the

most, telling them that it is their fault if they do not assimilate well into the industry.

Still, women who stick with it and lead/found tech companies, and who have demonstrated that their ventures perform three times better, on average, than those led by CEOs who are men, received only 2.1 percent of venture capital (VC) funding in 2023. Accessing capital is such a major challenge for women founders that they accounted for only 15 percent of US technology startups between 2016 and 2022. This lack of investment in female founders is being reflected in AI, where male-founded artificial intelligence companies are sweeping VC funding while female-founded ones are being left behind. The discrepancies only continue as women are largely excluded and missing from the c-suite and from executive boards. In tech, especially in AI, American patriarchy takes the form of what is often referred to as "bro culture." This term describes spaces that prioritize and reward men who are self-centered and ego-driven, who are dominant, who are focused on winning and who do not care if this comes at the expense of others. Bro cultures are smaller versions of our national patriarchy that replicate the hierarchy in the makeup of a company and the way the company is run. These cultures often follow the same trajectory we have become familiar with in this book, where white cisgender men are in power and others are reminded of "their place" below said white men. Again, such reminders come in the form of toxic work environments where crimes like assault and harassment are commonplace with few consequences, if any. Furthermore, high usage of drugs and alcohol, and the encouragement of these behaviors in order for people to be included, create even more dangerous situations for those seen as subordinates. If diverse women and people are not on the teams creating the technologies that will inform our future, and instead bro cultures, filled with toxicity, harassment, and American patriarchy, continue to be at the forefront of technological advances, it will be impossible to fight the reproduction of our current power dynamics. Regarding artificial intelligence, it will only continue to be trained and based on the minds and motivations of the hegemony.

One might be led to think that tech has always been dominated by such cultures that center white men, but the reality is that computer programming was originally seen as "women's work" here in the United States. As we discussed briefly in chapter 18, during World War II, women were encouraged to take on jobs while men were overseas, and one of these jobs included calculating ballistic trajectories by hand. According to the article "When Computer Coding Was a 'Woman's' Job," "this meant determining the angle soldiers should fire at based on how far away the target was, what the weather conditions were that day, and other factors. By 1945, they were part of nearly 100 female mathematicians working as 'computers.'" These kinds of computations took a very long time, but even when a machine called the Electronic Numerical Integrator and Computer (ENIAC) was invented by John Mauchly and J. Presper Eckert to make the math faster, it was still women who performed calculations with it. These women led the development of computer storage and memory. Since they were the first modern coders, they were also the ones who taught others how to code. As the article states, "Mauchly and Eckert were introduced to the press as the ENIAC's designers. The women were never introduced, and they weren't invited to the Army dinner celebrating the debut either. . . . Because they were women, it was assumed that the work they did must not have been very difficult."

In the early 1940s, the field, highly feminized, was underappreciated and did not receive much attention. Nor were careful records kept of the women who performed calculations and wrote some of our oldest coding. At a time when software seemed secondary to hardware and coding was considered tedious, computer programming was rendered invisible. Furthermore, the women doing the coding were underpaid and undervalued. This trend continued for several years. In *Hidden Figures: The American Dream and the Untold Story of the Black Women Mathematicians Who Helped Win the Space Race*, by Margot Lee Shetterly, the book that was turned into a box office hit, we see how "computers" at NASA in the 1960s were actually largely Black women.

The shift to men leading in technological fields took place for a number of reasons but was mostly due to the growing importance and profitability of the industry. Male executives began purposefully excluding women, especially women of color, through their hiring criteria and by sending the message internally and externally that the field was for white men. Hiring criteria included aptitude tests and personality profiles that favored and described white men. Commercials and ads started featuring computers as "boys' toys"; one ad even featured a man teasing a woman for trying to use one. The rising importance of coders and mathematicians aligned with the belief that men were always better suited for important roles. The realization of the importance of such work all along resulted in the strategic erasure of women's historical participation in such fields. The story of tech was manwashed and whitewashed to keep young girls and women from knowing that they were once the brains behind it all. As more men entered the field, they were paid far more than their female counterparts, and this ability for men to make fortunes also allowed for them to rise in the industry and recruit to the field others who looked just like them. Hence why the coders who were supported and invested in the most were white men, and, over time, women have been told they are no longer welcome in the industry they built.

Patriarchal technology is not only a problem because of how it pushes women, nonbinary people, and people of color further into the margins; it is also dangerous because it possesses violent consequences for us all. Lensa is only the tip of the iceberg of the sexualization and violence used against marginalized groups. The issues run much deeper and become scarier when we think of innovations in online pornography, to people using virtual reality to harass and assault women, to the continued misogyny and racism present in the gaming industry, and much more. All these sources influence their users to normalize and justify abusive actions even more, because the artificiality of it all desensitizes people and gives them room to explore their temptations without limits.

A study by the National Center on Sexual Exploitation showed that pornography, made readily accessible by technological advances, fosters aggression by making violence seem enjoyable to its victims: "Aggressive acts against women in pornography occur in roughly 87% of the scenes, and 95% of the time when these acts are committed, women respond with expressions of pleasure or neutrality." There are direct links between online porn consumption and the normalizing of rape and other forms of sexual abuse. Now with AI, pornography has entered a new stratosphere with the possibility of deepfake porn. This pornography is created using artificial intelligence technology and can produce whatever users dream up, including horrible atrocities like sex with children as well as other forms of violence and rape. Furthermore, images created based on the likeness of real people have already been used as a new form of revenge porn, the practice of distributing sexual images of people without their consent.

In the realm of virtual reality, where people can interact in seemingly real and physical ways to computer-generated simulations, we have also seen the furthering of the most violent and disturbing products of American patriarchy. In cases where virtual reality allows people to interact with others, people have been more abusive because such platforms aren't technically "real" and therefore carry lower stakes for abusers. People have reported hearing racial slurs targeted at them, and others have reported being groped and raped in the metaverse. The gaming industry, where virtual reality is having its largest impact, has long been notorious for its gross representation of women and people of color, and online communities have only seemed to grow in violence as more "connection" has been made possible with technological advances. A researcher using Horizon Worlds, an online VR game, was "led into a private room at a party where she was raped by a user who kept telling her to turn around so he could do it from behind while users outside the window could see—all while another user in the room watched and passed around a vodka bottle." It becomes clear yet again that such atrocities will persist in a virtual world that is built to replicate and not to improve. While it isn't technically real, those who experience the abuse report many of the same post-traumatic responses as those who have experienced abuse in "real life."

With every year that passes, digital technology takes more control of our lives and our minds and tells us what is accepted and what is the norm. Yet it has been proven repeatedly that with more advances and little change to the people behind these, humans, machines, and computers will continue to favor, replicate, and protect American patriarchy, making them do far more harm than good. Our discussion of artificial intelligence, virtual reality, and augmented reality leads us to a discussion of the harm being done beyond negative impacts on humans. As is the case with all modern advances, there must come a discussion concerning impacts on our environment; American patriarchy also appears intent on destroying Mother Earth.

24

NOR ITS DESIRE TO SEVER

✦

first noticed something was wrong when I started to feel light-headed even before I could see the cause; the air felt slightly too thick to breathe. My first thought was that I was imagining the problem; maybe I simply needed to take a break. I was working with students at the time, helping them prepare their college applications at a school that primarily served low-income families of color, and the door to my shared office was almost always open to let fresh air in and allow us to greet students walking by. As the day went on, the sky progressively changed, making it clear that the problem was not in my imagination. I was sensing the air pollution ahead of it becoming visible. The other counselors, teachers, and I called parents to come pick up their children. We learned from news reports that a fire had broken out somewhere miles away, and the air around us was becoming too dangerous to breathe.

After having doubted my instincts and breathing in contamination for hours, I was worried what this meant for the baby forming inside me, and when I got home I could not help but research the adverse effects of inhaling wildfire smoke for anyone, and particularly for pregnant women. It was in this search that haunting images of ruin emerged. Whole houses and buildings were now ash; scorched cars—sometimes abandoned and others still holding the remains of their terrified travelers—sat lined up in the streets. The skies were lit red and orange but not in a beautiful way; instead they evoked horror and destruction threatening all breathing beings: humans, animals, and plants both near and far. The images were accompanied by messages warning that these kinds of fires would only grow without massive course correction to save our environment and to intervene in climate change that led to the hotter temperatures and droughts necessary for such monstrous fires to begin.

As with every other natural disaster, wildfires reveal both the similarities between all human beings affected by the same crisis as well as the differences that certain privileges make. The similarities are easier to list: People all over from different walks of life have been put in harm's way as a result of wildfires; people have lost their lives and properties, and they have felt the terror of seeing catastrophic scenes like the ones I describe above. However, as fires rage on, some people have access to the best masks and protective equipment they can find for themselves and their family members; some choose to travel away, waiting to return when things are back to normal, while the air continues to fill with toxins; others keep themselves safe and comfortable in their homes with filtered air conditioners. While many lose their properties, some can easily rebuild with the insurance money they will receive, and will simply have to deal with the inconveniences of waiting for a few years while their homes or second homes are rebuilt, this time even better than before. This group is overwhelmingly rich, male, and white. On the opposite side of the coin, many have difficulties finding masks that can actually filter out harmful smoke particles, people without housing are left unprotected from the fumes, others with poor ventilation in their homes will endure the heat as they avoid opening their windows, caretakers will watch as their loved ones, including children and the elderly, grow sick or their health concerns like asthma grow worse, workers in outdoor settings—especially farmers—and other essential workers will be asked to continue to do their jobs despite hazardous conditions, and people who are incarcerated will fight the fires alongside recognized fire-fighters but will be compensated only one or two dollars per hour for risking their lives. This group looks much different from the first. And even worse is the fact that the first group is likely the reason the fire started to begin with.

In part 5 we have been discussing how many technological advancements are sadly being used to maintain American patriarchy and reproduce the cycles of American patriarchy that make it feel unavoidable and almost unnoticeable. We have explored how things like social media and artificial intelligence in the wrong hands not only reify the status quo but also make it that much stronger. Here in chapter 24 we continue our discussion of such "advancements," with a topic that is inextricably linked to American patriarchy: climate change and our dying planet. Patriarchy across the world, especially American patriarchy, is to blame for the fact that Earth is now warming up faster than it ever has before. Wildfires are not only a useful metaphor to discuss the way American patriarchy impacts all of us while certain privileges provide the protection and escape plans necessary for those in power to survive, they are also a product of everything we have learned in this book so far.

Regarding part 1, the story of American patriarchy—that says the masculine must dominate the feminine and white culture must dominate the practices of people of color—leads to a dying planet. White American men have taken the belief that they should dominate everything around them, nature most of all, to the most extreme levels. Regarding part 2, taking people's land, exposing certain groups to harmful waste, and denying people access to clean air all follow the "reminders of our place" and punishments of American patriarchy. Other examples include overhunting animals, overfishing without any regard for the balance of the ocean or for the sharing of resources with others, putting pollutants into the air in order to maximize production and profit without caring about the consequences, and contaminating the water being consumed by less privileged populations in order to expand an individual company's profits. Regarding part 3, interrupting nature's reproduction by saying we humans can make the processes faster and more efficient through genetic modifications of animals and food speaks to another arm of reproductive control. Furthermore, studies show that climate change also makes it harder for people to have children; groups that are exposed to higher temperatures and pollution report more health complications related to infertility and pregnancy loss. Regarding part 4, the denying of evidence that points to climate change shows the power of misinformation, disinformation, and illusory truths once again. All those who claim that global warming is a hoax only worsen things for the rest of us. In summary, the disrespect of Mother Nature is an intentional part of American patriarchy and therefore must be included in all our antipatriarchal agendas. We cannot say that we want to dismantle American patriarchy if we do not believe protecting our planet is part of that dismantling.

Again, while advancements in technology have the potential to do good, something I will discuss more in depth in the final part of this book, the negative will outweigh the positive if we do not get the risks under control. If we do not see what checks must be in place to limit the expansion of American patriarchy through the expansion of technology, we will suffer while those with the most power will use all their resources to try to leave the planet they played a role in destroying. We have seen the richest in our nation, like Elon Musk, put their resources toward their own trips to space, an obvious signal that they will use their money to make sure that they are okay rather than making sure our planet is. For example, segueing from our past chapter in particular, the technology needed for the training and running of artificial intelligence systems alone requires an immense amount of computing power and electricity, which results in exponential carbon dioxide emissions. These emissions only grow depending on what the AI system is built for and how it will be used beyond its initial training. For example, according to an article in *Scientific American*, "when OpenAI trained its LLM [large language model] called GPT-3, that work produced the equivalent of around 500 tons of carbon dioxide." Such emissions blanket Earth, trapping the sun's heat, and lead to global warming and climate change.

Moreover, several studies have shown that protecting the environment or showing any care for the sharing of resources, including with our nonhuman sentient companions, is actually seen as unmanly and even queer by American men. These men, especially those who are antifeminist and homophobic, reject eco-friendly behavior because they find it to be emasculating and a threat to their identity. One study even showed that both male and female participants described using plastic bags as masculine, while bringing a reusable tote to the grocery store was described as feminine. Other data shows that women litter less than men, eat far less meat, and are more likely to lead vegan and vegetarian lifestyles, recycle more, and purchase electric vehicles. The *New York Times* article "The Climate Crisis Is Worse for Women" quotes Katharine Wilkinson: "Men have a larger carbon footprint than women, by 16 percent. . . . And the top 1 percent of income earners globally, who are overwhelmingly male, are responsible for more carbon emissions than the bottom 50 percent of earners."

Women are impacted more by climate change because they face higher risks and heavier burdens that come with the responsibilities of their cultural "role." For example, as caretakers of our children and the elderly, who are most vulnerable to increased sickness as a result of something like rising temperatures, women will see and face the consequences first. In fact, several scholars believe that sustainability and eco-friendly practices are more likely to be developed by girls and women because they are taught, from the moment they are born, that they are caretakers and that what they do impacts others; they therefore become more selfless and socially responsible. Men, on the other hand, are taught that altruism and regard for others, especially weaker beings and Mother Nature, will make them less powerful. Men will go so far as to deny scientific facts and purposefully engage in environmentally harmful activities to reassert their manhood.

In comparison to other nations, including China, Argentina, Italy, Spain, France, India, Brazil, Canada, Australia, and the UK, the United States has the highest rate of climate-change deniers, and the issue of climate change causes more debate here than anywhere else across the world. The data also shows that not only is there a gendered divide but a racial and ethnic one when it comes to those willing to protect our environment. A 2023 study by the Chicago Council on Global Affairs found that "56 percent of Americans consider climate change a critical threat to the United States. Concern is highest—at solid majorities—among Hispanic Americans (70%), Asian Americans (65%), and Black Americans (65%). Asian Americans (66%) and Hispanic Americans (62%) are the most likely to view climate change as a serious and pressing problem that needs action now, even if it involves significant costs to the United States. Majorities of Asian Americans (64%), Hispanic Americans (62%), and Black Americans (54%) say the United States should take a leading role in the international effort to limit climate change." In other words, these groups are more likely to be concerned about climate change than white people. They also put global warming higher on their list of issues when voting in elections than white people do. Again, people of color are less likely to be climate-change deniers because they tend to be more affected by the consequences. It is harder to ignore something when you are facing the damages of the problem.

The ones who are perhaps the most aware of the dangers of climate change in the United States, because of how much their livelihood is impacted by it, are Indigenous people. After being pushed off their land, they have been forced to live in areas that are most exposed to hazards like extreme heat and droughts. One example that is referenced in a multiyear study published in the journal *Science* in 2021 is the Mojave tribe (along the Colorado River), which experiences "an average 62 more days of extreme heat per year than [they] did on [their] historical lands. . . . Nearly half of tribes experienced heightened wildfire hazard exposure." This American patriarchy–driven theft of land from Native Americans has not only put tribes in danger but has come back to affect us all; because they know best how to protect our relationship with nature, they should have been allowed to remain the stewards of this relationship. Across the many different Indigenous populations of the United States is the understanding of our deep-rooted connection to nature as human beings and the need to practice judiciousness in order to live in harmony with our ecosystem. With these sentiments at the heart of Indigenous practices we find a list of concrete ways to restore balance in the relationship between humans and Mother Earth, such as regenerative agriculture, intercropping, polycultures, controlled burns, intentional hunting, and cutting down or getting rid of diseased trees and plants only if methods to cure them have failed. These are all techniques that lessen carbon emissions, build symbiotic relationships across different plant species, and produce sustainable ecosystems.

Climate change is happening globally; it is not taking place only in the US. But as the most powerful nation in the world, it is very telling that many Americans, mostly white Republican men, are convinced the issue does not exist. Although a 2010 analysis by *Slate* found that the typical single man in the US was responsible for about 6 percent more carbon emissions than the typical single woman, many American men still tie actions to save our planet to the feminine, and therefore reject changing their habits and taking responsibility. Tom Stuker, for example, the world's most famous frequent flier, has flown upward of 23 million miles in the past three decades and has been quoted as saying that he is unconcerned about his carbon footprint because the planes will fly with or without him. For Stuker, this may have simply been an offhand remark. However, on a broader level, this kind of American patriarchal attitude is not only detrimental to US citizens, it is contributing to catastrophes across the entire planet.

The Environmental Protection Agency classifies wildfires as natural disasters even though only 10 to 15 percent of wildfires are attributed to natural causes. While some wildfires occur naturally, such as by lightning striking a tree, most are the result of human actions that can be intentional, accidental, or negligent. More than 80 percent of wildfires in the US are man-made, caused by reckless human activities. I think of the continuance of American patriarchy as a series of wildfires that produce poison in our air that is sometimes invisible and other times completely blinds our vision. It's something that we can be tricked into thinking exists purely in our imagination until we are suffocating, plants and animals die en masse, and we are facing apocalyptic scenes all around us. Our relationship with American patriarchy shares similarities with wildfires and the smoke they give rise to. While wildfires have become almost normal as a result of their frequency—on average, more than a hundred thousand wildfires clear 4 to 5 million acres of land in the US every year—it does not change the fact that they are toxic, that they destroy everything in their path, that they ob-scure our view, that they are hurting us oftentimes before we notice the more obvious changes in the air around us, and that they are preventable. Stopping them starts with change on both personal and larger scales that require us to care more about the collective than the self, to switch from a mentality of "every man for himself" to every living being working in harmony for our shared desire to continue residing on planet Earth. A recent report published by the UN predicts that wildfires will increase by 50 percent by the end of the century, based on current trends. I am left wondering if our inability to see clearly through the smoke will only continue, if our normalizing of breathing harmful fumes will only make it less noticeable, if our numbness to carnage will allow it to perpetuate, or if there is hope yet to clear the smolder once and for all if only we, as well as those who are coming after us, can listen and follow those who have shown us a different way historically.

As I scrolled through the articles that day in 2019 listing all the harmful effects of wildfire smoke on children, reading terms like "higher risk," "preterm birth," "low birth rate," "morbidity," and more, I felt my child kicking inside me. All at once I experienced a feeling of fear of what would come if we continued down this road of disregarding our planet, a feeling of shame for the dying Earth I was bringing my child to, but also a feeling of hope and inspiration, imagining all the future activists yet to be born. I thought of the students I had spent my morning with and remembered the power of our youth, who always taught me more than I could ever teach them because they so often asked how everything could be done differently.

25

OUR VISION OF NEW POSSIBILITIES

✦

I am a member of Generation Y; we have also come to be known as millennials. We are the generation of people who were the last to experience parts of the analog world before everything became digital. For example, our baby pictures were printed and put in photo albums; we remember using disposable cameras and watching memories on VHS tapes. We also experienced the complete transition into a digital world; we grew up with the Internet, cell phones, and social media, and we helped to teach our parents and grandparents how to use them. The digital world became so second nature to us that we were the first generation referred to as "digital natives," a term that is now used for successive generations as well. But the fact that we still remember the way things once were has allowed us to see digital technology differently than Generation Z, who have integrated this technology into every aspect of their lives and who were given access to things like phones and social media at the youngest ages before their parents fully knew the potential dangers of such decisions. While there are many positive characteristics associated with Generation Z, those born between 1996 and 2010, such as their embrace of change and diversity, when it comes to technology usage they have become a case study of its adverse effects.

Generation Z has reported an increase in depression and anxiety largely due to the many issues we have discussed in part 5 that each day appear to get more severe. Other examples, in addition to what we have covered thus far, include teenagers finding easier access to drugs by using online platforms. Right now, dozens of parents are suing social media platforms for enabling drug dealers to sell their products to young people. Most of these families lost their children to overdoses and they are trying to find clarity in the changing landscape young people find themselves in today. Another example comes in online users being classified as domestic terrorists when they go so far as to coerce young users to perform degrading acts online through blackmail. As described in the *Washington Post*, one girl in Oklahoma was pressured to send a nude photo to someone she chatted with online, and when she obliged, he and other online predators threatened to share the picture unless she "live-streamed degrading and violent acts. . . . They coerced her into carving their screen names deep into her thigh, drinking from a toilet bowl, and beheading a pet hamster—all as they watched in a video chatroom on the social media platform Discord." The article describes these online abusers as part of a growing network of sadistic social media users who target thousands of young people each day.

Throughout this book I have interwoven my mapping of American patriarchy with my personal life trajectory. In the first part, I discussed the founding fathers and original crafters of American patriarchy while I also reflected on my mother's upbringing and her desire to break free from the story she had heard growing up. In part 2, as we explored the Supreme Court and other authority figures who uphold the laws of American patriarchy and use these to ratify the system, I simultaneously reflected on my life as a child and teenager. I questioned the place I was taught to inhabit as a Black girl in the United States. In part 3, while we analyzed the role of doctors and scientists, and the way these authorities have robbed women of their power, especially over our own bodies, I also spoke about my identity as a wife and my becoming a mother. I reflected on the ways in which these growths in my identity made me even more aware of strategies to make me feel reliant on others, rather than trusting my own intuition. Part 4 was a reflection on both the stories we are taught and the stories we teach through media, particularly news stories but also movies, books, TV shows, and songs. This reflection came alongside my thoughts about having young kids who are forming their identities with such inputs from the moment they are born. Here in part 5 I have continued my political and personal journey as we covered the darker sides of technology, primarily digital technology, revealing its potential to ensure the indomitability of American patriarchy. In this chapter I think about the future of the country and world my children will become teenagers and adults in. I ask what their future will look like because I fear that it has the potential to be much the same, if not worse than what we have already experienced. If we do not intervene, and if we do not catch the reproduction of American patriarchy in our advancements, our algorithms, and our codes, our mission to create a more equitable nation will become futile. With everything we have explored thus far, I would be lying if I said I was not afraid.

What we have witnessed in several regards is the replication of everything we have studied in this book so far. We have seen in the examples presented in part 5 that white men continue their rule through their dominance in technological advancements; we have seen that these have become means for them to maintain their power and uphold the status quo. We have seen that women and girls have not only been pushed out of such fields but have also been dissuaded from ever returning. We have seen how all women, especially women of color, have purposefully not received the credit they deserve for their contributions to such advancements. We have seen that hatred has been allowed to live freely and build in new ways. We have seen that computers are following the dictates of the system they were informed by and the minds of the people who built them. We have seen more clearly than anywhere else in the book how horrible American patriarchy is for our young people, where they either learn to hate themselves or to hate others or both. We have seen that the growth of untruths has risen to uncontrollable levels where it is even difficult for a researcher like myself, who is highly trained in media literacy, to distinguish between what is propaganda and what is verified.

As a mother, I am very afraid. I do not know how to make decisions for my children and their future with the dangers that await them beyond our door, and even within our home, depending on when they will begin to understand how our digitized world works and how much they have access to at their fingertips. I am scared that the battle for our basic rights continues each time I see Donald Trump, Elon Musk, and those like them use the things that should take us forward only to drag us back. It is daunting to think about the conditions of our environment each time we experience clear indications of climate change, such as the extreme heat waves we endure in Southern California as I write this book.

I would also be lying if I said I did not have hope. The reality is that we cannot defeat something unless we fully understand the extent to which it exists and what it relies on to stay alive. It is for this reason that I have spent part 5 in this conversation that makes me feel so scared and vulnerable. I have been committed to explaining just how horrific American patriarchy has already become in digitized spaces, and showing just how influential these are on all our experiences. At a time when these forms of technology are no longer a relatively small part of our lives like they were when I was a child, but are instead intertwined with every aspect of our existence, we must make sure we understand their potential and that we are using them carefully and for good. We must not be swept away by the lure of it without checks in place; we must be especially cautious of what our children interact with and what they will come to see as their norm.

Digital technologies can also result in more inclusion by giving people access to knowledge and resources they were previously excluded from; they can create community for the best of us and not solely for those with ulterior motives; they have the potential to lessen biases rather than magnifying them; and they can actually help reduce carbon emissions. It all depends on who is behind such advances and how these will be used to make their vision of what the world should look like a reality.

We must make sure that we are fully aware of the need for girls, people of color, nonbinary people, and all others who have traditionally been subjugated by American patriarchy to be equally encouraged to not only understand every advancement in this space, but to be the ones ushering in new technologies and leading the charge. This is not simply because it is the "right" thing to do, or because it is fair to do, but because we will all be better off as a result. We have to do what each of us can to ensure that with the furtherance of digital media, AI, and beyond, we are bringing more acceptance, equity, and healing, more of the antipatriarchal agenda that seeks to combat the hierarchy, the violence, and the pain of things as they are. We must demand regulations and checks to ensure that attacks online and offline are contained and stunted. We must recognize how the examples we have discussed in part 5 are all connected to one another, all products and feeders of American patriarchy. Furthermore, we must always consider how to make the good outweigh the bad; we can experience the positives of development and innovation while ensuring that our planet is taken care of and protected.

As a mother, I feel very hopeful because we know more now than we did when I was a child; we know more than we did when members of Generation Z were children too. We know that there are tactics in place to reproduce and magnify the things that have hurt us, and we can protect ourselves with this level of consciousness. By analyzing how hard the maintainers of American patriarchy are working to reproduce the system that benefits them, we also become aware of the things they are so afraid of. They are afraid of us loving ourselves and one another, they are afraid of us coming together rather than being divided, they are afraid of us being informed rather than being willing to blindly follow where they want us to go, and they are afraid of us implementing our vision of the world into the code. We can see more clearly what they are trying to keep from us and exactly why; we can make decisions with the knowledge we've gained, and we can be brave. We can ask which digital technologies can ensure the safety of girls and women, which digital technologies can bring more joy and self-acceptance to people, which ones might help us understand and celebrate differences, and which ones will ensure that young people can access resources they need without becoming vulnerable to predators. We should ask how AI can help us envision and work toward a nation where all people are considered human and treated as such regardless of sex, gender, race, sexuality, and more.

After Generation X, Generation Y, and Generation Z there was a question as to what to name the next group. Why not simply go to the beginning of the alphabet already in use especially since we didn't start naming generations until the 1970s? The children born in 2010 and beyond could have been Generation A, but by starting with a different alphabet entirely came a symbol that I hope will define my children's generation, a representation not of recycling the present but of beginning something new. My children, all born between the years 2019 and 2023, are members of Generation Alpha, the first generation to be fully raised in the twenty-first century. It is predicted that Generation Alpha will not only be tech savvy with artificial intelligence becoming their norm, but that they will also be environmentally conscious and become the most diverse and interconnected generation thus far. With these factors, they carry the potential to bring the changes we have wanted for so long. It is for these reasons that they will be strategically targeted by American patriarchs intent on keeping them from using innovation for good. It is no coincidence that those invested in upholding the status quo have targeted young people, have tried to keep them from accessing information about their people's histories in addition to making them doubt themselves whenever possible, because young people can take it all apart with the right tools used in the right ways. It is up to us to make sure they are aware of what has led to our current reality, of the dangers they might confront, but more important, that they are aware of the power they hold. This is the greatest gift we can give them and ourselves.

Part 6

OUR
INTERCONNECTEDNESS
AND
COURAGE

26

REGARDLESS, I BELIEVE

■

Black women are the only people in the United States who historically, by law, have been deemed the birthers of nonlife despite the fact that the economy of our nation depended on our re-creation; told that we were not human and that our children were not human, but instead were someone else's property. Yet Black women have created life in infinite ways through our children, through our creativity, through our art, through our activism, and through our stories because we have never believed what the law said to be the truth. We know we are precious beings and that our children are the most precious of us all. As a collective, we have never accepted circumstances as they are but have instead pushed for things to be as they should be, because we have had no other option. To succumb to what our country has told us about ourselves, to simply agree to the terms of our dehumanization, to allow our children to be taught that they are not worthy of humanity, would mean death and eradication. But to see beyond what was readily available to us, to envision a world that did not yet exist, to push others to align with our vision that at its core simply states that we are all human and our descendants are too, means revolution, hope, and life. In no way is this persistent hope born out of ignorance of the risks resistance poses to our lives, or ignorance of what those in opposition to us are capable of. It is born and sustained out of necessity and faith.

The first step in achieving radical change is shifting our mindsets from believing it is possible to accepting nothing less. While part 5 came with warnings about how the cycles of American patriarchy are multiplying and gaining strength, part 6 shows how such cycles are not inevitable and, in fact, are weaker than they appear. What we must know is that it is largely fear that drives American patriarchy, and it is for this reason that the protectors of the system strategically try to make us all fearful of one another. The system of American patriarchy is alive because a group of people created it out of feelings of insecurity and their desire to keep a tight grip on their resources. The cycles are a product of these mentalities that enforce hierarchy and justify inequity out of constant fright of losing it all. The opposite would be a nation that is organized based on bravery, optimism, a sense of security, and a comfort that comes with everyone having their needs met and therefore not being tricked into feeling the need to withhold all your power and wealth for yourself. In order for us to break a system and its cycles of fear that result in oppressive rule that denies the humanity of many, we must simply become more equipped.

Now that we know what we are up against we can find hope, inspiration, and strategy by studying those who have come before us. It is a common saying that we do not want history to repeat itself, but I often say it depends what history you see yourself as being part of. As a Black American woman, knowing the stories of Black women before me is what brings me the most optimism and allows me to believe in the possibility of radical change. Replicating their strategies and building upon them is where I find a path forward for our nation that is brave and that stems from minds more concerned with safety than with violence, more concerned with the collective than with the individual, and more concerned with balance than with a ranking system. Before we can move to a collective mind shift, we must first find that mentality in ourselves. Here I will share one of the life stories that brings me the most inspiration and that speaks to the personal mind shifts that take place for all of us on our journey of realizing our bravery, in working for change, and in arriving at a place where we cannot accept anything less.

She was born in the summer of 1947 in Flushing, Queens. Brilliant from an early age, the girl spoke in full sentences before most other children can even master one word at a time. Her grandmother would build her up with affirmations. "Who is better than you?" she would ask; "Nobody," little JoAnne would reply. "I want that head held up high, and I don't want you taking no mess from nobody, you understand?" her grandmother would continue. Her grandparents even forbade her from saying "Yes, ma'am" and "Yes, sir," or to look down when talking to white people, because they believed she shouldn't be obligated to respect anyone who did not respect her back. When JoAnne was three years old she moved to Wilmington, North Carolina, where her grandmother had inherited land and where her grandparents started a business right by the beach. Their success and their pride made them a target for white supremacists who often paid visits to their establishment to harass JoAnne's family, always yelling racial slurs and sometimes shooting guns in the air. JoAnne saw her grandfather calmly retrieve his own gun and wait patiently, ready to shoot if need be; she also saw her grandmother tell off a white man who tried to trespass on their property.

While we are often told the stories of Black people who chose to stay silent in order to protect themselves and their loved ones, we are less often told the stories of Black people who were willing to risk their lives by standing up for themselves and making their disdain of the social order obvious. JoAnne's upbringing speaks to a legacy of fighters in her own family who showed her from early on that the way our nation operated was wrong, and that they wanted her to avoid feeling limited by the dictates in place that would try to tell her she was less worthy of dignity and respect. Through their actions, her grandparents displayed what they were willing to sacrifice in order for her to live freely, yet it would take more years for JoAnne to fully see what role she had to play in continuing that legacy and building upon it. Similarly, for many of us, especially those who did not have the same grandparents as JoAnne, there is an awareness of the inequity that surrounds us, but we are nascent in our understanding of where we fit in creating something new. We are still learning what it is we have to add to the fight. Perhaps we are still fearful of those trying to enforce the codes of American patriarchy on us, and we allow others to do the work of fighting for us.

When JoAnne later returned to New York and went to community college in Manhattan, she initially hoped to go into marketing or advertising, fields she thought she could earn a decent living in. Her grandparents had taught her that being "just as good" as white people meant having things white people had like power and money. They told her school would allow JoAnne to have a nice house, nice clothes, and a nice car. They wanted her to ascend the ranks of American patriarchy. But she found she was much more passionate about subjects like sociology, history, and psychology. She was now learning that she could build on the foundation her grandparents gave her, one filled with bravery and a refusal to bow down, with a new layer of thinking that was more intent on tearing down the structure rather than ascending it. She was on her journey to finding courage for herself and a vision of the world she hoped to help create. In this same vein, a step for each of us to take is to become more aware of what has been done in times past while reflecting on how we can take our commitment to justice to a new level.

JoAnne was on a campus filled with other Black students both from the United States and abroad during a time when Black consciousness and Black nationalism were on the rise. Fellow students were demanding that their college hire more Black faculty and introduce more Black courses, and they organized concerts, poetry readings, and celebrations filled with love for their Black identity. JoAnne's understanding was continuing to grow; she was identifying that the fight for freedom was not only one she shared with generations past but one she could carry forward with her peers. We can all find inspiration in knowing who among us shares our imaginations for our nation.

Her first experiences with organizing came through a student group, the Golden Drums, that provided a safe space for members from the African diaspora to explore their identities while also educating others through programming and lectures. It was at one of these lectures that JoAnne learned the story of Nat Turner, an enslaved man who had plotted and fought for freedom by leading one of the largest slave revolts in US history. She had always loved and admired Harriet Tubman for running to liberation and returning to free countless others, and hearing about Nat Turner added a new layer to JoAnne's understanding of what Black people throughout history had been willing to do to change the United States: They would outwit white supremacists by running *and* they also fought their oppressors directly.

Her formation as an activist was continuing; her peers were teaching her stories she was unaware of and, with their help, she was learning in real time while simultaneously building on her wisdom of the past that would inform her future approach. She immersed herself in learning more about Black freedom movements and realized something important: White people had not freed Black people from slavery; Black people had done everything imaginable to claim freedom with their own hands, hearts, and minds. This step in her gradual transformation was her arrival at her cognizance that she too could create change with her hands, heart, and mind. She came to understand something that we all must accept: Those in power are not going to be the ones who dismantle a system that works for them; it would take the rest of us for that to happen. Furthermore, it had been done before; it could be done again.

With this awareness, JoAnne started questioning everything she knew of herself up until that point. She first wondered what history her name held, and she felt the urge to change it. She wanted a name that reflected the revelation she was experiencing of seeing herself as a contributor to the fight, one who each day was becoming more informed of her history, who each day was becoming more prepared to contribute in her own ways. She decided she wanted a name that, in her words, "had something to do with struggle, something to do with the liberation of [her] people."

Before telling you the name we all now know her by, I want to pause to reflect on her, right before she took a step that would lead to her becoming one of the most famous freedom fighters, and think about how we might each relate to her journey of coming fully into her awareness. JoAnne now understood that to engender change meant to not only recognize when things were unfair, it was not only having the courage to try to protect yourself when the enforcers of such unfairness showed up at your door, it was not only about claiming power for yourself, it was not only about knowing the celebrated stories in our history, it was not only about equipping yourself with knowledge for the sake of it; it was about knowing how the injustices came to be, it was about changing power structures, it was about searching for the stories that were strategically being kept from us, it was about camaraderie, it was about taking our knowledge of those before us and claiming our rightful place in the legacy so that we could finish the work, it was about introspection, and it was about committing to being on a journey of change on both a personal and a political level.

The first name she chose was Assata, meaning "she who struggles"; the second was Olugbala, "love for the people," two sentiments that she is still known for to this day. Her last name, Shakur, meant "one who is thankful." Assata Olugbala Shakur. The ultimate struggle and love for her people came when she stepped into her identity as a revolutionary and became a leader in the Black Panther Party and the Black Liberation Army in Harlem, where she helped to provide free breakfast for children and organized free clinics, among other important work. She would come to find out, however, that her becoming a person who would take her mental shift and create system shifts would at times be a dangerous endeavor.

On May 2, 1973, Assata Shakur and two other members of the Black Liberation Army were pulled over by troopers James Harper and Werner Foerster. The traffic stop turned into a shootout that resulted in the deaths of one of Shakur's peers and Officer Foerster. While the full details of the shooting remain unclear and Shakur argued that she was wounded in the shooting herself, making her unable to hurt Foerster, she was arrested and charged with murder. She was placed in solitary confinement for more than a year in a men's facility, where she was harassed and tortured. She was mistreated even while she was pregnant and was forced to give birth behind bars to her only child. She maintained that she was innocent despite being sentenced to life in 1977. She spent two more years in prison after that. As we know from what we have studied thus far, we can read the imprisonment and torment of Assata Shakur as a punishment for her attempts to challenge the structure of American patriarchy. We must acknowledge the risks of such work because it allows us to see how willing our foremothers have been to do whatever it takes to challenge the system holding us back. When we speak to the pain she experienced, we also then better appreciate her ability to continue fighting.

What happened next is what has made the name Assata Shakur so renowned and awe-inspiring to many like me, and hated among others. She found a way to escape the bars that held her. Her escape from prison, her avoidance of a life sentence, and her safe arrival in Cuba made her a target of (primarily male) white supremacists who have not waned in their hatred of her. So great is the threat of a Black woman defying the rules that years later, in 2013, she became the first woman ever to be placed on the FBI's Most Wanted Terrorists list, and several politicians have continued to call for her extradition from Cuba, even offering rewards of up to $2 million for her return.

After her escape, Assata Shakur published her autobiography, which began with a poem, "Affirmation." In it she writes,

> I have been locked by the lawless.
> Handcuffed by the haters.
> Gagged by the greedy.
> And, if i know any thing at all,
> it's that a wall is just a wall
> and nothing more at all.
> It can be broken down.

This stanza is the most famous one as it speaks to our ability to tear structures apart and the power that comes with simply knowing we have that ability, knowing they are just walls and nothing more at all.

Assata Shakur's incredible life teaches us many lessons, but chief among them is that American patriarchs are deeply afraid of the message free people who are not brainwashed by oppressive doctrine send to the entire world, afraid of what someone like Assata Shakur is teaching those who keep telling her story: we can fight, our lives can be testament to the weaknesses of the entire system, and we can show the unlimited power of what we're willing to do.

For Black women, pessimism is not a luxury we or our children can afford. There may be times when we fall; there have certainly been many times when we have lost sisters in the battle, but we will always be able to picture more, to know our lives have not been lost in vain, to regroup, to try new strategies, and to keep on fighting. The fight includes declaring our rights; rewriting laws; disrupting the norm through our marches, boycotts, and sit-ins; loving ourselves and our children; speaking through our talks and books and shows; keeping our histories alive; providing essential resources in our communities, especially when the state will not; challenging powerful American patriarchs by running against them in office; organizing to gain and keep our right to vote; and more. But before any of this, there must first be a belief in what is possible, an awareness of our capabilities, and an incomparable commitment to create the world of our imagination. These facts are what keep me confident; they are why I will leave you with a reminder in this final section of the book, that we must continue to believe that we can and will take down the American patriarchy that threatens us all. While the past few chapters showed that the oppressive cycles of our country will continue to repeat themselves, these next chapters will complete the sentence: The oppressive cycles of our country will continue to repeat themselves unless each of us who reads this fill ourselves with the optimism, resolve, and action of people who cannot afford anything else. What will it take for us to defeat American patriarchy once and for all?

You should be hopeful and confident too, believing fully in the power of these sentiments that is only proven by the ways in which those who oppose us respond to our gains of freedom and our commitment to keep fighting for more. Moments that feel like national regression in recent years, such as the election and reelection of Donald Trump, the overturning of *Roe v. Wade*, the reintroduction of antigay and anti-trans bills, the killing of protesters without any consequences, the very public reappearance of neo-Nazi groups, the growth in hate crimes, the countless cellblocks that are disproportionately filled with Black and Brown bodies, all signal an acknowledgment of our power and a fear of the fact that times are changing.

This first chapter has spoken to the shifts in mindset we must have on an individual level to create change. In the next chapter we explore how such shifts can happen in our collective mentality, especially in spaces that have tasked themselves with being the messengers of truth for centuries.

27

WE CAN WIN TOGETHER

✦

The book of Genesis, the story of the "beginning," is one that is known by most humans, even if they identify with different religions or do not consider themselves religious at all. It goes like this: God created the universe by separating light from darkness, heaven and earth, and formed the first human from the dust of the earth, naming him Adam. From Adam's rib, God created Eve. Adam and Eve lived in an abundant paradise with access to everything they needed and were told that they could eat anything they wanted except for the fruit from one particular tree. Eve was persuaded by the devil, in serpent form, to disobey God's orders and eat fruit from the forbidden tree. Adam then followed by doing the same. When God discovered what they had done, committing the first sin, they were banished from the Garden of Eden. The most commonly held interpretation of this origin story is that it shows that women are meant to be secondary to men; that women cannot be fully trusted; that women are weak, seductive, and evil; that women need to be watched and controlled or else their decisions will lead humankind astray. In summary, through this interpretation it is believed that women are the source of pain and have been made to pay for Eve's actions ever since. Hence the reason why many people say that the story of Adam and Eve is where patriarchy originated.

However, other interpretations of the text exist. There is the interpretation that the story is not meant to be taken literally, that
Adam and Eve were not real humans but were instead metaphors
to discuss themes of good (Adam and Eve) and evil (the serpent),
or the innocence we experience in youth versus the knowledge that
comes from growing and acting on our curiosity as we gain more
worldly wisdom and see our surroundings with clarity, or the danger of leaving nature behind in our pursuit of material things. There
are also other literalist interpretations, including feminist ones that
say Adam and Eve actually represent equality. These interpretations reveal that, in reality, Genesis presents two origin stories but
that one simply became more popular than the other. In the first,
less famous one, God created an ungendered being that was divided
into two equal humans. And even in the second story, a feminist interpretation might say that Eve being created after Adam signified
her superiority since Adam himself was created after the animals
and not before them, so maybe Eve was the pinnacle.

I tell you all this to say that it is not the story of Adam and Eve
that created patriarchy; it is patriarchs who have used the story to
advance their agenda, who have tried to bury evidence that suggests
alternatives, and who have made it a justification for inequity. One
might find it surprising that I left any discussion of religion to the
end of a book about a hierarchy that places men above women and
places white people above all others, but this was not by accident. I
have done this because while it is true that religion has played a role
in furthering inequity in our nation and across the world, I believe
it is wrong to say that it caused it. Collective mentalities that are
based in the fears we discussed in chapter 26 created purposefully
unjust systems, called their goals holy, and used organized religion
as a vehicle to spread the message of hate and enforce exclusion,
injustice, and violence in their most extreme forms. Religion has
been used as a tool of patriarchy, especially in the United States,
and not the other way around. Based on what we have come to

learn about American patriarchy, it should not come as a surprise that those who believe in maintaining it have interpreted religious texts to justify their sexism and racism.

These interpretations have been used to spread false messages and images of religion. For example, it is not because of ancient texts that images of Jesus as a blond-haired, blue-eyed, white man became popularized around the world. Take Warner Sallman, a white man born in Chicago, Illinois, in 1892, who in 1940 created the *Head of Christ*, the all-time most popular portrait of Jesus, which has sold over five hundred million copies. While it has historically been common for people to draw images of Jesus in their likeness across various cultures around the world, the *Head of Christ* became the accepted standard for American families and was distributed more universally during a time defined by World War II. Christ as the whitest man you could picture appeared in stained glass in churches, prayer cards, calendars, and on people's furniture, and it even accompanied soldiers into battle. Again, a white man's interpretation, one that he said came to him as a "miraculous vision" in response to his prayers in a "despairing situation," spread like a divinely ordained wildfire to bring a message to a suffering world: white men resembled God the most.

White Christian churches in the United States have a ripe history of racism and exclusion of people of color. Slavery itself was justified by religious leaders, and following the Civil War these same leaders enforced the racial hierarchy and segregation by participating in KKK rallies. According to the Equal Justice Initiative, "In 1959, nearly a century after slavery was abolished, less than two dozen of the South's 100,000 white churches were known to have any Black members." But what is more disappointing is to see how some Black churches that formed in response to such racism and exclusion replicated American patriarchy in their own ways. Black churches have a rich history of contributing to the fight for freedom and justice, but many have also gotten caught up in reproducing the hierarchies of the white churches that excluded them, again speaking to the belief that in order to be free we must aspire to what white people do rather than doing something else entirely. There are several Black churches that also spread sexist and homophobic rhetoric in the name of the Lord.

Within churches of all racial backgrounds in the US we find the replication of American patriarchy, and where we see this kind of replication we also find the same disturbing and disgusting issues we have studied throughout this book. We see examples of churches that do not allow women to be pastors; we see members who are men feel justified to abuse their spouses and children. Jocelyn Andersen, an author who writes about Christianity and women, says, "The practice of hiding, ignoring, and even perpetuating the emotional and physical abuse of women is . . . rampant within evangelical Christian fellowships and as slow as our legal systems have been in dealing with violence against women by their husbands, the church has been even slower." Furthermore, you will also see examples of church leaders who not only allow the abuse of women but who also create unsafe spaces for children. A recent study of over three hundred alleged child sexual abuse cases, "Child Sexual Abuse in Protestant Christian Congregations: A Descriptive Analysis of Offense and Offender Characteristics," found that the overwhelming majority took place on church grounds or at the offender's home, and were most frequently carried out by Caucasian, male clergy or youth pastors. Many scholars have pointed out that the abuse of children is more rampant in faith communities than in secular communities for a number of reasons, including a culture that easily allows for the abuse of those seen as subordinates and that also offers abusers forgiveness if they simply repent.

Fearful interpretations of the Bible have also been used to permit wreaking havoc and terror. Evangelical Christians are some of the strongest advocates for keeping our nation in a patriarchal state. They believe their interpretation of faith should take a foundational role in government, and also that the entire nation should live by their interpretation of Christianity. During the storming of the Capitol in 2021, not only were rioters carrying American flags, Confederate flags, Trump flags, and even nooses, many of them were also carrying crosses while chanting "Jesus is my savior, Trump is my president." Several pastors participated in the riot while others encouraged the behavior beforehand and defended the actions of the protesters afterward. One pastor by the name of Ken Peters preached at a rally on January 5 in DC about how the election was stolen. Then, during the riot, Peters sat comfortably in a hotel tweeting praise for the "patriots." Following the attack on the Capitol, Peters defended the riot as a patriotic mission to take the country back for God, who he said "has a special plan for this country." The Christian right feels threatened by the changing role of women in their families, women's rights to make decisions concerning their own bodies, immigration, the acceptance of different gendered identities and sexual orientations, and the teaching of evolution in schools, and it believes that critical race theory is somehow fundamentally at odds with Christian faith.

They have become violent on many occasions in the "name of the Lord." Evangelical Christians often state the need for all their members to arm themselves. According to an article in *Christianity Today* by Matthew Soerens, "White evangelicals are both more likely to own guns than the overall population and less likely to support stricter regulations on gun ownership, and most evangelical gun owners cite 'protection' (not hunting) as the primary motivator." Soerens continues by pointing out that politicians interested in gaining the support of Evangelicals often state that they stand for "God and guns." This stance on guns is unique to American Christians in comparison to Christians around the world, who mostly believe that guns do not align with their faith. Once again, this is an example of the fact that it is not the Bible that tells someone to pick up a gun as a testament to their faith; instead it is a person who believes they have something to protect and people to fear who uses the Bible to justify these beliefs. Evangelical Christians in the United States are just one example of how dangerous a collective mentality that grows out of fear and a desire for power can be.

Some Evangelical Christians argue that these are the things the founding fathers wanted; they also twist lessons from the Bible to fit their opinions and describe themselves as fulfilling a divine calling. On both of these points, however, they are incorrect. The founding fathers identified as men of faith but were men whom many historians now describe as deists. This means that while they believed a supreme being, God, had created the universe to operate by "natural" laws, God's people were meant to operate with human reason when thinking about social and political problems. The founding fathers believed in the separation of church and state. Of course their interpretation of natural laws included a belief that white men were naturally superior to others, and therefore they saw themselves as the most appropriate rulers of the nation, operating with God's blessing, but they likely would have been surprised to see how much religion plays a role in politics to this day. More important, however, is what other believers and religious scholars see as the mutilation of God's teachings by the Christian right, which distorts biblical lessons and creates a disconnection between religion and notions of acceptance, justice, and equality.

People of faith, usually white ones, often find themselves aligning against groups fighting for their rights because they think that their religious beliefs cannot align with messages of radical change, and this is a shame. One does not have to renounce religion in order to be anti–American patriarchy; in fact, there are many ways in which religion aligns with the dismantling of oppressive systems. To keep with our focus on Christianity we can return to a discussion of Jesus, sans the blond hair and blue eyes, especially considering he was more likely, according to both scientists and historians, to be a person of color. As Obery M. Hendricks Jr. writes in his book *The Politics of Jesus: Rediscovering the True Revolutionary Nature of Jesus' Teachings and How They Have Been Corrupted*, "Jesus was a political revolutionary. . . . The message he proclaimed not only called for change in individual hearts but also demanded sweeping and comprehensive change in the political, social, and economic structures in his setting in life: colonized Israel." Jesus's ministry was to radically transform unjust systems, to change the people in power who had contributed to the unequal distribution of resources, who had repressed others and caused them to suffer from poverty and hunger. Jesus was on a mission to heal individual pain and remove unjust structures that were causing the pain to begin with. As Jesus states in Luke 4:18–19, "The spirit of the Lord is upon me, because he has anointed me to bring good news to the poor. He has sent me to proclaim release to the captives and recovery of sight to the blind, to let the oppressed go free, to proclaim the year of the Lord's favor." Hendricks identifies Jesus as a voice for those previously silenced, a changemaker and a chain breaker.

Several feminist scholars have also pointed to examples of Jesus being feminist himself; even though the term is more modern, his actions would fall under the category of feminism today. The Bible is filled with examples of the ways Jesus treated women with the same dignity, care, and respect as men. One of the most famous is of a woman who was caught committing adultery. Those who apprehended her demanded that she be stoned to death, without much attention being paid to the man she was committing adultery with. However, Jesus did not punish the woman but instead said, in front of the growing and judging audience, that the only people who had a right to throw stones were those who had never done anything wrong themselves: "He that is without sin among you, let him first cast a stone at her." The crowd grew smaller and smaller until everyone scattered and the woman was left unharmed. Women played critical roles in the life of Jesus: They financially supported him and his twelve disciples, they followed and cared for Jesus closely, and they were the first he spoke to when he rose from the dead. Mary Magdalene was identified as an Apostle to the Apostles. The evidence is rich that Jesus was not only feminist but was concerned with loving all people equally and teaching human beings how to do the same.

There is far more that people concerned with social justice can claim in relation to Jesus than those who are opposed to such principles, and many people, churches, and Christian organizations display this in their antipatriarchal approaches. There is a rich tradition of women and nonbinary people of color using their faith to bring services and messages of hope to their people, and in recent years more of them have risen to positions of leadership through their dedication to remove the patriarchal traditions from their places of worship. Pauli Murray, an activist and attorney, was recognized as the first African American woman to be ordained a priest in the Episcopal Church, in 1977. Murray's groundbreaking work influenced the civil rights movement and expanded legal protections for gender equality; Murray saw faith as essential to activism. Churches like Trinity United Church of Christ in Chicago and Glide Memorial Church in San Francisco preach messages of love, inclusivity, and justice being inseparable in living a life of faith, and they back this belief with direct acts of service and acceptance in their cities. There is a growing list of churches, ashamed of the stances and actions of the Christian right, that denounce such messages of hate and identify themselves as standing in opposition, churches that led in the civil rights movement, churches that are currently fighting to save women's access to abortions, churches that participate in Pride parades, churches that provide housing and food to immigrants, and that all see these as fulfilling the mission God called them to fulfill. There are also feminist movements in Judaism and Islam that prove that the dominant practices of many religions have largely been because of how men in power interpreted the Word of God rather than necessarily being what the Word originally meant.

It is far too easy to blame religion for American patriarchy, and far too easy for patriarchs to claim that their actions are religious. It is for this reason I have left a discussion of faith for the last part of this book rather than the beginning. For far too long we've elevated the stories of religious bigots rather than balancing the scales with those who use their faith to create more freedom and justice. For far too long people of faith have felt that they have to stand against abortion, against gay rights, against women's freedoms, against people of color, when in reality there have always been people teaching us the opposite: To be a person of faith is to be a person who believes in the possibility of radical change and justice; to believe our country does not need to be hierarchical but can instead be egalitarian. Religion can actually be people's reason to be the most transformational fighters among us, interpreting the Word to help set people free instead of using it to judge them, instead of oppressing them, instead of excluding them from divinity.

In chapter 26 we discussed how we can each come into our identities as activists who are anti the system that is American patriarchy, and here we have explored the role of the church and religion as just one example of the dangers of mob mentality. But the opposite of this is the potential of growing our empowering individual beliefs by creating shifts in our collective mentalities that promote less insecurity and fear. Once we experience our personal realization of our bravery and our faith in a different way of doing things, we can strengthen these in larger groups. Our religious communities are one place where these shifts can happen, and they offer examples of potentially powerful coalitions. The next step is translating our coalitions' shared vision into action.

28

RECOGNIZE ONE ANOTHER

■

The day is April 4, 1969. It's been four years since Martin Luther King Jr. saw the slums of the Windy City for himself. Reflecting on the immense segregation and brutality he witnessed during his visit he stated, "I've been in many demonstrations all across the South, but I can say that I have never seen—even in Mississippi and Alabama—mobs as hostile and as hate-filled as I've seen here in Chicago." April 4, 1969, also marks one year since the date of MLK Jr.'s assassination, a tragedy that spurred Black Chicagoans to riot in pain, pain that was answered with more police brutality and heightened segregation. It is not only Black Chicago residents who are suffering from immense poverty and police violence as a result of rampant discrimination; Latinx groups that are largely Puerto Rican are facing hunger as well, while being kicked out of their neighborhoods in the name of redevelopment. Alongside them also exists a group of white people who have come to Chicago from the poverty of Appalachia, looking for better economic opportunities but finding continued struggle. Because each of the members of these individual groups are poor, they are treated similarly despite the fact that they are of different races. They are harassed by law enforcement and are denied basic services.

Up until this date they have all tried to meet their direct needs separately. The Black Panthers launched survival projects; they started educational programs for Black children, they offered tuberculosis testing, transportation services, ambulance services, free food for those who could not afford to buy their own; and they even distributed free shoes, all on the West Side. On the North Side, in the Latinx community, a group called the Young Lords focused on initiatives to meet the necessities of their people. They used a church building and transformed it into a health clinic, where parents could take their children for day care, and where people could have access to food. In the poor white community, a group called the Young Patriots followed similar models with their own clothing drives and breakfast programs in addition to organizing themselves to monitor police activities in Uptown. But on April 4, 1969, all three groups, who had been divided along the lines of race and city geography, realized their shared struggles and tried to do something revolutionary together.

With palpable agony and desperation for relief from the inequities they had been plagued with for far too long, a mixed crowd gathered to listen to their leaders speak about what could change if they could all come together to demand better treatment from police officers and access to resources that would meet their basic human needs. Their poverty was their shared experience, and it brought them a revelation of their shared humanity. They dared to dream of the potential strength of unifying their efforts. The Rainbow Coalition was established by Fred Hampton of the Black Panthers, Jose Cha Cha Jimenez of the Young Lords, and William "Preacherman" Fesperman of the Young Patriots. They would go on to include groups like Students for a Democratic Society, the Brown Berets, the American Indian Movement, and Mothers and Others (MAO). While the leading men have received more coverage in our historic understandings of the Rainbow Coalition, the women of each of these groups are largely to thank for the implementation of programs meeting the direct needs of community members. The Black Panther Party, for example, was two-thirds female by the early 1970s. This powerful coalition supported one another in actions against poverty, racism, substandard housing, and police brutality, and they even worked together to reduce crime and gang violence.

Members of these groups knew that the most important practice in creating change on a massive scale was coalition building—people coming together from different walks of life and declaring that the issues they are individually impacted by are more likely to change when fought for together. In chapter 26 we discussed how in order for us to begin dismantling American patriarchy, we first must be aware of our individual mindset concerning what is possible for our nation and discover how committed we are to that vision. In chapter 27 we explored how that shift in our mindsets must also happen on a collective level where individuals come together with the faith that we can and should do things differently. While we focused on the messages of religious groups and leaders as one key example, this cultural shift applies to all messengers who influence our collective knowledge. Here in chapter 28 we focus on the next step in bringing the vision to reality, which is through action. We specifically look at action that does not wait for national policy changes to occur, but focuses on meeting the direct needs of human beings first. Through these kinds of interventions, groups in the past have created minisocieties that display the possibilities available for our nation as a whole if we are able to scale the solutions. The most impactful of these groups have been those who came together across differences without attempting to erase their differences, instead using their sometimes universal and sometimes more unique needs to cover more ground and bring healing to all their communities. They remind us that sometimes we can actually create the world we envision for ourselves even before major shifts take place on a national level. If people are hungry, we can feed them; if people are unhoused, we can provide housing; if people need access to doctors, we can bring the doctors to them. By doing this we display the simplicity of the solutions, we can demonstrate the effects on people's lives of us coming together to meet everyone's essential necessities, and we can envision what policy change might be necessary for these to be met on a national scale.

Studying such coalitions throughout American history brings immense hope and inspiration, which is what this concluding part of the book is concerned with. In the example of the Rainbow Coalition, we see a commanding and revolutionary antiracist, anticlass, multicultural movement. Three distinct groups came together on common ground in Chicago, one of the most segregated cities in the United States at the time, to confront their shared issues and implement change. Regarding the immense segregation and divisiveness in Chicago, MLK Jr. also said, "If we can break the system in Chicago, it can be broken in any place in the country." This allows one to understand the incredible feat of the coalition even more. These different groups had previously been taught to fear one another, told they were too different to work together, but through their exhaustion of coming up against a state that tried to suppress them all, they united their efforts. People of different races were linked arm in arm as they marched, children from the different groups shared meals with one another, and they came together in organizing meetings to dream of all they could accomplish as a unit. Beautiful images of the Rainbow Coalition and their programs fill me with inspiration and remind me that it can be done.

The study of historic coalitions like this one also provides important lessons, especially in the way it makes us familiar with the tactics those in opposition to such coalitions have used to dismantle transformative collective action. By knowing these tactics, we protect ourselves from being defeated by destructive strategies moving forward. The Rainbow Coalition's incredible feat of looking past what they had been told all along, and redefining the way the country could work, caused extreme fear and retaliation from those who wanted to keep things as they were. They became one of the primary targets of a national counterintelligence program often called COINTELPRO, which was run by the FBI with an agenda of discrediting and neutralizing groups that were considered subversive to US political stability. In the context of this book we can conclude that any groups seen as disrupting American patriarchy, i.e., any groups that stood for the sharing of resources, the dismantling of hierarchy, and the establishment of justice, would be viewed as being subversive to the organization of our nation that we have now studied extensively. Members of the Rainbow Coalition were being watched closely, informants were planted among them, and they were constantly harassed by local and federal law enforcement. This harassment included heightened police brutality as well as an increase in arrests. Despite attempts to create dissonance among the group, such as through forged statements on behalf of the FBI that appeared to be written by members of the coalition and sought to divide them, the coalition continued to grow in strength. Our nation's leaders could not accept the message of unity the Rainbow Coalition was spreading, the potential for working-class people across the country to rise together, meet the needs of their communities, and show what was possible on a national scale. The leaders needed to be taken down. *The power they held needed to be stopped.*

This fear speaks to the power of the coalition above all else, as well as the clear statement that "US political stability" relied on factors like white supremacy, inequality, and power imbalances. This was not hidden, in fact it never has been, and we must be clear on this fact when speaking about what our current national system stands for. Otherwise, why would children being fed, people having access to day care, a reduction of crime, and a coming together of people of different races be deemed a threat by the Federal Bureau of Investigation? When we're talking about dismantling the system of American patriarchy, we are talking about this. Our nation is one that currently relies on some children going hungry, on people of different races fighting against one another, on mothers not having a safe and affordable place for their children to go so that they themselves cannot reach their full potential, on a continuance of crime and a growth of us fearing one another. Anyone who tries to share a different vision for our country, especially anyone who demonstrates how changeable it is by bringing people together and meeting those needs, will become a target.

On December 3, 1969, only eight months after the official formation of the Rainbow Coalition, Fred Hampton fell asleep while talking to his mother on the phone. A few hours later, local police burst into the building, shooting in the chest an eighteen-year-old who was standing watch, before riddling the walls with a hundred rounds as they looked for Hampton. Hampton was asleep next to his pregnant fiancée, Deborah Johnson, who woke up from the noise and tried desperately to wake him up as well, but she couldn't. It was later discovered that Hampton had been drugged. When the cops reached their room, they dragged Johnson out and shot Hampton twice as he slept. After Hampton's tragic death, the surviving members of the Rainbow Coalition continued to experience police harassment. The breakfast programs, the health clinics, the housing units were subject to random searches. Officers would enter these spaces and take medicine away from sick people. The coalition was forced to fall apart, as community members were afraid to access the resources being offered and the leaders of the movement were arrested and held on charges like "mob action" and "resisting arrest."

The first Rainbow Coalition was largely left out of our history lessons with hope that it would fade from our shared knowledge. But for those who know of this historic coming together of forces, the Rainbow Coalition lives on, inspiring continued visions of the power of collective action. Many of the original members of this Rainbow Coalition, still alive today, have continued to fight for the vision they had in 1969, building on it with more solidarity. Hy Thurman, who was a member of the Young Patriots, says he continues to fight, in his seventies, for the progressive agenda that also includes LGBTQ+ rights. Billy "Che" Brooks, who was a member of the Black Panthers, says he believes women's access to abortion and trans rights are an essential part of the revolution. In an interview for *Teen Vogue*, Brooks says, "We can't give up. What Fred and the Black Panther Party exemplified was a struggle against injustice. It's a struggle that always needs to go on. . . . You can murder a revolutionary, but you can't murder a revolution." The revolution was never killed; instead, it has continued in different forms. The first Rainbow Coalition inspired several other movements that pushed the needle further. Many similarly began by meeting the direct needs of people, and progressed into national movements focused on changing laws and policies that not only brought acknowledgment of those who had previously been ignored by American patriarchy but also brought punishment for American patriarchs, something we will discuss more extensively in the next chapter.

You see, the study of coalitions is not the study of perfect movements but instead means building our armory of hope and our understanding of those who have dared to unite before us and believing that we can learn from the past to come together stronger than ever before. I know a powerful movement exists in our near future where we can concretely identify our shared enemies, and we can sustain unity on such a large scale that we will no longer be tricked by forced historical amnesia or scare tactics. We are stronger than we have ever been, our coalition larger than ever before; we now need only to recognize that.

29

CREATE JUSTICE, AND

✹

I have always loved superhero stories. Since I was a little girl they have excited and inspired me. I remember leaving theaters feeling as though I suddenly had superpowers too. I would run around my room in an imaginary fight scene, wielding a weapon or spreading my arms wide as if I could fly. My children love the genre too; they pretend to shoot webs from their wrists and call themselves Spin, Ghostie, and Spidey. There is something so engrossing about the storylines no matter how repetitive they ultimately turn out to be across different characters in different times, spaces, universes, and told for audiences of different ages. We are inspired by them because they are entertaining but also because they make us feel optimistic. We relate to the characters' desires to make the world a better place, to defeat evil forces, to be able to protect ourselves and our loved ones in dangerous situations. Beyond this, they help us navigate dilemmas such as what to do when your unique talents are not enough, or when you cannot seem to accomplish everything for everyone. The villains are also often based on real people throughout history who have thought themselves the deciders of other people's fates, the holders of drastic answers and inhumane tactics that can "save humanity"; they are often people responsible for imposing rules that limit others' opportunities, and the messengers of these rules call them divine.

The genre recycles certain messages: Good generally wins over evil, we are more effective when we come together with others who possess different strengths than our own, superheroes suffer losses and heartbreak too but they turn these into opportunities to help others, and perhaps most important, the genre tells us that change is possible, that we must never give up but always believe we are capable of making a difference. The superheroes who teach us this have their powers for different reasons: Some are regular humans who gave themselves power through science and technology; others were born with different abilities, while others gained them through a life-altering event.

Despite how entertaining I find the genre, I also know it is flawed. Quite often, the same villains seem to appear over and over again as a result of the fact that in versions for kids, at least, and in some adult ones too, superheroes do not punish the bad guys; often they actually help to save them from themselves. Furthermore, the genre purposefully presents us with one-off interventions when a problem appears, rather than sustained commitment to systemic change. The characters we look up to respond to situations as they come, rather than preventing them and shifting structures that make the danger appear in the first place. And of course, despite progress, most superheroes are still straight white men, the few women who do appear are often hypersexualized, and there are virtually no nonbinary characters.

I would love for the genre to move closer to being based on people in real life who better represent our many different life experiences: people who also intervene beyond individual moments when something is temporarily going wrong; people who are actively doing work to prevent bad things from happening again and even prevent many of the origin stories of villains who were born out of inequity, in addition to responding in moments of crisis by meeting people's immediate needs; people who work with others and remind us what we are each capable of, who spark moments of hope even without any supernatural strength or abilities. The moments in recent history that give me the same feeling of flying and power like I used to feel as a teenager when I stepped out of an X-Men movie provide yet another source of optimism and belief in the ultimate defeat of American patriarchy.

I bring our minds to heroism here because I know how daunting the beast that is American patriarchy can be, how undefeatable it can seem. But I believe that with a comparison to storylines many of us have come to love and feel inspired by in worlds that are loosely based on reality, we can find applicability to our current battle. We can find the team members we must assemble with. We can bring stories from our reality to the forefront of our minds that show our power and that arm us with bravery. In chapter 26 we discussed an individual's hero journey, particularly focusing on the mindset that is required to commit ourselves to fight for freedom because we will no longer be willing to accept anything else. In chapter 27 we spent time critiquing how some have used systems of faith to turn collectives of people into defenders of inequity, while we imagined what might happen if these spaces that hold such influence shifted their message to be of acceptance, love, and justice. In chapter 28, we studied a real-life example of people using their collective mind shifts concerning their views of one another and turning their new understandings into action, particularly action that met the direct needs of their community members. Here in chapter 29, we explore how all these steps—individual mind shifts, collective mind shifts, coalition building to meet direct needs—lead to punishment for those upholding American patriarchy rather than the other way around, to policy shifts, statewide change, and, ultimately, national change. When we witness these changes, when we realize the heroism that exists all around us, we move closer to winning.

Our study of American patriarchy throughout this book has made it clear that real-life monsters and villains do live among us. While I would not consider everyone who upholds, protects, and contributes to American patriarchy in this harsh category, Harvey Weinstein, Larry Nassar, R. Kelly, and others like them all scare and disgust me more than fictional characters do. Similarly, I feel fear when thinking of the suffocating grasp of the NRA on our nation and the growing incidences of mass shootings and other forms of gun violence. Furthermore, it can be paralyzing to consider all the policy reform we need, and all the states that seem like they will continue to be led by officials who defend the status quo. All of it can feel like too much to take on, too great of a fight for us to win, until we remember there are heroes among us too.

I think of the people who brought Harvey Weinstein, Larry Nassar, and R. Kelly to justice. In all three cases we witnessed how men with power could abuse others for decades with little repercussion until brave bands of people came forward. Survivors of Weinstein's abuse built on the MeToo movement started by Tarana Burke when they courageously reported horrific incidents ranging from rape, being forced into other sexual acts with him, and being made to look at him naked. When these accusations started coming to light I remember feeling a sense of defeat at the beginning. We had seen in our country's history many times before how women were not believed. Despite their courage, they were called liars and punished for coming forward. I didn't think they would be able to build enough power to take him down, and I was already grieving what they had gone through as well as what they would endure in the national spotlight. Yet the accusations kept coming; the women he had injured were rising and powerfully declaring that they would not be silenced any longer. Allies were taking up the charge as well, and Weinstein was eventually sentenced to spend the rest of his life in prison. This was nothing short of heroism by and on behalf of the survivors.

Larry Nassar molested young girls while pretending he was giving them medical treatment or conducting medical studies, sometimes while they were alone in his care, other times in front of their parents and guardians. Over one hundred survivors and counting have come forward with statements against him. Many of them had told people before, but they had either been dismissed or led to believe they couldn't do anything about it. However, in 2016, a spark was ignited when one survivor told Detective Andrea Munford about what she'd endured and Munford acted immediately. Together they started building an army and a wave of change that led to the conviction of Nassar for up to 175 years in prison for his heinous crimes.

R. Kelly was finally sentenced in 2022 after twenty years of accusations that he was abusing children and holding girls and women hostage in his home. The singer used his fame to trap women in abusive relationships, separate them from their families, and force them to perform sexual acts. One of the most effective strategies used against R. Kelly came from the storytelling of Dream Hampton, who documented R. Kelly's abuse in her docuseries *Surviving R. Kelly*. Hampton brought the stories of survivors, which had been told for decades, to a national audience. The series was released in January 2019, and R. Kelly was sentenced in February 2021.

It is awful that these acts happened at all; it is even more devastating that for many years they took place without any repercussions. But it is hopeful that consequences are now being faced as a result of survivors rising, investigators believing them, and storytellers bringing their truth to the light.

I also find hope when I think of groups like Everytown for Gun

Safety and Moms Demand Action: grassroots movements of people fighting for public safety measures to protect us all against gun violence and to take on villains as large and powerful as the NRA. They formed when Congress failed to pass federal legislation in the wake of the tragic Sandy Hook school shooting in Newtown, Connecticut, when twenty-year-old Adam Lanza shot and killed twenty-six people on December 14, 2012. Twenty of the victims were children between six and seven years old, and the other six were adult staff members. While our national leaders did virtually nothing in response to the loss of these lives, Everytown and Moms Demand Action dedicated themselves "to take on and take down the gun lobby." Over the past twelve years the ever-growing groups have been able to achieve victories that were previously thought to be impossible. These changes include California's implementation of an Office of Gun Violence Prevention, resolutions addressing the secure storage of guns, the reporting by credit card companies of dangerous gun purchases, gun safety laws, and state lawmakers and governors across the nation blocking 95 percent of the gun lobby's agenda. These coalitions are alive and well and are dedicated to ending gun violence in our nation.

Even in the arena of politics that can often feel hopeless and a repetition of the same cycles, I remind myself of epic moments that once again seemed impossible. In 2020, the country was left stunned and in complete awe of a woman who had a vision for her state that very few others believed could ever be realized. Stacey Abrams, alongside her network of activists largely composed of other Black women, knew that they could flip Georgia in favor of Democratic candidates. She had already shown the nation that change was on the horizon when she narrowly lost her race for governor in 2018, but what she accomplished just two years later was extraordinary. By engaging new voters who had previously been strategically pushed out of the political process through various barriers in their way, Abrams and her Fair Fight and New Georgia Project teams were able to register more than eight hundred thousand new voters and secure a historic win for President Joe Biden. That same year, as a result of years of organizing by a growing Latinx population, paired with growing involvement by Native Americans in the same region, and allyship from some white Republicans, Arizona also went with a Democratic candidate for only the second time in more than seven decades. Then in 2022, when everyone, including Democrats, expected major losses during the midterm elections and messages of doom for our nation rang on the news, Democratic victories surprised us all as young people, especially young women, and racially diverse voters carried the party and voted for pro-choice, diverse, and inclusive candidates. While the Democratic Party as a whole has a long way to go to fulfill its promises to all members of our nation, and I believe there might be more freedom waiting beyond what our two-party system can offer us, these wins for democracy and the people who secured them remind us that we are moving closer to our goals. They show us that when we come together in coalition, meet our shared needs, and translate these into systemic shifts, we approach victory. Although President Donald Trump was re-elected in 2024, which can signal regression and feel like defeat, I believe it also signals an opportunity for us to refocus and rebuild.

We are often taught that such movements and organizations are a thing of the past, and asked what people are doing today to keep the momentum that civil rights heroes dedicated themselves to. Young people are often accused of not doing their part, people of color often told they do not participate in the political process enough. We direct our focus to fictional stories of inspiration, sometimes unsure of where they exist in our reality. But I daresay these messages and our actions are often incorrect and misguided. There are numerous current, real, and epic movements taking place led by survivors, elected officials, detectives, storytellers, organizers, and heroes, a word that is now seen as a gender-neutral term, who are unwilling to give up, who continue to believe that good can triumph over evil, who meet immediate needs while also addressing necessary monumental change. They are the examples that make us all feel power coursing through us and are even more inspiring than fantasy ever could be.

30

RECOVER ALL THAT
HAS BEEN HIDDEN

◼

T hings do not have to be this way" is a saying that has driven my entire life trajectory. It is a sentiment that was passed to me from my parents and one that has rung throughout all my experiences of becoming who I am today. These are the words I want to end part 6 with as we approach a conclusion filled with concrete steps and guidance on where we go from here, where we go when we fully understand American patriarchy and see how it no longer serves us, how in fact, by design, it never did.

I started this book by telling you about the little girl from Clarkston, Washington, who wanted to pursue a career in law. A little girl who was told that she was meant to do something else simply because that's how things had supposedly always been done. The people who gave her this message did not do so out of hatred; they often thought they were communicating out of love how things were, perhaps so she wouldn't get hurt or face worse disappointment moving forward when she ran into the rules over and over again. Yet she questioned this and believed in something more for herself. She dared to think she was capable of taking control of her destiny and that she might find a path to her dreams away from her small town. I told you that this little girl became my mother as well as the lawyer she once only dreamed of being. She held a truth in her heart that she shared with her children and others she worked with and mentored, others who had also been told, somewhere along the way, that they did not deserve to be treated equally. She built an epic life for herself and her family by always believing in the bold truth of "things do not have to be this way."

My father has also always lived with the same mindset. He was born in Ghana, a beautiful nation with a rich history of rebellion against colonial rule. Right around the time that my father was born, Ghana became the first African nation to gain independence, under the leadership of Kwame Nkrumah. Nkrumah inspired freedom fighters around the world, including Malcolm X. However, in the 1980s, when my father was in his late twenties and early thirties, Ghana was facing some of its most difficult years. Many Ghanaians were experiencing extreme poverty and searching for better lives in neighboring nations like Nigeria but were often met with deportation. At the same time, President Jerry Rawlings came into power after a coup that resulted in the executions of the previous president and hundreds of Ghanaians. My father knew he needed to leave, and through a courageous journey he eventually found asylum as a political refugee in Sweden. This is where he would meet my mother. My father has always been driven by the history of resistance that he inherited as well as an intolerance for discrimination, inequality, and violence. He too has lived his life declaring "things do not have to be this way."

My parents led their family with this lesson at the forefront. In retrospect it is easy to identify the many ways they taught my siblings and me to never accept the dominant stories without questioning them, to seek truth for ourselves and see beyond what was readily available to us, to be aware of our history and to be equipped with knowledge. Every day my parents would watch the news together and they would discuss each news story with information from their own background, experiences, and degrees. They watched multiple news channels and discussed historic events that led to current issues around the world. At one point I found myself frustrated with what felt like their monopoly over our limited TV time, but as I grew up with this routine in place I became familiar with world history and modern events. In addition to their consistent engagement with material from news sources, and their modeling of dialogue and debate, they knew there was no knowledge that compared to the experience of seeing things firsthand. They believed that the more we were able to experience for ourselves, the more we could move through our lives with the tools we needed to be citizens of the world who sought freedom for ourselves and for others. Hence why they wanted us to travel from country to country. In reality, they could have had a much easier life had they stayed in one place, but it was almost as if they couldn't sit still, and they could not allow us to get too satisfied or small-minded, either; we needed to keep seeing and learning more, seeing and learning all the other ways of doing things.

Both of my parents had been made aware of blatant unfairness in their own experiences growing up. While it might feel as though these are the only people who should seek to correct injustice in the world, because they feel more urgency to do so, it is just as important for us to notice unfairness even in cases when we don't yet realize how it impacts us. You may relate to my mother's experience of being told that girls and women were not allowed to do something. You may relate to my father's experience of dealing with heartache that colonialism still causes decades after a country's independence. Or you might not relate to having experienced the injustices of discrimination in your own life yet. If you are in this last category, this next story is for you.

When I was a sophomore in high school and we were back in the United States, my parents insisted on sending me to a boarding school away from everything I had come to know over the previous four years because they worried I was becoming too comfortable, too complacent with what was, and would have continued being, an unchallenging life in the small town where we lived. School was too easy for me there; I was not being pushed and was almost effortlessly a straight-A student. Virtually all my friends and their parents had lived there their whole lives and my peers planned on staying there for college. I had a boyfriend whom my parents worried I would become too serious with. They feared I would become content trying to fit in with women in a white, homogenous, heavily Republican state that prioritized marriage and family and made it easy to accept and adopt myopic views, views that directly countered what my parents had tried to instill in us. They often spoke about everything they hoped my siblings and me would take from our experiences of growing up nomadically abroad. They wanted us to see the world for ourselves, to witness different ways of living with our own eyes, to question the stories being told by those in charge or those with more power, and to learn of different histories of resistance, as I have already mentioned. They also wanted us to see all the possibilities as well as pros and cons of each of the cities we visited, to feel uncomfortable in places that were not diverse and question them, to return to the United States with fresh eyes, and to spread the message they lived their life by: "Things do not have to be this way."

I was heartbroken when my parents sent me to boarding school and they moved abroad again. I wanted the comforts and familiarity of that unchallenging all-American life, where I was assimilating well enough. Immediately, my college preparatory school challenged me in ways I hadn't been challenged before; I could not sail by anymore and I had to wake up. My teachers encouraged me to be better. It was still largely white and in another red state, but there were students from across the world, some well-off in life, others on financial aid. I made friends who came into their identities while there. Girls talked openly about their sex lives, friends proudly declared that they were bi or gay, and I had teachers who were willing to take us to rallies for Barack Obama. We lived in a little melting pot that put me back in the mindset my parents wanted for me, especially as I began applying for college and visiting places that all had the potential to be my home for the following four years. I had been reminded that while it is usually easier to live in the rigid comforts of the status quo, to assimilate and become as homogenous as possible, to be unchallenged and unchallenging, it is much more beautiful to grow, to question, to take part in and create spaces where people can be themselves, where people are active and dedicated to change when it is necessary, where when inequity exists or a painful lack of diversity stifles even the air we breathe, or you are being made to forget and overlook what needs correcting in the world around you, you can say, "Things do not have to be this way."

When I write about possibility and hope, especially for a country that divorces itself from American patriarchy, I do so from the perspective of someone who was raised by a mother who always wanted more for herself, her children, her mentees, her small town, and her nation, and also by a father with an anticolonial mindset who called out all forms of injustice and constantly reminded us to connect current events to history, to equip ourselves with pride and knowledge of the past. I also write from the perspective of someone who is not solely imagining what is possible, but who has seen much of it with my own eyes, as well as from the perspective of understanding how bizarre some propositions can seem to those who have been taught to avoid and fear what they did not grow up with, those who have lived in the ease and comfort of an existence where they and their families have been able to thrive peacefully with little interruption. At the same time, as a mother myself now, especially of Black children, I also know what my mom came to know well: It is ultimately not a choice but a necessity for me to keep pushing and moving for our country to be better. I may have been able to push it to the back of my mind as a teenager, accepting the microaggressions like people saying that in their eyes, I "wasn't really a Black girl" because I was seen as pretty and smart, but when I look at my kids I cannot sit still either. I understand my parents' seeming restlessness. My only choice as I watch our country allow all the horrible things we have discussed in this book so far is to say, "Things do not have to be this way," and fight until they are no longer so.

These are some of the gifts my parents granted me by not allowing me to stay put. For me it is not too soon for our nation to elect an antipatriarchal woman to the highest office, not only because I believe the revolutionary ripple effects of what we know from the data around female leadership, but also because I have seen it in other places around the world. For me it is not a wild prospect to think that all citizens of the United States should have access to healthcare because I believe it is a human right, but also because I have seen it in action before and reaped the benefits of such healthcare systems. For me it is not too ambitious to declare that women should not be dying from preventable issues during pregnancy and childbirth, that they should all have access to midwives and doulas, that their bodies and power should be respected and admired rather than feared, because I believe it is necessary for our collective survival and thriving, and because I have seen it in action before; I even considered having my children abroad. For me it is not a pipe dream to declare that guns should be virtually eradicated from our country so that even our officers do not have to carry firearms to "protect" us, because I believe they lead only to more harm and devastation for all, and also because I have seen it in action abroad, where officers in many nations do not carry guns. For me it is not an impossible hope to fight for a national reconciliation process for past wrongs against groups that have been oppressed and marginalized, through a countrywide education initiative that faces its poor decisions and promises not to repeat them, as well as through reparations, because I believe this is critical to our national healing and because I have seen it in action before. I can declare these visions because of the evidence that already exists from places across the world: "Things do not have to be this way."

In part 5, I told you about many of the fears I have for my children's future in the United States. Here in part 6 I have told you about what brings me hope and calms those fears in my mind. I did it this way because while it is tempting to stay stuck where we are with our perils and fears for our children's futures, either at the forefront of our minds or tucked away in denial, it is imperative that we bravely imagine and work toward the promises of a different country our children will help us to create. In parts 1 through 5, I also identified the different authorities who have done their job in upholding American patriarchy, and in part 6 I have left that commentary for here at the very end. After experiencing our own growth—in realizing our bravery like Assata Shakur, in transforming institutions that influence our collective mindsets like churches, in coming together with others to address our immediate needs and create the realities we seek right in front of us like the Rainbow Coalition, in transforming our national dialogue and policy and taking down the worst American patriarchy has to offer with real consequences—by speaking up and organizing, we realize that we are the ones with authority over our own lives. We are the protagonists. It is our view of our nation that can become our reality.

Like my parents, I take from my knowledge of the past and can imagine more beyond what's already in existence. I picture possibilities that do not exist anywhere else, but could in the United States as a result of our richness in difference. The opposite of our current American patriarchy is a United States where humanity and community are at the center of our decisions, and where we achieve an egalitarian democracy for all. Where we each possess the same courage, belief, and unwillingness to stay stuck. Where we all repeat the mantra "Things do not have to be this way," where we become resolute that things no longer can continue to be this way, and we do what it takes to ensure that things are never this way again.

CONCLUSION

Not Least of All: Our Power

In the introduction, I told you of my goal to make American patriarchy as obvious to you as it is to me, so that together we could put our hands on it and take it apart. I told you that I wanted us to define American patriarchy accurately and to see it clearly in all the stages of our lives. With these primary goals in mind, we have journeyed through my life of coming to full awareness of what I believe to be the narrative that currently dictates our nation. We have come to understand how even when the story is not always read out loud, it still exists in our minds and informs our interactions with each other. We have seen how the made-up tale has been translated into a system, how what the founding fathers believed about their own superiority was translated into their building of a country that would confirm that superiority. We have witnessed how their opinions concerning themselves and others became laws, and how such laws have upheld their opinions.

American patriarchy tries to disguise itself as democracy, in which state power is vested in the people, where human rights and fundamental freedoms are respected, and the will of the people is exercised. But when we know the definition of American patriarchy, it becomes clear that it is misaligned with ideals of democracy. American patriarchy is based on the narrative that white, able-bodied, cisgender, straight men should hold all the power in our society, that white women are to help white men retain power by doing what they are told, most specifically by reproducing white power. The narrative tells us that those who fall out of these categories not only are separated from the power afforded to whiteness, they are also separated from the humanity that comes with being gendered and that is reserved for white men and their dependents. Gender in the United States is defined with power in mind; to be a man is to be dominant, aggressive, and willing to do whatever it takes to provide for yourself without considering others. To be a woman is to be docile, fragile, and to be concerned with reproducing the hierarchy. White women are seen as subordinates to white men in American patriarchy, and people of color are viewed and treated as something less than human, more as animals who should serve their purpose of building more power and wealth for their white superiors. In other words, while the organization of the gender binary in the US sets up an imbalance between white men and white women, it also affords white women some protections and encourages the rest of us to see it as our path to being recognized, to our families being protected, and to our basic needs being met.

When we understand that these are the roles American patriarchy offers each of us, we better understand how we have arrived where we are as a nation today, where Project 2025 is not an outlandish agenda but an actual possibility. Where a man like Donald Trump was elected, not once but twice, as president of our nation. American patriarchy is the reason why some white women find themselves voting against what we would assume are their interests in health and well-being and reflects instead a greater interest in white power; why some men of color find themselves taking their inability to achieve white power out on women of color; why family relationships among people of color are often disrespected and interrupted by the state; why women of color experience extreme forms of objectification and dehumanization; why people who do not identify neatly with the

gender binary face violence and face it even more if they are also people of color; why some parents who see their children display any sign
of wanting to live beyond the binary are terrified because they believe
their children will have no chance of being seen as human; why girls
are taught at young ages that they are caretakers and boys are taught
at young ages that they cannot display vulnerability; why women and
girls are told to focus more on how they can make themselves attractive, usually by making themselves appear thinner, smaller, and
weaker, while boys are told to focus more on how to make themselves
bigger, stronger, and angrier. The truth is, we can all be tricked into
upholding American patriarchy because we believe that within it lies
a path to equality and safety for all if we can just contort ourselves to
fit its dictates and steadily climb up the ladder. However, the lower
you start on the ladder, the more clearly you see the steps are thin as
rope, they are spread farther apart, and if you slip even once, you will
fall without anyone to catch you. If you are able to stay the course and
keep on climbing, there are still many who will take it upon themselves to push you down when they see you approaching.

There are countless examples of the ways in which American patriarchy plays out in our lives to this day, and while I could not possibly include all of them in this book, I hope moving forward when
you notice them, you can see which of these chapters each instance
might fit into. This book can be used as a guide to detecting American patriarchy's poisonous fruit all around us. It can be scary to realize how embedded these original white supremacist men's views
are in the fabric of the United States, how they dictate our daily experiences through our laws, our law enforcement, our interactions
with healthcare systems, the messages we hear, even the quality of
the air we breathe. It can feel daunting to discover how each stage of
our lives is affected by such myopic visions. It can be disappointing
to find that both parties in our two-party system carry remnants of
the visions, one much more than the other, but both leaving many
voters with a desire for more options. However, hope lies in the fact

that when you study it you realize that your view of what is possible can actually be reflected and supported by collective action, and by law and policy as well. A beautifully inevitable product of studying American patriarchy is learning of those who have seen it for what it is all along and have left the rest of us clues of its fabrication and fragility. It is empowering to become aware that at every stage of our lives we can profess a different vision, and we can usher our nation into a new era with our enlightenment. We can reverse it all with our own views, organizing, strategies, and teamwork. We must no longer ignore the effects of American patriarchy on our lives or allow them to go unnoticed; we must call them out and offer alternatives. We must no longer see all the different ways in which it currently exists as separate, but instead as symptoms of the same disease.

We must no longer reduce our understanding of American patriarchy to a fight for power between men and women, but instead recognize that this is a fight between those who believe in the dictates of American patriarchy—inequity, injustice, fear, violence, dehumanization, power in the hands of white supremacists—and those who do not, those who instead believe in fairness, security, humanity, and opportunity for all. It is not the case that all men are the problem and all women need liberation from men; it is not the case that all white men are the enemy, either; it is also not the case that all rich people are culpable; it is not the case that all women are currently allies in the fight, nor that all people of color are committed to dismantling an unjust system. Instead, it is a case of some people who are pro–American patriarchy and some who are anti–American patriarchy, and there are varying degrees to which we might currently relate to the former or the latter. However, in order to simplify it, those who believe in and uphold American patriarchy subscribe to a belief in hierarchy, a belief that white men should be at the top of that hierarchy, that white women serve the purpose of re-creating said hierarchy and that all others are subjects in keeping the hierarchy alive. Those who do not believe in American patriarchy and who stand against it believe in the principle that all people in the United States are equal in worth and status, and that they deserve equal rights and opportunities and the ability to make choices for themselves, rather than simply being told to play their part in a nation that won't honor the beautiful complexity of their humanity. The variance we might experience when we consider ourselves as standing in opposition to American patriarchy comes with complexities that will arise when we offer new laws and policies to rid ourselves of hierarchy. It won't always be a straightforward path— it never has been—but if we can focus on the basic principle that all humans possess inherent worth and dignity and we aim to accomplish a nation that professes and respects that, we will find our way.

To continue with the same structure I have employed throughout the book, we can explore what our nation would look like at each stage of life we have discussed to realize how much more in reach this vision is than it may seem. We would begin with each of us becoming informed and aware of our histories, the good and the bad on a familial level, on a group level, and on a geographic level. We should each be aware of how the family we come from became what it is today. If we are wealthy, we should know where that wealth came from; if we are struggling, we should be allowed to learn what factors led to that struggle; we should be cognizant of the lands we inhabit and who the people who lived there before us were so that we may honor them, and also so that we may learn of their ways and reflect upon what practices we may benefit by returning to. If there are parts of our family or group histories that have contributed to the mistreatment of other people, that have contributed to the maintenance of American patriarchy, we should seek to repair what we can, knowing that there is collective healing on the other side of that positive action. These actions cannot fully fix past wrongdoings, but they can interrupt a cycle of pain and violence with reconciliation and the dawn of a new chapter. I am not arguing that wealthy people should not have access to their riches, but I do believe they are uniquely positioned to help ensure that others have access to the resources every human inherently deserves. Another way of putting this is that I am not as concerned about building a ceiling in the United States; what I am discussing is the need for a foundation that recognizes us all.

In an antipatriarchal vision all babies in the United States would be given the same support, including access to healthy meals, time with their parents/guardians, and a space where they can learn, grow, and be cared for if and when their parents return to work. They will be told from the moment they are born that they are not limited by their genitalia or the color of their skin, but that these qualities make them all special and unique. They will be told that the factors their nation is invested in are their joy, well-being, and safety. Our national systems would aim to keep children with their loved ones by supporting their diverse family units with resources that fill in the gaps for families dealing with the inequities caused by the histories of our nation we already discussed. These interventions would range from basic necessities like free diapers to having access to mental health therapists and counselors who can help caretakers of children to achieve their healthiest states. In the rare cases of parents being unable to provide well for children even with the right support, children would be with members of their extended family and still have opportunities to form relationships with their more immediate loved ones. And in the even rarer cases where extended family placement is not possible, children would be adopted by loving families of all different kinds.

School-age children would have these messages of love from their nation reinforced through the lessons they learn in the classroom. They would be told that they were accepted in their uniqueness and would be met in the ways they learn differently. Their teachers would be paid sufficiently so that the most talented of us all could also bring their best selves to the classroom as they shape the minds of our next generation. Teachers would be vetted to ensure that they are aware of any existing biases and are able to learn how to grow from these and encourage students to celebrate their differences together. As children grow and move through different grade levels, they would be taught tools for analyzing all the many materials they might encounter in their lives, rather than having books kept away from them that allow them to better understand themselves, their own histories, and other people. At school and at home they would be told, yet again, that while their differences are loved and appreciated, these differences do not predict their abilities. They will be encouraged to explore and play in a variety of ways that show them that they can all cook, clean, take care of dolls, and choose whatever colors they like. They will hear over and over again that they are each capable of becoming leaders, scientists, artists, of becoming whatever they would like to become. Again, in the name of equity, when clear results of inequality present themselves, or when children have unique needs and abilities, it would be up to our government to provide access to what children need, if their families cannot afford it, to even the playing field whether these be tutors, safe buses, mental health therapists, wheelchairs, or hearing aids, so that our next generation of leaders has everything they need to reach their full potential. We would also ask if our current educational spaces are meeting our diverse needs or if they need to be reimagined to fit different children rather than solely intervening to make children fit the spaces.

Children in middle school and high school would be taught, both at home and at school, about the changes taking place in their bodies, in empowering ways where they are encouraged to ask questions and reflect openly about their identities. They will not be taught through fear tactics that keep things a mystery and shame them, making them feel like something is wrong with them for experiencing puberty, but instead they will be wrapped in acceptance and given resources to learn about themselves. They will be celebrated for going through a stage of growth while also learning about all the different changes that can take place. For example, all children would be taught about menstruation even if they won't be experiencing it, in ways that speak to it as an ability and not a deficiency. All girls and other menstruating people would have access to menstrual hygiene products and support with affording them, if need be, without being subject to the "pink tax." All children would also learn what it means to respect other people's bodies and would be able to define and identify consent as well as anything less than consent. With lessons concerning healthy interactions with others, children would also be told whom to turn to if they ever experience unhealthy interactions with other children or adults.

We would not have to do away with competition such as through sports; in fact, we would encourage such team building and healthy living without needing to replicate extreme forms of aggression or locker-room culture. The ripple effects of messages filled with acceptance, celebration of difference, and team building from the moment they are born would begin to reshape spaces that have traditionally reproduced mini–American patriarchies. Instead of sexist, racist, and homophobic banter, sports teams could build on unity, encouragement, and acceptance that are all already naturally associated with winning together as a team. We would encourage engagement in activities like dance, and arts such as school plays, just as much as we encourage sports for all kids. Similarly, debate teams and robotics teams would not be solely for a specific set of teens but instead activities that are open for all to explore. As children find what they are inspired by and gifted with, they will specialize their involvements over time. States would make opportunities available to those who cannot afford to pay for them on their own so that all children have the potential to become the next great athlete, artist, coder, or all of the above. Our country will only benefit from each child being given the chance to reach their potential. For those graduating from high school, there will be opportunities for them to pursue higher education whether through college or through trade schools, where they can continue to build on their own vision for their lives with financial support from individual donors, through scholarships, or from the state and nation when needed.

With guidance on how to understand and process material they encounter, both within and beyond school, from a perspective of self-love and acceptance, young adults would not only seek such messages, they would become creators of them on online platforms. They would also know how to identify when others are aiming to make them feel unsafe and insecure; they will have built relationships of trust with their caretakers and teachers and will feel able to discuss messages they encounter with the adults in their lives. Sadly, the reason many teens are vulnerable to bullying is because they are familiar with others telling them what they should do and who they should be; they have been told before that they were not good enough or that they couldn't be themselves, and they were often told this in one way or another by their parents. Yet, in the nation we're imagining here, parents couldn't be less afraid of what their children might face through technology because the parents will have already established bonds of openness and understanding rather than rigidity and unfair expectation. With this kind of love, the threat of online platforms not only becomes less dangerous, it also becomes less prevalent. The same would take place with the messages young people hear in the media; they will be more equipped to question the messengers and the purpose behind each story they hear, each show they watch, and each book they read. With the foundations of security and celebration of difference from the youngest stages of life, as well as their human needs being met and their family units being strengthened and seen as equal members of our larger nation, young people will no longer be seeking entertainment, nor people, nor groups that feed their fears and insecurities. Without being stifled from the beginning and being told they must either be dominant or dominated, the mental health of young people will flourish. Boys will not believe that girls owe them anything, for example. They will not believe that they are supposed to assert their power; they will all find power within themselves and remember that they are to respect the choices of others.

For adults who enter into romantic and/or sexual relationships with others, they will approach their partners with respect and a desire to achieve equality and security together. Again, what we often see in partnerships and sexual relationships is the reproduction of American patriarchy on a mini scale but, instead, in our alternative reality, these partnerships could be testaments to acceptance and equity, whether they constitute onetime interactions or build into lifelong bonds where people choose to merge their lives together. In these moments of coming together, it will be important for members of the relationship to process their own lives and histories, to know what they are carrying with them that might challenge those feelings of safety, acceptance, and equity, and to seek support with a commitment to engendering more good through their relationships rather than more pain. If these partners choose and are able to bring children into their relationship, whether biologically or differently, they will lead their households with the mission of moving away from hierarchy and instead exemplifying love and embrace. All people will be given access to reproductive healthcare and family planning that suits their needs. Both contraceptives and fertility treatments would be available to everyone rather than being an option only for those who can afford it.

For people in these relationships who might choose the journey of pregnancy, they will be met with messages that build on the empowerment they heard when they were little. Before proceeding, while I am primarily speaking to the experiences of women and mothers in this section, it should be noted that not all birthing people identify as women or mothers and that each person should still be given the same supports I am calling our attention to. Mothers will be asked what their vision is for their labor, they will be told about their options, they will be reminded that they have nothing to fear because they will be supported in working with doctors, or midwives, or doulas, or hospitals, or birth centers that are covered equally so that each person can choose what works best for them, where they feel most affirmed, protected, and respected. Doctors would no longer view themselves as the authorities whom everyone should blindly trust, but instead as medically knowledgeable partners in each of our unique life journeys, as resources who are also willing to honor and consider the wisdom of our intuition and traditional healing practices. Partners would not fear the abilities of the person carrying and delivering the child, nor would they try to degrade or minimize the experience as a result of any feelings of inadequacy, but instead would honor pregnancy and birth while doing their part to alleviate any additional stresses or pressures for mothers. After labor and delivery, mothers and other birthing people would not be ignored while all attention shifts to the baby, but instead their well-being will be prioritized with the knowledge that the better they are doing, the better the child will do. Also covered by insurance or a universal healthcare plan would be home checkups from each mother's chosen provider to prevent the many instances of maternal mortality that take place in the days, weeks, and months following childbirth.

The primary caretakers of children, namely mothers, will hear messages from their family members as well as their nation that their role is honorable, wonderful, and also difficult, but that they are not alone. The primary caretaker and one support person, whether a partner or someone else, especially in the case of single parents, would have paid parental leave for a minimum of six months, and in cases where families cannot afford baby essentials, they will be provided them by their state. In addition to access to physical healthcare, insurance companies should also cover the cost of mental health therapists, including relationship counselors, especially for new parents.

For parents returning to work after paid leave, they will also have choices as to where they can take their children to be cared for in a place that is safe, clean, and promotes the healthy development of their children. These could be provided by employers so that children and parents can travel to the same location and parents can rest assured that their children are still close to them. Nursing mothers could even nurse their children during the work day. Another option includes day-care centers that are well maintained and available at different costs, depending on each family's budget, where staff are paid above minimum wages. Yet another option includes the ability of stay-at-home moms to open their homes to more children, where they are given opportunities to become certified as professional caregivers and given grants to provide quality care to other children if they desire to. We could also provide free training programs for women who have come to the United States seeking better opportunities for their own families to become professional caregivers, earn work visas, and be matched with families needing support with childcare and/or elder care. We would see the raising and care of all children as a community effort that we are each invested in, rather than a game of survival of the fittest where children are left to face unsafe situations if their families cannot afford quality care.

A country divorced from American patriarchy is kinder for aging people as well. Currently our nation is one that tells us all, but most harshly tells women, to fear getting older and to do everything in our power to keep ourselves from even looking older, from Botox to plastic surgery. The hatred of ourselves that we are taught from childhood extends into the latest years of our lives, and through every one of our transitions, not only are we told to be ashamed of natural occurrences like cellulite and stretch marks, we are also made to be terrified of normal wrinkles in our skin. But when we move away from seeing women's primary role as the reproducers, we also move away from discarding them when they are no longer of reproductive age. In our alternative reality, women would not only feel prepared to age, they will embrace it, and they will know what to expect in phases of perimenopause and menopause. Up until very recently these were two words that created shame; women experiencing menopause have been told to hide their symptoms, and they have been left not knowing where to turn for support. There is extremely limited research on this unavoidable stage of life. But just like celebrating puberty and providing resources for those experiencing it, in our new reality, we would do the same for our aging Americans. It is not only women who experience hormonal changes in their forties and fifties; men experience what is called "andropause," which consists of decreased testosterone, mood swings, irritability, erectile dysfunction, and a decline in their general well-being. In our antipatriarchal country, we would educate everyone on experiences of aging so that they are not so surprised by them, and we would encourage them to honor their changing bodies, celebrate the close of one chapter and the start of a new one where they still have much more life to live.

While American patriarchy promotes individualism and an "every man for himself" mentality, an alternative nation would prioritize community. This shift will be especially beneficial for our older citizens, who currently are at an increased risk of loneliness and isolation. In our new country, we would build more spaces for older people to spend time together while also helping to make our homes and public spaces more accessible. Our nation would support the caretakers of older people with better pay and provide time away from work for those in charge of caring for loved ones. We would reap the proven benefits of children spending time with their elders; we would avoid an epidemic of disconnection facing millions of Americans.

This is the vision I offer you, and it is one that is not impossible to bring to life with some changes on individual levels, interpersonal levels, and national levels. The different American patriarchs I have discussed throughout this book, such as politicians, parents, law-enforcement officers, doctors, researchers, journalists, writers, founders, coders, church leaders, and more can also all be members of this shared vision, and many of them have been historically. Politicians can create and implement policy that works toward and protects all of the above; they can put money toward the goal of allowing people to reach their full potential from the moment they are born so that our nation can reach new heights. Parents can lead their homes with equity and acceptance at the center, no longer fooled by narratives that try to make them replicate American patriarchy, instead allowing their children to feel safe and included for who they are. Law enforcement can stand against American patriarchy rather than being the upholders of it; they can issue consequences for those who actually rob the safety of others, while exploring possibilities for restorative justice. Doctors can provide medical advice that is separate from a hierarchical structure and that sees each human in their unique needs. We can put stories and messages forward that no longer try to grow fears, insecurities, and jealousies but instead promote our celebration of difference, our shared humanity, and all our inherent worth, while also highlighting our unique histories and cultures. We can build technologies that protect our well-being, that make resources more accessible, and that promote reconciliation and unity.

At the beginning of part 6 I asked one final reflection question: What will it take for us to defeat American patriarchy once and for all? As it stands today, we are trapped in an oppressive system that was made up by the limited views of white men from the 1700s. These views, the laws, and the systems that resulted from them are kept alive by the fears of those who believe they will lose something if they do not try to keep things as they were originally designed to be. This fear takes form in control, manipulation, violence, exclusion, division, dehumanization, self-hatred, selfishness, depression, inequity, confusion, injustice, denial, ignorance, and erasure. So overwhelming are these negative feelings and so heavy is the pain we are collectively feeling, it is no wonder so many Americans are addicted to numbing themselves with opioids and other substances. The way we heal and defeat all these burdens is by embracing everything the creators and maintainers of American patriarchy have tried so desperately to keep from us, themes that stand in opposition to the ones above. While we've reviewed all their horrific tactics in our quest to make American patriarchy undeniable, we have also done something much more important. We have inevitably revealed the weaknesses and the tools we each have available to us to use the vulnerabilities of American patriarchy to our advantage.

Here I will make the necessary tools of dismantling as obvious as we have made the system that tries to rob us of them. In order to defeat American patriarchy we must believe in our ability to imagine, create, and test alternative possibilities; we must listen to our intuition, seek knowledge, and reject attempts to limit us from learning; we must unify, collaborate, and celebrate our differences; we must protect our rights to choice and self-determination; we must offer one another respect, affirmation, and recognition; we must balance the scales and share our access to resources so that our collective needs are met and our collective capabilities grow; we must reclaim our energy, no longer willing to waste it asking whether American patriarchy is at play, or feeling shocked when it tightens its grasp upon us, but using our energy to embody everything American patriarchy previously made us believe we had lost; we must be courageous.

I often say that the way we achieve a new nation is through trusting, listening to, and electing Black women. I do not say this because I believe Black women should be in charge of everything, or because I think Black women want to be. I say it because in our current American patriarchy, Black women have historically been cast as the furthest from being able to achieve the status of humanness. Through this expulsion from what it means to be a person in the United States—an experience that requires the denial of other people's humanity, an ignoring of other people's needs, a delusion that allows one to be blind to our interconnectedness—most Black women have successfully rejected that definition, to the benefit of everyone. We Black women know that the opposite of American patriarchy is not necessarily a nation where women have power over men, it is simply a nation where power over others is no longer the goal we are told to aspire to. Instead we are focused on feeling whole no matter what body parts and hues we are born with. We are focused on having our needs met and helping to meet those of our loved ones. We are focused on reducing our own suffering as well as the suffering of others. We are focused on everyone being treated as the human beings we are. It is worth repeating: power over others is no longer the goal we are told to aspire to. The goal is instead to honor the power within you.

The thing American patriarchy fears most is the inherent power we each possess when we know what we are capable of, when we know what legacies we carry, and when we come together. Its fathers and its cultivators tried to erase us, to erase traditional practices, to erase our ability to hear ourselves, to erase our ancestors, to erase our history, to erase examples of our interconnectedness, and even to erase evidence of their own strategies to make themselves undetectable, but they have not succeeded. They did not delete these things; they simply covered them up. With this knowledge, I hope you feel seen and better able to see. I hope you choose to write a different story, to resist, to reconnect with what you know to be true about yourself, to walk alongside our children as we build something new together. Finally, if at any point while reading this book you recalled a moment or multiple instances when the system of American patriarchy tried to erase your power from you, whether as a child, a teenager, or an adult, I hope you now feel it returning to you.

In my introduction, I told you that the day my daughter was born I wondered what new world had begun with her. I will conclude by saying that I believe it is a world where we each remember our inherent power is indelible and permanently imprinted, a world where it is never hidden nor denied ever again.

AFTERWORD

I write this on Friday, November 7, 2024, just a few days after Donald Trump's reelection. Once again, millions of Americans have chosen a man who is openly sexist, racist, xenophobic, homophobic, transphobic, ableist, and more to lead our nation. And once again, millions are shocked and confused; they cannot understand how we arrived here. I find myself wanting to tell them about American patriarchy and how we have in fact not arrived anywhere new—we just haven't moved very far from where we began. Not for a lack of trying but a lack of fully understanding what we have been up against that has led to a cycle of action and reaction rather than sustained forward momentum.

I want to tell them that we can no longer be surprised by American patriarchy; we can no longer waste our time explaining from scratch how it came to be each time it rears its head, solely presenting parts of the definition and not its full form. We cannot keep acting only in response to it and continuing this exhausting tug-of-war. We must instead be intent on coming together and building a movement that is more connected and sustained than ever before. If you are still unsure how American patriarchy is hurting you, or you still don't see the limited and detrimental choices it offers you, I am sad to say that Donald Trump's second term will make it painfully obvious.

However, as scary as they will be, these next four years and beyond also offer us the opportunity to fully step into our role of dismantling American patriarchy. We can turn our visions into reality; we can find our inner power and refuse to let anyone else limit it, and we can dedicate ourselves to callings that fulfill us and serve this larger purpose as we divide the work ahead of us. Although our founding fathers carried problematic views of themselves and others, they still intended for the Constitution to be amended to adapt to the changing needs of our nation. They purposefully ensured that our branches of government would have checks and balances so that none of them could become too powerful. That's the beauty of the nation we find ourselves in. Even if our founders did not recognize all our humanity, even if the narrative and system they left us with have brought painful results, we still always have a path to create something new. Now it is time to do just that.

ACKNOWLEDGMENTS

I must begin by thanking the woman who gave me life and who nurtured my dreams day in and day out. Mom, I miss you dearly, and I thank you for always believing in me and teaching me to believe in myself. I am grateful to my dad for instilling a sense of social justice in me and always reminding me that change is not only possible but necessary. My parents laid a powerful foundation for me to be the storyteller and mother I am today. I am grateful to live life alongside my wonderful husband. Michael, it is a treasure to dream, parent, and grow with you. Our children bring me the utmost inspiration and joy. Malakai, Nehemiah, and Ezra, thank you for filling my heart with love and for being the reason I feel more resolute and braver than I ever have before. Being your mother is the greatest honor of my life. I cannot speak about my three precious children without thanking the woman who cares for them like her own in the moments when I am focused on work. Nuri, I could not accomplish everything I do without you, and I will forever be indebted to you. I also must thank the women who supported me as I brought my children into the world and who consistently reminded me of my power: my midwife and doulas. Debbie, Julia, Mika, Samsarah, and Kathleen, I am so grateful for each of you.

I am always supported by my siblings and extended family, no matter how far apart we may be. My sister and brother have been my role models ever since I can remember. They both encouraged, loved, and protected me with their whole hearts and they continue to do so. Lydia and Isak, thank you for your guidance, humor, and steadfast love that lifts me up. To my aunt Kathryn, thank you for being my cheerleader, confidante, and safe space. You are always the one who reminds me to pause and take care of myself. I am also blessed by my in-laws, who support me in countless ways. To my mother-in-law, Racole; Auntie Tasha; Nana; Uncle Craig; Anthony; Mariah; Marc; Scharlyce; and Shaleeka, thank you for helping us with our kids, for watching my talks, for checking in on me, for your prayers, and much more.

I am always grateful for the many deep friendships and mentor-mentee relationships that sustain and inspire me. I must give a special shout-out to my best friend, Jessica, for always being there for me. Thank you for traveling across the country with me on multiple occasions to help with the kids. Thank you for always listening to me and believing my biggest ideas are possible to achieve. I am also grateful to Christie and Joe Marchese for your never-ending belief in all my projects and the countless ways in which you inspire me by being examples of what it means to be great and to do good in this world. To Desiree Gruber, Anne Walls, SaraJane Simon, and Ally Bernstein, I cannot thank you enough for your mentorship and the roles you have played in sharing my work with others. Much of my success has come as a result of your belief in me.

I could not have written this book without the fellowships that made it possible for me to complete my research and focus on writing while also providing for my family. Thank you to Carol Tolan for always believing in the importance of my work. Thank you to Patty Quillin, Lateefah Simon, and the Meadow Fund for recognizing the impact *Erased* could have and backing it with a yearlong fellowship. Thank you to USC's Center on Communication Leadership and Policy for making me a senior fellow and connecting me with the wonderfully talented Dominique Fluker, who was my research assistant in the earliest stages of my writing process.

To my fabulous agent, Julia Kardon, thank you for representing me with such love. I am grateful for your wisdom and our friendship. To my editors, Lee Oglesby and Bryn Clark, thank you for having faith that I could pull off such an audacious project and for building it with me. To my entire HG Literary and Flatiron families, thank you for helping to turn my ideas into reality more than once.

To every single person who picks up this book, I cannot thank you enough. If you read *The Three Mothers* too, I am sending you the deepest gratitude for your time and your continued engagement with my words; please know that I do not take these things for granted.

In closing, I must also thank the people who have comforted me as I navigate the immense grief of losing my mother. In addition to everyone I have mentioned above who has held me through this, I am forever grateful to my grief support group and my therapist, who help me to keep going by giving me space to reflect on my mom's life and legacy.

Lastly, I thank my ancestors and I thank God.

BIBLIOGRAPHY

Abouzahr, Katie, Matt Krentz, John Harthorne, and Frances Brooks Taplett. "Why Women-Owned Startups Are a Better Bet." BCG Global, June 6, 2018. www.bcg.com/publications/2018/why-women-owned-startups-are-better-bet.

Abrams, Stacey. *Our Time Is Now: Power, Purpose, and the Fight for a Fair America*. Henry Holt and Company, 2020.

Ackmann, Martha. *Curveball: The Remarkable Story of Toni Stone, the First Woman to Play Professional Baseball in the Negro League*. Lawrence Hill Books, 2010.

Adams, Abigail. Abigail Adams to John Adams, March 31, 1776. Founders Online, National Archives. https://founders.archives.gov/documents /Adams/04-01-02-0241. Originally published in *The Adams Papers: Adams Family Correspondence*, vol. 1, *December 1761–May 1776*, edited by Lyman H. Butterfield, 369–71. Harvard University Press, 1963.

Adams, Diana. "Why US Laws Must Expand Beyond the Nuclear Family." TED Talk, Palm Springs, CA, December 2021. 18 min., 12 sec. https://www .ted.com/talks/diana_adams_why_us_laws_must_expand_beyond_the _nuclear_family.

Adams, John. John Adams to Abigail Adams, April 14, 1776. Founders Online, National Archives, https://founders.archives.gov/documents/Adams /04-01-02-0248. Originally published in *The Adams Papers, Adams Family Correspondence*, vol. 1, *December 1761–May 1776*, edited by Lyman H. Butterfield, 381–83. Harvard University Press, 1963.

Adams, John Quincy. "Argument of John Quincy Adams, Before the Supreme Court of the United States, in the Case of the United States, Appellants, vs. Cinque, and Others, Africans, Captured in the Schooner Amistad, by Lieut.

Gedney, Delivered on the 24th of February and 1st of March, 1841." S. W. Benedict, 1841. Yale Law School, Lillian Goldman Law Library, https://avalon.law.yale.edu/19th_century/amistad_002.asp.

Ahmed, Imran. *Deadly by Design: TikTok Pushes Harmful Content Promoting Eating Disorders and Self-Harm into Users' Feeds*. Center for Countering Digital Hate, December 15, 2022. counterhate.com/wp-content/uploads/2022/12/CCDH-Deadly-by-Design_120922.pdf.

Alamillo, Rudy. "Hispanics para Trump? Denial of Racism and Hispanic Support for Trump." *Du Bois Review: Social Science Research on Race* 16, no. 2 (2019): 457–87. https://doi.org/10.1017/S1742058X19000328.

Alemi, Farrokh, and Kyung Hee Lee. "Impact of Political Leaning on COVID-19 Vaccine Hesitancy: A Network-Based Multiple Mediation Analysis." *Cureus* 15, no. 8 (August 2023): e43232. https://doi.org/10.7759/cureus.43232.

All-American Girls Professional Baseball League (AAGPBL) Players Association. "AAGPBL League History." AAGPBL, 2014. www.aagpbl.org/history/league-history.

American Bar Association. "Demographics: Growth of the Legal Profession." *ABA Profile of the Legal Profession*. 2023. www.abalegalprofile.com/demographics.html.

American Civil Liberties Union. *The Unequal Price of Periods*. American Civil Liberties Union (ACLU), November 6, 2019. www.aclu.org/wp-content/uploads/publications/111219-sj-periodequity.pdf.

American Indians of the Pacific Northwest Collection. University of Washington Libraries. content.lib.washington.edu/aipnw/index.html.

American Psychological Association, Task Force on the Sexualization of Girls. *Report of the APA Task Force on the Sexualization of Girls*. American Psychological Association, 2007. http://www.apa.org/pi/women/programs/girls/report-full.pdf.

Anderson, Carol. *The Second: Race and Guns in a Fatally Unequal America*. Bloomsbury, 2021.

Andronik, Catherine M. *Copernicus: Founder of Modern Astronomy*. Rev. ed. Enslow, 2009.

Armstrong, Ken. "Draft Overturning Roe v. Wade Quotes Infamous Witch Trial Judge with Long-Discredited Ideas on Rape." ProPublica, May 6, 2022. www.propublica.org/article/abortion-roe-wade-alito-scotus-hale.

Aspinwall, Cary, Brianna Bailey, and Amy Yurkanin. "They Lost Their Pregnancies. Then Prosecutors Sent Them to Prison." The Marshall Project, September 1, 2022. https://www.themarshallproject.org/2022/09/01/they-lost-their-pregnancies-then-prosecutors-sent-them-to-prison.

Atske, Sara. "Teens, Social Media and Technology 2023." Pew Research Center, April 14, 2024. https://www.pewresearch.org/internet/2023/12/11/teens-social-media-and-technology-2023.

Auchter, Bernie. "Men Who Murder Their Families: What the Research Tells Us." *National Institute of Justice (NIJ) Journal* 266 (June 2010): 10–12. www .ojp.gov/pdffiles1/nij/230412.pdf.

Azhar, Sameena, Antonia R. G. Alvarez, Anne S. J. Farina, and Susan Klumpner. "'You're So Exotic Looking': An Intersectional Analysis of Asian American and Pacific Islander Stereotypes." *Affilia* 36, no. 3 (2021): 282–301.

Balachandra, Lakshmi. "How Gender Biases Drive Venture Capital Decision-Making: Exploring the Gender Funding Gap." *Gender in Management* 35, no. 3 (2020): 261–73. https://doi.org/10.1108/GM-11-2019-0222.

Barkin, Shari L., Elena Fuentes-Afflick, Jeffrey P. Brosco, and Arleen M. Tuchman. "Unintended Consequences of the Flexner Report: Women in Pediatrics." *Pediatrics* 126, no. 6 (December 2010): 1055–57. https://doi.org /10.1542/peds.2010-2050.

Bedecarré, Kathryn. "Of Vigils and Vigilantes: Notes on the White Witness." *Cultural Dynamics* 34, no. 1–2 (2022): 82–99. https://doi.org/10.1177 /09213740221075292.

Belmonte, Laura A. *Selling the American Way: U.S. Propaganda and the Cold War*. University of Pennsylvania Press, 2008.

Bernard, Diane. "The Creator of Mount Rushmore's Forgotten Ties to White Supremacy." *Washington Post*, July 2, 2020. https://www.washingtonpost.com /history/2020/07/03/mount-rushmore-gutzon-borglum-klan-stone-mountain.

Bessey, Sarah. *Jesus Feminist: An Invitation to Revisit the Bible's View of Women*. Howard Books, 2013.

"Betsy Ramos." Survivor Series. Survived & Punished NY, May 1, 2020. www .survivedandpunishedny.org/betsy-ramos.

Bian, Lin, Sarah-Jane Leslie, and Andrei Cimpian. "Gender Stereotypes About Intellectual Ability Emerge Early and Influence Children's Interests." *Science* 355, no. 6323 (January 2017): 389–91. https://doi.org/10.1126 /science.aah6524.

Bigman, Dan. "What the NRA's Wayne Lapierre Gets Paid to Defend Guns." *Forbes*, December 22, 2012. www.forbes.com/sites/danbigman/2012/12/21 /what-the-nras-wayne-lapierre-gets-paid-to-defend-guns.

Bill of Rights Institute. "John Quincy Adams and the Gag Rule." Bill of Rights Institute. https://billofrightsinstitute.org/essays/john-quincy-adams -and-the-gag-rule.

Black, Amy E., and Jamie L. Allen. "Tracing the Legacy of Anita Hill: The Thomas/Hill Hearings and Media Coverage of Sexual Harassment." *Gender Issues* 19 (2001): 33–52. https://doi.org/10.1007/s12147-001-0003-z.

Blee, Kathleen M. "Women in the 1920s' Ku Klux Klan Movement." *Feminist Studies* 17, no. 1 (1991): 57–77. https://doi.org/10.2307/3178170.

Bloodhart, Brittany, Meena M. Balgopal, Anne Marie A. Casper, Laura B. Sample McMeeking, and Emily V. Fischer. "Outperforming Yet Undervalued:

Undergraduate Women in STEM." *PLoS ONE* 15, no. 6 (2020): e0234685. https://doi.org/10.1371/journal.pone.0234685.

Boburg, Shawn, Pranshu Verma, and Chris Dehghanpoor. "On Popular Online Platforms, Predatory Groups Coerce Children into Self-Harm." *Washington Post*, May 13, 2024. www.washingtonpost.com/investigations /interactive/2024/764-predator-discord-telegram.

Bonaparte, Alicia D. "Physicians' Discourse for Establishing Authoritative Knowledge in Birthing Work and Reducing the Presence of the Granny Midwife." *Journal of Historical Sociology* 28, no. 2 (2014): 166–94. https://doi .org/10.1111/johs.12045.

Bowman, Emma. "As States Ban Abortion, the Texas Bounty Law Offers a Way to Survive Legal Challenges." NPR, July 11, 2022. www.npr.org/2022 /07/11/1107741175/texas-abortion-bounty-law.

Bracewell, Lorna. "Gender, Populism, and the QAnon Conspiracy Movement." *Frontiers in Sociology* 5 (2020): 615727. https://doi.org/10.3389/fsoc .2020.615727.

Bresnahan, Mary, Jie Zhuang, Jennifer Anderson, Yi Zhu, Joshua Nelson, and Xiaodi Yan. "The 'Pumpgate' Incident: Stigma Against Lactating Mothers in the U.S. Workplace." *Women & Health* 58, no. 4 (2018): 451–65. https://doi .org/10.1080/03630242.2017.1306608.

Broome, Avery. "Menstrual Product Deprivation in Prison: A Sex-Neutral Litigation Strategy." University of Chicago Legal Forum, University of Chicago Law School, 2023. legal-forum.uchicago.edu/print-archive /menstrual-product-deprivation-prison-sex-neutral-litigation-strategy.

Brown, Lee. "Sperm Donor Wins Custody of Child After Youngster's Two Oklahoma Moms Split." *New York Post*, February 17, 2023. nypost.com /2023/02/16/sperm-donor-wins-custody-of-child-after-two-moms-split.

Budd, Kristen M., PhD. "Incarcerated Women and Girls." The Sentencing Project, August 26, 2024. https://www.sentencingproject.org/fact-sheet /incarcerated-women-and-girls.

Burlingame, Michael. *Abraham Lincoln: A Life.* Johns Hopkins University Press, 2008.

———. *An American Marriage: The Untold Story of Abraham Lincoln and Mary Todd.* Pegasus Books, 2021.

Burnett, John. "Christian Nationalism Is Still Thriving—and Is a Force for Returning Trump to Power." NPR, January 23, 2022. www.npr.org/2022/01 /14/1073215412/christian-nationalism-donald-trump.

Burt, Larry W. "Roots of the Native American Urban Experience: Relocation Policy in the 1950s." *American Indian Quarterly* 10, no. 2 (1986): 85–99. https:// doi.org/10.2307/1183982.

Byerly, Carolyn. "Why White Male Dominance of News Media Is So Persistent." Women's Media Center, October 8, 2021. womensmediacenter

.com/news-features/why-white-male-dominance-of-news-media-is-so
-persistent.

Carlisle, Linda V. *Elizabeth Packard: A Noble Fight*. University of Illinois Press, 2010.

Carlson, Andrew. "Not Just Black and White: 'Othello' in America." American Theater, December 27, 2016. www.americantheatre.org/2016/12/27/not-just-black-and-white-othello-in-america.

Carpenter, Morgan. "Intersex Variations, Human Rights, and the International Classification of Diseases." *Health and Human Rights* 20, no. 2 (December 2018): 205–14. https://www.ncbi.nlm.nih.gov/pmc/articles/PMC6293350.

Cassino, Dan. *Fox News and American Politics: How One Channel Shapes American Politics and Society*. Routledge, 2016.

Chandler, Robert W. *War of Ideas: The U.S. Propaganda Campaign in Vietnam*. Routledge, 1981.

"Chief Justice John Roberts." Justia Law. supreme.justia.com/justices/john-g-roberts-jr.

Choudhury, Sharmila. Review of *Suppressed, Forced Out and Fired: How Successful Women Lose Their Jobs*, by Martha E. Reeves. *Gender Issues* 20 (2002): 84–86. https://doi.org/10.1007/s12147-002-0009-1.

Clark, Ella E., and Margot Edmonds. *Sacagawea of the Lewis and Clark Expedition*. University of California Press, 1979.

Clarke, Edward H. *Sex in Education, or, A Fair Chance for the Girls*. Osgood, 1873.

Coe, Alexis. *You Never Forget Your First: A Biography of George Washington*. Viking, 2020.

Coker, Calvin R. "Replacing Notorious: Barret, Ginsburg, and Postfeminist Positioning." *Rhetoric and Public Affairs* 26, no. 1 (March 2023): 101–30. https://doi.org/10.14321/rhetpublaffa.26.1.0101.

Coleman, Jude. "AI's Climate Impact Goes Beyond Its Emissions." *Scientific American*, December 7, 2023. www.scientificamerican.com/article/ais-climate-impact-goes-beyond-its-emissions.

Conner, Christopher T. "QAnon, Authoritarianism, and Conspiracy Within American Alternative Spiritual Spaces." *Frontiers in Sociology* 8 (2023): 1136333. https://doi.org/10.3389/fsoc.2023.1136333.

Contrera, Jessica. "She Was Pregnant When NASA Offered to Send Her to Space. Anna Fisher Didn't Hesitate." *Washington Post*, May 11, 2019. www.washingtonpost.com/history/2019/05/11/she-was-pregnant-when-nasa-offered-send-her-space-anna-fisher-didnt-hesitate.

Conway, Martin. "A Head of Christ by John van Eyck." *Burlington Magazine for Connoisseurs* 39, no. 225 (December 1921): 253–60. http://www.jstor.org/stable/861530.

Cooney, Samantha. "The Number of Women Who Direct Hollywood Movies Is Still Embarrassingly Small." *Time*, January 4, 2018. time.com/5087673 /film-directors-diversity-report.

Craft, William, and Ellen Craft. *Running a Thousand Miles for Freedom: The Escape of William and Ellen Craft from Slavery*. University of Georgia Press, 1999.

Curtin, Sally C., Kamiah A. Brown, and Mariah E. Jordan. "Suicide Rates for the Three Leading Methods by Race and Ethnicity: United States, 2000–2020." Centers for Disease Control and Prevention, National Center for Health Statistics, NCHS Data Brief No. 450, November 2022. www.cdc.gov/nchs /products/databriefs/db450.htm.

Daniels, Doris Groshen. "Theodore Roosevelt and Gender Roles." In "Reassessments of Presidents and First Ladies," special issue, *Presidential Studies Quarterly* 26, no. 3 (Summer 1996): 648–65. http://www.jstor.org/stable /27551623.

Davidson, Mena. "Transgender Legal Battles: A Timeline." JSTOR Daily, May 12, 2022. daily.jstor.org/transgender-legal-battles-a-timeline.

Davis, Angela Y. *Women, Race & Class*. Vintage, 1983.

Dekker, Sanne, Nikki C. Lee, Paul Howard-Jones, and Jelle Jolles. "Neuromyths in Education: Prevalence and Predictors of Misconceptions Among Teachers." *Frontiers in Psychology* 3 (October 18, 2012): 429. https://doi.org /10.3389/fpsyg.2012.00429.

Delli Carpini, Michael X., and Ester R. Fuchs. "The Year of the Woman? Candidates, Voters, and the 1992 Elections." *Political Science Quarterly* 108, no. 1 (Spring 1993): 29–36. https://doi.org/10.2307/2152484.

Denhollander, Rachael. *What Is a Girl Worth? My Story of Breaking the Silence and Exposing the Truth About Larry Nassar and USA Gymnastics*. Narrated by the author. Recorded Books, 2019. 11 hr., 11 min.

Denney, Andrew S., Kent R. Kerley, and Nickolas G. Gross. "Child Sexual Abuse in Protestant Christian Congregations: A Descriptive Analysis of Offense and Offender Characteristics." In "Religion and Crime: Theory, Research, and Practice," special issue, *Religions* 9, no. 1 (2018): 27. https://doi .org/10.3390/rel9010027.

Dennis, Brady, and Chris Mooney. "Neil Gorsuch's Mother Once Ran the EPA. It Didn't Go Well." *Washington Post*, February 1, 2017. www .washingtonpost.com/news/energy-environment/wp/2017/02/01/neil -gorsuchs-mother-once-ran-the-epa-it-was-a-disaster.

DeSanto, Barbara. "Moms Demand Action: Using Public Relations to Combat Gun Violence." In *Public Relations Cases: International Perspectives*, 3rd ed., edited by Danny Moss and Barbara DeSanto. Routledge, Taylor & Francis Group, 2023.

Dickerson, Caitlin, Seth Freed Wessler, and Miriam Jordan. "Immigrants Say

They Were Pressured into Unneeded Surgeries." *New York Times*, September 29, 2020. www.nytimes.com/2020/09/29/us/ice-hysterectomies-surgeries-georgia.html.

Domestic Violence Services Network. "The Long History of Domestic Violence and the Development of DVSN." DVSN, August 21, 2023. www.dvsn.org/august-2023-the-long-history-of-domestic-violence-and-the-development-of-dvsn.

Donald, David Herbert. *Lincoln.* Jonathan Cape, 1995.

Dorsey, Leroy G. "Managing Women's Equality: Theodore Roosevelt, the Frontier Myth, and the Modern Woman." *Rhetoric and Public Affairs* 16, no. 3 (Fall 2013): 423–56.

Draper, Robert. "The Problem of Marjorie Taylor Greene." *New York Times*, October 17, 2022. www.nytimes.com/2022/10/17/magazine/marjorie-taylor-greene.html.

Duffy, Thomas P. "The Flexner Report—100 Years Later." *Yale Journal of Biology and Medicine* 84, no. 3 (2011): 269–76.

Dyett, Jordan, and Cassidy Thomas. "Overpopulation Discourse: Patriarchy, Racism, and the Specter of Ecofascism." *Perspectives on Global Development and Technology* 18, no. 1–2 (2019): 205–24. https://doi.org/10.1163/15691497-12341514.

Easterbrook-Smith, Gwyn L. E. "'Not on the Street Where We Live': Walking While Trans Under a Model of Sex Work Decriminalisation." *Feminist Media Studies* 20, no. 7 (2020): 1013–28. https://doi.org/10.1080/14680777.2019.1642226.

Edmonds, Casey. "'Diff-ability' Not 'Disability': Right-Brained Thinkers in a Left-Brained Education System." *Support for Learning* 27, no. 3 (2012): 129–35. https://doi.org/10.1111/j.1467-9604.2012.01524.x

Eisenstein, Zillah. "Antifeminism in the Politics and Election of 1980." *Feminist Studies* 7, no. 2 (Summer 1981): 187–205. https://doi.org/10.2307/3177521.

Ellison, Betty Boles. *The True Mary Todd Lincoln: A Biography*. McFarland, 2014.

Epstein, Randi Hutter. "Emotions, Fertility, and the 1940s Woman." *Journal of Public Health Policy* 24, no. 2 (2003): 195–211. https://doi.org/10.2307/3343513.

Everbach, Tracy. "Breaking Baseball Barriers: The 1953–1954 Negro League and Expansion of Women's Public Roles." *American Journalism* 22, no. 1 (2005): 13–33. https://doi.org/10.1080/08821127.2005.10677622.

Faith, Ian. "Voices of Authority: The Rhetoric of Women's Insane Asylum Memoirs During Nineteenth Century America." Master's thesis, University of Akron, 2014. http://rave.ohiolink.edu/etdc/view?acc_num=akron1396362453.

Federici, Silvia. *Witches, Witch-Hunting, and Women*. PM Press, 2018.

Fitzpatrick, John L., Charlotte Willis, Alessandro Devigili, et al. "Chemical

Signals from Eggs Facilitate Cryptic Female Choice in Humans." *Proceedings of the Royal Society B Biological Sciences* 287, no. 1928 (June 2020): 20200805.

FOX News Network. "Fox News Channel Makes Cable News History as the First Network to Mark 22 Consecutive Years at Number One." News release, January 30, 2024. press.foxnews.com/2024/01/fox-news-channel -makes-cable-news-history-as-the-first-network-to-mark-22-consecutive -years-at-number-one.

Freeman, David B. *Carved in Stone: The History of Stone Mountain*. Mercer University Press, 1997.

Fried, Joseph P. "Prison Term Imposed for Helping Man Get Gun to Kill Officer." *New York Times*, March 23, 1999. www.nytimes.com/1999/03/23 /nyregion/prison-term-imposed-for-helping-man-get-gun-to-kill-officer .html.

Fry, Richard, Carolina Aragão, Kiley Hurst, and Kim Parker. "In a Growing Share of U.S. Marriages, Husbands and Wives Earn About the Same." Pew Research Center, April 13, 2023. www.pewresearch.org/social-trends/wp -content/uploads/sites/3/2023/04/Breadwinner-wives-full-report-FINAL.pdf.

Ganeva, Tana. "Black Panther Fred Hampton Created a 'Rainbow Coalition' to Support Poor Americans." *Teen Vogue*, July 25, 2019. www.teenvogue.com /story/fred-hampton-black-panthers-rainbow-coalition-poor-americans.

Garelick, Rhonda. "Brooke Shields and the Curse of Great Beauty." *New York Times*, April 3, 2023. www.nytimes.com/2023/04/03/style/brooke-shields -pretty-baby.html.

Gaudet, Janice Cindy, and Diane Caron-Bourbonnais. "It's in Our Blood: Indigenous Women's Knowledge as a Critical Path to Women's Well-Being." *AlterNative: An International Journal of Indigenous Peoples* 11, no. 2 (2015), 164–76.

Gerstle, Gary. "Theodore Roosevelt and the Divided Character of American Nationalism." *Journal of American History* 86, no. 3 (December 1999): 1280–307.

Ghandakly, Elizabeth C., and Rachel Fabi. "Sterilization in US Immigration and Customs Enforcement's (ICE's) Detention: Ethical Failures and Systemic Injustice." *American Journal of Public Health* 111, no. 5 (May 2021): 832–34. https://doi.org/10.2105/AJPH.2021.306186.

Ginsburg, Ruth Bader, Mary Hartnett, and Wendy W. Williams. *My Own Words*. Simon & Schuster, 2016.

Goldberg, Carole. "Finding the Way to Indian Country: Justice Ruth Bader Ginsburg's Decisions in Indian Law Cases." *Ohio State Law Journal* 70, no. 4 (2009): 1003–35.

Gordon-Reed, Annette, and Peter S. Onuf. *"Most Blessed of the Patriarchs": Thomas Jefferson and the Empire of the Imagination*. Liveright, 2016.

Gorski, Philip. "Why Evangelicals Voted for Trump: A Critical Cultural Sociology." In *Politics of Meaning/Meaning of Politics: Cultural Sociology of the 2016 U.S. Presidential Election*, edited by Jason L. Mast and Jeffrey C. Alexander. Cultural Sociology. Palgrave Macmillan, 2019. https://doi.org/10.1007/978-3-319-95945-0_10.

Gorsuch, Neil, Jane Nitze, and David Feder. *A Republic, If You Can Keep It*. Crown Forum, 2019.

Graham, Ruth, and Sharon LaFraniere. "Inside the People of Praise, the Tight-Knit Faith Community of Amy Coney Barrett." *New York Times*, October 8, 2020. www.nytimes.com/2020/10/08/us/people-of-praise-amy-coney-barrett.html.

Gramlich, John. "5 Facts About Fox News." Pew Research Center, April 8, 2020. www.pewresearch.org/short-reads/2020/04/08/five-facts-about-fox-news.

Green, Denise Nicole, Frances Holmes Kozen, and Catherine Kueffer Blumenkamp. "Facemasking Behaviors, Preferences, and Attitudes Among Emerging Adults in the United States During the COVID-19 Pandemic: An Exploratory Study." *Clothing and Textiles Research Journal* 39, no. 3 (July 2021): 216–31. https://doi.org/10.1177/0887302X211006775.

Greenwood, Shannon. "The Enduring Grip of the Gender Pay Gap." Pew Research Center, May 3, 2024. https://www.pewresearch.org/social-trends/2023/03/01/the-enduring-grip-of-the-gender-pay-gap.

Gross, Kali Nicole. "The Historical Truth About Women Burned at the Stake in America? Most Were Black." *Washington Post*, February 25, 2022. www.washingtonpost.com/opinions/2022/02/25/black-women-history-burned-at-stake.

Gumbs, Alexis Pauline, China Martens, and Mai'a Williams, eds. *Revolutionary Mothering: Love on the Front Lines*. PM Press, 2016.

Halberstam, Jack. *Female Masculinity*. Duke University Press, 1998.

Hampton, Deon J., Jonathan Dienst, Ken Dilanian, and Corky Siemaszko. "What We Know About the Slain Texas Mall Massacre Suspect, Mauricio Garcia." NBC News, May 8, 2023. www.nbcnews.com/news/us-news/mauricio-garcia-allen-texas-mall-shooting-suspect-what-know-rcna83242.

Han, Tan Cheng. "Marital Rape—Removing the Husband's Legal Immunity." *Malaya Law Review* 31, no. 1 (July 1989): 112–28. http://www.jstor.org/stable/24865602.

Hansen, Casper Worm, Peter Sandholt Jensen, and Christian Volmar Skovsgaard. "Modern Gender Roles and Agricultural History: The Neolithic Inheritance." *Journal of Economic Growth* 20 (2015): 365–404. https://doi.org/10.1007/s10887-015-9119-y.

Hartley, Florence. *Ladies' Book of Etiquette, and Manual of Politeness*. G. W. C. Cottrell, 1860.

Hassan, Aumyo, and Sarah J. Barber. "The Effects of Repetition Frequency on the Illusory Truth Effect." *Cognitive Research: Principles and Implications* 6 (2021): 38. https://doi.org/10.1186/s41235-021-00301-5.

Hearne, Brittany N., and Michael D. Niño. "Understanding How Race, Ethnicity, and Gender Shape Mask-Wearing Adherence During the COVID-19 Pandemic: Evidence from the COVID Impact Survey." *Journal of Racial and Ethnic Health Disparities* 9, no. 1 (2022): 176–83. https://doi.org/10.1007/s40615-020-00941-1.

Henderson, Emma L., Daniel J. Simons, and Dale J. Barr. "The Trajectory of Truth: A Longitudinal Study of the Illusory Truth Effect." *Journal of Cognition* 4, no. 1 (2021): 29. https://doi.org/10.5334/joc.161.

Hendricks, Obery M., Jr. *The Politics of Jesus: Rediscovering the True Revolutionary Nature of Jesus' Teachings and How They Have Been Corrupted.* Doubleday Religion, 2006.

Hiatt, Suzanne R. "Pauli Murray: May Her Song Be Heard at Last." *Journal of Feminist Studies in Religion* 4, no. 2 (Fall 1988): 69–73. http://www.jstor.org/stable/25002082.

Hill, Anita. *Speaking Truth to Power: A Memoir.* Knopf Doubleday Publishing Group, 1998.

Himelhoch, Myra Samuels, and Arthur H. Shaffer. "Elizabeth Packard: Nineteenth-Century Crusader for the Rights of Mental Patients." *Journal of American Studies* 13, no. 3 (December 1979): 343–75. https://doi.org/10.1017/S0021875800007404.

Hird, Myra J., and Kimberly Abshoff. "Women Without Children: A Contradiction in Terms?" *Journal of Comparative Family Studies* 31, no. 3 (Summer 2000): 347–66.

Hollis-Brusky, Amanda, and Celia Parry. "'In the Mold of Justice Scalia': The Contours & Consequences of the Trump Judiciary." *The Forum* 19, no. 1 (2021): 117–42. https://doi.org/10.1515/for-2021-0006.

Holmes, Marian Smith. "The Great Escape from Slavery of Ellen and William Craft." *Smithsonian Magazine*, June 16, 2010. www.smithsonianmag.com/history/the-great-escape-from-slavery-of-ellen-and-william-craft-497960.

hooks, bell. *We Real Cool: Black Men and Masculinity.* Routledge, 2004.

Hout, Michael, and Joshua R. Goldstein. "How 4.5 Million Irish Immigrants Became 40 Million Irish Americans: Demographic and Subjective Aspects of the Ethnic Composition of White Americans." *American Sociological Review* 59, no. 1 (February 1994): 64–82. https://doi.org/10.2307/2096133.

Hubbert, Jessica. "70+ Women in Technology Statistics (2024)." *Exploding Topics* (blog), November 14, 2023. explodingtopics.com/blog/women-in-tech.

Inskeep, Steve, and Odette Yousef. "Social Justice Group Examines How Deeply the Far-Right Has Penetrated State Politics." NPR, May 26, 2022.

www.npr.org/2022/05/26/1101423586/social-justice-group-examines-how
-deeply-the-far-right-has-penetrated-state-poli.

Jackson, Lauren. "The Climate Crisis Is Worse for Women. Here's Why."
New York Times, August 24, 2021. www.nytimes.com/2021/08/24/us/climate
-crisis-women-katharine-wilkinson.html.

Jackson, Rebecca, and Steve Coll. "How the Proud Boys Are Prepping for a
Second Trump Term." *The Economist*, July 22, 2024. www.economist.com
/1843/2024/07/22/how-the-proud-boys-are-prepping-for-a-second-trump
-term.

Jefferson, Thomas. Thomas Jefferson to Martha Jefferson, December 22,
1783. Founders Online, National Archives. https://founders.archives.gov
/documents/Jefferson/01-06-02-0322. Originally published in *The Papers of
Thomas Jefferson*, vol. 6, *21 May 1781–1 March 1784*, edited by Julian P. Boyd,
416–17. Princeton University Press, 1952.

Jefferson, Thomas. Thomas Jefferson to Anne Willing Bingham, May 11,
1788. Founders Online, National Archives. https://founders.archives.gov
/documents/Jefferson/01-13-02-0076. Originally published in *The Papers of
Thomas Jefferson*, vol. 13, *March 1788–October 1788*, edited by Julian P. Boyd,
151–52. Princeton University Press, 1956.

Jhally, Sut, and Justin Lewis. *Enlightened Racism: The Cosby Show, Audiences,
and the Myth of the American Dream*. Routledge, 1992.

Johnson, Akilah, and Dan Keating. "Whites Now More Likely to Die from
Covid than Blacks: Why the Pandemic Shifted." Princeton University, Department of African American Studies, October 30, 2022. aas.princeton.edu
/news/whites-now-more-likely-die-covid-blacks-why-pandemic-shifted.

Johnson, Candace. "Drafting Injustice: Overturning *Roe v. Wade*, Spillover
Effects and Reproductive Rights in Context." *Feminist Theory* 25, no. 1
(2024): 122–27. https://doi.org/10.1177/14647001221114611.

Johnson, Corey G. "Female Inmates Sterilized in California Prisons Without Approval." Reveal, July 7, 2015. revealnews.org/article/female-inmates
-sterilized-in-california-prisons-without-approval.

Johnston, G. A., Jr. "The Flexner Report and Black Medical Schools." *Journal
of the National Medical Association* 76, no. 3 (March 1984): 223–25.

Jones-Rogers, Stephanie E. *They Were Her Property: White Women as Slave
Owners in the American South*. Yale University Press, 2019.

Joseph, K. S., Amelie Boutin, Sarka Lisonkova, et al. "Maternal Mortality in
the United States: Recent Trends, Current Status, and Future Consider-
ations." *Obstetrics and Gynecology* 137, no. 5 (May 2021): 763–71.

"Justice John Roberts Joins the Supreme Court's Liberal Wing in Some Key
Rulings." *The Economist*, July 2, 2020. www.economist.com/united-states
/2020/07/02/justice-john-roberts-joins-the-supreme-courts-liberal-wing-in
-some-key-rulings.

Kajstura, Aleks, and Wendy Sawyer, "Women's Mass Incarceration: The Whole Pie 2024." Prison Policy Initiative. https://www.prisonpolicy.org /reports/pie2024women.html.

Kann, Mark E. *A Republic of Men: The American Founders, Gendered Language, and Patriarchal Politics.* New York University Press, 1998.

Keegan, Cáel M. "On the Necessity of Bad Trans Objects." *Film Quarterly* 75, no. 3 (2022): 26–37. https://doi.org/10.1525/fq.2022.75.3.26.

Kendall, Mikki. *Hood Feminism: Notes from the Women That a Movement Forgot.* Bloomsbury, 2021.

Kendi, Ibram X. *Stamped from the Beginning: The Definitive History of Racist Ideas in America.* Nation Books, 2017.

Kerr, Dara. "Meta Failed to Address Harm to Teens, Whistleblower Testifies as Senators Vow Action." NPR, November 7, 2023. www.npr.org/2023 /11/07/1211339737/meta-failed-to-address-harm-to-teens-whistleblower -testifies-as-senators-vow-act.

Kessler, Donna Barbie. *The Making of Sacagawea: A Euro-American Legend.* University of Alabama Press, 2019.

Kessler, Glenn. "Brett Kavanaugh and Allegations of Sexual Misconduct: The Complete List." *Washington Post*, September 27, 2018. https://www .washingtonpost.com/politics/2018/09/27/brett-kavanaugh-allegations -sexual-misconduct-complete-list.

Kim, Mimi E. "Challenging the Pursuit of Criminalisation in an Era of Mass Incarceration: The Limitations of Social Work Responses to Domestic Violence in the USA." *British Journal of Social Work* 43, no. 7 (October 2013): 1276–93.

King, Tania L., Anna J. Scovelle, Anneke Meehl, Allison J. Milner, and Naomi Priest. "Gender Stereotypes and Biases in Early Childhood: A Systematic Review." *Australasian Journal of Early Childhood* 46, no. 2 (2021): 112–25.

Kirchgaessner, Stephanie. "FBI Interviewed Individuals Who Accuse Amy Coney Barrett Faith Group of Abuse." *The Guardian*, October 3, 2023. www .theguardian.com/us-news/2023/oct/03/fbi-people-of-praise-amy-coney -barrett-faith-group-abuse-allegations.

Kirksey, Kristen. "A Social History of Racial Disparities in Breastfeeding in the United States." *Social Science & Medicine* 289 (November 2021): 114365. https://doi.org/10.1016/j.socscimed.2021.114365.

Kitts, Margo. "Proud Boys, Nationalism, and Religion." *Journal of Religion and Violence* 9, no. 1 (2021): 12–32. https://www.jstor.org/stable/27212335.

Kizy, Kaitlyn. "Anna Lee Fisher Was the First Mom in Space; She Now Embarks on a New Mission: USC Viterbi." USC Viterbi School of Engineering, March 22, 2023. viterbischool.usc.edu/news/2023/03/anna-lee-fisher-was -the-first-mom-in-space-she-now-embarks-on-a-new-mission-usc-viterbi.

Kochhar, Rakesh. "The Enduring Grip of the Gender Pay Gap." Pew Research Center, March 1, 2023. www.pewresearch.org/social-trends/2023/03 /01/the-enduring-grip-of-the-gender-pay-gap.

Kolbert, Kathryn. "The End of Roe v. Wade—and What Comes Next for Reproductive Freedom." TED Talk, Palm Springs, CA, December 3, 2021. 16 min., 51 sec. https://www.ted.com/talks/kathryn_kolbert_the _end_of_roe_v_wade_and_what_comes_next_for_reproductive_freedom ?subtitle=en.

Kuck, Kevin. "Generative Artificial Intelligence: A Double-Edged Sword." In *2023 World Engineering Education Forum, Global Engineering Deans Council (WEEF-GEDC)* (Monterrey, Mexico, 2023), 1–10. https://doi.org /10.1109/WEEF-GEDC59520.2023.10343638.

Kukla, Jon. *Mr. Jefferson's Women*. Vintage Books, 2008.

Kwon, Sarah. "Was Racism a Factor in Death at Centinela Hospital? California Is Ill-Equipped to Investigate." *Los Angeles Times*, August 8, 2023. www .latimes.com/california/story/2023-08-08/racism-death-centinela-hospital -inglewood-childbirth-black-women.

Lamb, Sharon, Tangela Roberts, and Aleksandra Plocha. "Body Image, Sexy, and Sexualization." In *Girls of Color, Sexuality, and Sex Education*. Palgrave Macmillan, 2016. https://doi.org/10.1057/978-1-137-60155-1_2.

Lapchick, Richard E. "The 2021 Sports Media Racial and Gender Report Card: Associated Press Sports Editors." Institute for Diversity and Ethics in Sport, September 22, 2021. https://www.tidesport.org/_files/ugd/138a69 _e1e67c118b784f4caba00a4536699300.pdf.

Law, Tara. "Home Births Became More Popular During the Pandemic. But Many Insurers Still Don't Cover Them." *Time*, February 11, 2022. time.com /6145726/home-births-insurance-coverage.

Lempinen, Edward. "Loss, Fear and Rage: Are White Men Rebelling Against Democracy?" *UC Berkeley News*, November 9, 2024. https://news.berkeley .edu/2022/11/14/loss-fear-and-rage-are-white-men-rebelling-against -democracy.

Lepore, Jill. "The Invention of the Police." *New Yorker*, July 13, 2020. www .newyorker.com/magazine/2020/07/20/the-invention-of-the-police.

Leung, Rebecca, and Robert Williams. "#MeToo and Intersectionality: An Examination of the #MeToo Movement Through the R. Kelly Scandal." *Journal of Communication Inquiry* 43, no. 4 (2019): 349–71.

Levsky, Danielle. "Life as a Form of Art: Meditations on Alok Vaid-Menon and LaSaia Wade's Femme in Public." *Scapi Magazine*, June 20, 2018. scapimag.com/2018/06/20/life-as-a-form-of-art-meditations-on-alok-vaid -menon-and-lasaia-wades-femme-in-public.

Lewis, Meriwether, and William Clark. *The Journals of Lewis and Clark*. Edited by Bernard DeVoto. Penguin Books, 1989.

Lincoln, Abraham. Abraham Lincoln to the editor of the *Sangamo Journal*,

June 13, 1836. In *The Collected Works of Abraham Lincoln*, edited by Roy P. Basler, 1:48. Rutgers University Press, 1953.

Lindberg, David C. "2. Galileo, the Church, and the Cosmos." In *When Science and Christianity Meet*, edited by David C. Lindenberg and Ronald L. Numbers, 33–60. University of Chicago Press, 2003.

Lins, Karl V., Lukas Roth, Henri Servaes, and Ane Tamayo. "Sexism, Culture, and Firm Value: Evidence from the Harvey Weinstein Scandal and the #MeToo Movement." *Journal of Accounting Research* (2024). https://doi.org/10.1111/1475-679X.12573.

Liszewski, Walter, J. Klint Peebles, Howa Yeung, and Sarah Arron. "Persons of Nonbinary Gender—Awareness, Visibility, and Health Disparities." *New England Journal of Medicine* 379, no. 25 (2018): 2391–93. https://doi.org/10.1056/NEJMp1812005.

Little, Becky. "When Computer Coding Was a 'Woman's' Job.'" HISTORY, A&E Television Networks, February 9, 2021. www.history.com/news/coding-used-to-be-a-womans-job-so-it-was-paid-less-and-undervalued.

Loizos, Connie. "'When You Spend $100 Million on Social Media,' It Comes with Help, Says Trump Strategist." TechCrunch, November 8, 2017. techcrunch.com/2017/11/08/when-you-spend-100-million-on-social-media-it-comes-with-help-says-trump-strategist.

Lorde, Audre. "The Transformation of Silence into Language and Action." In *Sister Outsider: Essays and Speeches*. Crossing Press, 1984.

Lu, Denise, Jon Huang, Ashwin Seshagiri, Haeyoun Park, and Troy Griggs. "Faces of Power: 80% Are White, Even as U.S. Becomes More Diverse." *New York Times*, September 9, 2020. www.nytimes.com/interactive/2020/09/09/us/powerful-people-race-us.html.

Mack, Ashley Noel, and Bryan J. McCann. "Recalling Persky: White Rage and Intimate Publicity After Brock Turner." *Journal of Communication Inquiry* 43, no. 4 (2019): 372–93.

Madden, W. C. *The All-American Girls Professional Baseball League Record Book: Comprehensive Hitting, Fielding, and Pitching Statistics*. McFarland, 2000.

Mandler, C. "What Happened to Nex Benedict?" NPR, March 22, 2024. www.npr.org/2024/03/15/1238780699/nex-benedict-nonbinary-oklahoma-death-bullying.

Margaret C. Smith: A Midwife Remembered. Video, WTTO-TV, c. 2005. In *Reclaiming Midwives: Pillars of Community Support*, audiovisual records (2014). Anacostia Community Museum Archives, Smithsonian Institution. Exhibition catalog.

Marshall Project Staff. "RBG's Mixed Record on Race and Criminal Justice." Marshall Project, September 23, 2020. www.themarshallproject.org/2020/09/23/rbg-s-mixed-record-on-race-and-criminal-justice.

Martin, Emily. "The Egg and the Sperm: How Science Has Constructed a Romance Based on Stereotypical Male-Female Roles." *Signs: Journal of Women in Culture and Society* 16, no. 3 (1991): 485–501.

Matsui, Amy, and Sarah Lipton-Lubet. "Judge Neil Gorsuch's Record on Women's Legal Rights." National Women's Law Center, March 29, 2017. nwlc.org/judge-neil-gorsuchs-record-on-womens-legal-rights.

Matsumoto, Kendall. "Orientalism and the Legacy of Racialized Sexism: Disparate Representational Images of Asian and Eurasian Women in American Culture." *Young Scholars in Writing* 17 (January 2020): 114–26. https://youngscholarsinwriting.org/index.php/ysiw/article/view/305.

McAndrew, Tara. "The History of the KKK in American Politics." JSTOR Daily, January 25, 2017. daily.jstor.org/history-kkk-american-politics.

McIntire, Mike, Glenn Thrush, and Eric Lipton. "Gun Sellers' Message to Americans: Man Up." *New York Times*, June 18, 2022. www.nytimes.com /2022/06/18/us/firearm-gun-sales.html.

McLaren, Jackson Taylor, Susan Bryant, and Brian Brown. "'See Me! Recognize Me!' An Analysis of Transgender Media Representation." *Communication Quarterly* 69, no. 2 (2021): 172–91. https://doi.org/10.1080/01463373 .2021.1901759.

McLaughlin, Elliott C., Casey Tolan, and Amanda Watts. "What We Know About Robert Aaron Long, the Suspect in Atlanta Spa Shootings." CNN, March 18, 2021. https://www.cnn.com/2021/03/17/us/robert-aaron-long -suspected-shooter/index.html.

McLaughlin, Heather, Christopher Uggen, and Amy Blackstone. "Sexual Harassment, Workplace Authority, and the Paradox of Power." *American Sociological Review* 77, no. 4 (August 2012): 625–47.

McLeod, Carolyn, and Julie Ponesse. "Infertility and Moral Luck: The Politics of Women Blaming Themselves for Infertility." *International Journal of Feminist Approaches to Bioethics* 1, no. 1 (2008): 126–44. http://www.jstor .org/stable/40339215.

McNamara, Haley. "Three Ways Domestic Violence Is Connected to Pornography." National Center on Sexual Exploitation, October 1, 2018. end sexualexploitation.org/articles/three-ways-domestic-violence-is-connected -to-pornography.

McPherson, Craig. "You Can't Kill Chairman Fred: Examining the Life and Legacy of a Revolutionary." *Journal of African American Studies* 23 (2019): 276–98. https://doi.org/10.1007/s12111-019-09436-8.

McQuigg, Ronagh J. A. "Domestic Violence and the Inter-American Commission on Human Rights: *Jessica Lenahan (Gonzales) v United States*." *Human Rights Law Review* 12, no. 1 (March 2012): 122–34.

Merson, Molly. "This Is Not About Nex Benedict." *Studies in Gender and Sexuality* 25, no. 2 (2024): 143–47. https://doi.org/10.1080/15240657.2024.2346459.

Mihaila, Sorina. "Women's Health Content Censored and Blocked on Social Media." FemTech World, February 27, 2024. www.femtechworld.co.uk /news/lifesaving-womens-health-content-censored-and-blocked-on-social -media.

Miller, Chanel. *Know My Name: A Memoir*. Viking, 2019.

Mind. Unsigned review of *The Physiology of Mind*, by Henry Maudsley. Vol. 2, no. 6 (April 1877): 235–39. http://www.jstor.org/stable/2246379.

Mitchell, Paul Wolff. "The Fault in His Seeds: Lost Notes to the Case of Bias in Samuel George Morton's Cranial Race Science." *PLoS Biology* 16, no. 10 (October 2018): e2007008. https://doi.org/10.1371/journal.pbio.2007008.

Moga, Diana A., and Cosima Rughiniş. "Idealized Self-Presentation Through AI Avatars. A Case Study of Lensa AI." In *2023 24th International Conference on Control Systems and Computer Science (CSCS)*, 426–30, Bucharest, Romania, 2023. https://doi.org/10.1109/CSCS59211.2023.00073.

Monea, Alexander. *The Digital Closet: How the Internet Became Straight*. MIT Press, 2022.

Moraga, Cherríe L., and Gloria E. Anzaldúa, eds. *This Bridge Called My Back: Writings by Radical Women of Color*. Third Woman Press, 2002.

Morgan, Thomas D. "Native Americans in World War II." *Army History* 35 (Fall 1995): 22–27. http://www.jstor.org/stable/26304400.

Moss-Racusin, Corinne A., Casey A. Schofield, Sophie S. Brown, and Kerry A. O'Brien. "Breast Is (Viewed as) Best: Demonstrating Formula Feeding Stigma." *Psychology of Women Quarterly* 44, no. 4 (2020): 503–20. https://doi .org/10.1177/0361684320947647.

"Mrs. America: Women's Roles in the 1950s." *The Pill*, PBS. Accessed October 1, 2024. www.pbs.org/wgbh/americanexperience/features/pill-mrs-america -womens-roles-1950s.

Nakamura, David, and Anu Narayanswamy. "President Trump Names Longtime Aide Brad Parscale as Campaign Manager for 2020 Reelection Effort." *Washington Post*, February 27, 2018. https://www.washingtonpost .com/news/post-politics/wp/2018/02/27/trump-names-longtime-aide-brad -parscale-as-campaign-manager-for-2020-reelection-effort.

National Park Service. "Wildfire Causes and Evaluations." National Park Service, U.S. Department of the Interior. Accessed October 1, 2024. www .nps.gov/articles/wildfire-causes-and-evaluation.htm.

Neely, Mark E., and R. Gerald McMurtry. *The Insanity File: The Case of Mary Todd Lincoln*. Southern Illinois University Press, 1986.

Ng, Stephanie V. "Social Media and the Sexualization of Adolescent Girls." *American Journal of Psychiatry Residents Journal* 11, no. 12 (December 1, 2016): 14. https://doi.org/10.1176/appi.ajp-rj.2016.111206.

Novak, Nicole L., Natalie Lira, Kate E. O'Connor, Siobán D. Harlow, Sharon L. R. Kardia, and Alexandra Minna Stern. "Disproportionate Sterilization of Latinos Under California's Eugenic Sterilization Program, 1920–1945." *American Journal of Public Health* 108, no. 5 (May 2018): 611–13.

Oh, Chong, and Savan Kumar. "How Trump Won: The Role of Social Media Sentiment in Political Elections." *PACIS 2017 Proceedings*, 2017.

Oluo, Ijeoma. *Mediocre: The Dangerous Legacy of White Male America*. Seal Press, 2020.

Orloff, Leslye E., and Paige Feldman. "Domestic Violence and Sexual Assault Public Policy Timeline: Highlighting Accomplishment on Behalf of Immigrants and Women of Color." National Immigrant Women's Advocacy Project (NIWAP), American University Washington College of Law, August 2016. niwaplibrary.wcl.american.edu/wp-content/uploads/Herstory-2016-1.pdf.

"Paid Family Leave: Maternity, Paternity, and Other Parental Benefits in Tech." Techpoint, September 17, 2023. https://techpoint.org/paid-family-leave.

Paltrow, Lynn M., Lisa H. Harris, and Mary Faith Marshall. "Beyond Abortion: The Consequences of Overturning Roe." *American Journal of Bioethics* 22, no. 8 (2022): 3–15. https://doi.org/10.1080/15265161.2022.2075965.

Peffer, George Anthony. "Forbidden Families: Emigration Experiences of Chinese Women Under the Page Law, 1875–1882." *Journal of American Ethnic History* 6, no. 1 (Fall 1986): 28–46. http://www.jstor.org/stable/27500484.

Perry, Brea L., Kathi L. H. Harp, and Carrie B. Oser. "Racial and Gender Discrimination in the Stress Process: Implications for African American Women's Health and Well-Being." *Sociological Perspectives* 56, no. 1 (2013): 25–48.

Peterson, Cathy Norman. "Grappling with the Image of Jesus." Evangelical Covenant Church, January 16, 2024. covchurch.org/2024/01/16/grappling -with-the-image-of-jesus.

Peterson, Jillian, and James Densley. Violence Prevention Project Research Center, Hamline University. Accessed September 13, 2024. www .theviolenceproject.org.

Phillips, David J. "Negotiating the Digital Closet: Online Pseudonymity and the Politics of Sexual Identity." *Information, Communication & Society* 5, no. 3 (2002): 406–24. https://doi.org/10.1080/13691180210159337.

Pierson, Michael D. "'Slavery Cannot Be Covered Up with Broadcloth or a Bandanna': The Evolution of White Abolitionist Attacks on the 'Patriarchal Institution.'" *Journal of the Early Republic* 25, no. 3 (September 2005): 383–415.

"QAnon." Anti-Defamation League, December 14, 2022. https://www.adl .org/resources/backgrounder/qanon.

Rabin, Roni Caryn. "In N.Y.C., the Coronavirus Is Killing Men at Twice the Rate of Women." *New York Times*, April 7, 2020. www.nytimes.com/2020 /04/07/health/coronavirus-new-york-men.html.

"Racial Segregation in the Church." Equal Justice Initiative, January 1, 2016. eji.org/news/history-racial-injustice-racial-segregation-in-church.

Reich-Stiebert, Natalia, Laura Froehlich, and Jan-Bennet Voltmer. "Gendered

Mental Labor: A Systematic Literature Review on the Cognitive Dimension of Unpaid Work Within the Household and Childcare." *Sex Roles* 88 (2023): 475–94. https://doi.org/10.1007/s11199-023-01362-0.

Reumann, Miriam G. *American Sexual Character: Sex, Gender, and National Identity in the Kinsey Reports.* University of California Press, 2005.

Reyhner, Jon Allan, and Jeanne M. Oyawin Eder. *American Indian Education: A History.* University of Oklahoma Press, 2017.

Rich, Adrienne. *Of Woman Born: Motherhood as Experience and Institution.* W. W. Norton, 1976.

Richardson, Craig, and Zachary Blizard. "Benefits Cliffs, Disincentive Deserts, and Economic Mobility." *Journal of Poverty* 26, no. 1 (2022): 1–22. https://doi.org/10.1080/10875549.2020.1869665.

Roberts, Dorothy. *Torn Apart: How the Child Welfare System Destroys Black Families—and How Abolition Can Build a Safer World.* Basic Books, 2022.

Robinson, Margaret. "Two-Spirit Identity in a Time of Gender Fluidity." *Journal of Homosexuality* 67, no. 12 (2020): 1675–90.

Romo, Vanessa. "Last Living Mount Rushmore Carver Dies at 98." NPR, November 26, 2019. www.npr.org/2019/11/26/783091531/last-living-mount-rushmore-carver-dies-at-98.

Roth, Louise Marie, and Megan M. Henley. "Unequal Motherhood: Racial-Ethnic and Socioeconomic Disparities in Cesarean Sections in the United States." *Social Problems* 59, no. 2 (May 2012): 207–27.

Rothschild, Mike. *The Storm Is Upon Us: How QAnon Became a Movement, Cult, and Conspiracy Theory of Everything.* Blackstone Publishing, 2021.

Santana, María Cristina. "From Empowerment to Domesticity: The Case of Rosie the Riveter and the WWII Campaign." *Frontiers in Sociology* 1 (2016). https://doi.org/10.3389/fsoc.2016.00016.

Savage, Mark. "R. Kelly: The History of His Crimes and Allegations Against Him." BBC News, February 24, 2023. www.bbc.com/news/entertainment-arts-40635526.

Schofield, Mary Anne. "Miss America, Rosie the Riveter, and World War II." In *There She Is, Miss America*, edited by Elwood Watson and Darcy Martin. Palgrave Macmillan, 2004.

Schrobsdorff, Susanna. "Top 10 Breast-Feeding Controversies." *Time*, February 23, 2011. content.time.com/time/specials/packages/article/0,28804,2053230_2053229_2053225,00.html.

Seitz, Amanda. "White Supremacists Are Riling Up Thousands on Social Media." PBS News, June 10, 2022. www.pbs.org/newshour/politics/white-supremacists-are-riling-up-thousands-on-social-media.

Serrato, Jacqueline. "Fifty Years of Fred Hampton's Rainbow Coalition." South Side Weekly, September 27, 2019. southsideweekly.com/fifty-years-fred-hampton-rainbow-coalition-young-lords-black-panthers.

Serwer, Adam. "Why Fox News Lied to Its Viewers." *The Atlantic*, February 19, 2023. www.theatlantic.com/ideas/archive/2023/02/fox-news-dominion -lawsuit-trump/673132.

Shakur, Assata. *Assata: An Autobiography*. Lawrence Hill Books, 2001.

Shead, Sydney. "'Granny' Midwife to Nurse-Midwife: The Decline of Southern Black Midwifery in the 20th Century." *Historical Perspectives: Santa Clara University Undergraduate Journal of History, Series II* 27, no. 1 (2022): 9.

Sheikh, Knvul. "How 'The Lion King' Gets Real-Life Lion Family Dynamics Wrong." *New York Times*, July 21, 2019. www.nytimes.com/2019/07/21 /movies/lion-king-nature.html.

Shetterly, Margot Lee. *Hidden Figures: The American Dream and the Untold Story of the Black Women Mathematicians Who Helped Win the Space Race*. Harper Luxe, 2016.

Shmerling, Robert H. "Right Brain/Left Brain, Right?" *Mind & Mood* (blog), Harvard Health Publishing, Harvard Medical School, March, 24, 2022. www.health.harvard.edu/blog/right-brainleft-brain-right-2017082512222.

Sisson, Gretchen. *Relinquished: The Politics of Adoption and the Privilege of American Motherhood*. St. Martin's Press, 2024.

Smeltz, Dina, Craig Kafura, Candace Rondeaux, Heela Rasool-Ayub, and Deborah Avant. "Race, Ethnicity, and American Views of Climate Change." Chicago Council on Global Affairs, May 25, 2023. globalaffairs.org/research /public-opinion-survey/race-ethnicity-and-american-views-climate-change.

Smith, Lauren Reichart, and Ann Pegoraro. "Media Framing of Larry Nassar and the USA Gymnastics Child Sex Abuse Scandal." *Journal of Child Sexual Abuse* 29, no. 4 (2020): 373–92. https://doi.org/10.1080/10538712.2019 .1703233.

Smith, Rex Alan. *The Carving of Mount Rushmore*. Abbeville Press, 1985.

Soerens, Matthew. "This Love of Guns: It's Way Beyond Our Understanding." *Christianity Today*, 2022.

Spruill, Larry H. "Slave Patrols, 'Packs of Negro Dogs' and Policing Black Communities." *Phylon* 53, no. 1 (Summer 2016): 42–66. http://www.jstor.org /stable/phylon1960.53.1.42.

Staniunas, Sophia. "Misconduct and the Metaverse: Legal Prevention and Prosecution of Virtual Sexual Harassment." *Fordham Undergraduate Law Review*, 2024. undergradlawreview.blog.fordham.edu/criminal-justice /misconduct-and-the-metaverse-legal-prevention-and-prosecution-of -virtual-sexual-harassment.

"Statistics." Rape, Abuse & Incest National Network (RAINN). rainn.org /statistics.

Suarez, Alicia. "Black Midwifery in the United States: Past, Present, and Future." *Sociology Compass* 14, no. 11 (2020): e12829, 1–12. https://doi.org /10.1111/soc4.12829.

"Suicide Statistics." American Foundation for Suicide Prevention. afsp.org /suicide-statistics.

Switzer, Kathrine. "The Girl Who Started It All." Kathrine Switzer, Runner's World. March 26, 2007. kathrineswitzer.com/2007/03/the-girl-who-started -it-all.

Taber, Ronald W. "Sacagawea and the Suffragettes: An Interpretation of a Myth." *Pacific Northwest Quarterly* 58, no. 1 (January 1967): 7–13. http:// www.jstor.org/stable/40488221.

Thompson, Clive. "The Gendered History of Human Computers." *Smithsonian Magazine*, June 2019. www.smithsonianmag.com/science-nature /history-human-computers-180972202.

Tikkanen, Roosa, Munira Z. Gunja, Molly FitzGerald, and Laurie C. Zephyrin. "Maternal Mortality and Maternity Care in the United States Compared to 10 Other Developed Countries." Commonwealth Fund, November 18, 2020. www.commonwealthfund.org/publications/issue-briefs/2020/nov /maternal-mortality-maternity-care-us-compared-10-countries.

Traynor, Joleen. "Supreme Court Justice Brett Kavanaugh and Accusations of Sexual Assault in the Media." *Political Analysis* 20 (2019): 4.

Treisman, Rachel. "How Loss of Historical Lands Makes Native Americans More Vulnerable to Climate Change." NPR, November 2, 2021. www .npr.org/2021/11/02/1051146572/forced-relocation-native-american-tribes -vulnerable-climate-change-risks.

Trent, Judith. "The National Rifle Association: Credibility in a Propaganda Campaign." *Journal of the American Forensic Association* 7, no. 4 (1971): 216–23. https://doi.org/10.1080/00028533.1971.11951430.

Tyson, Alec, Cary Funk, and Brian Kennedy. "What the Data Says About Americans' Views of Climate Change." Pew Research Center, August 9, 2023. www.pewresearch.org/short-reads/2023/08/09/what-the-data-says -about-americans-views-of-climate-change.

Uggen, Christopher, and Amy Blackstone. "Sexual Harassment as a Gendered Expression of Power." *American Sociological Review* 69, no. 1 (2004): 64–92.

UN Environment Programme. "Spreading Like Wildfire: The Rising Threat of Extraordinary Landscape Fires." UN Environment Programme, February 23, 2022. www.unep.org/resources/report/spreading-wildfire-rising -threat-extraordinary-landscape-fires.

United States Attorney's Office, District of Columbia. "Proud Boys Leader Sentenced to 22 Years in Prison on Seditious Conspiracy and Other Charges Related to U.S. Capitol Breach." News release, September 5, 2023. www .justice.gov/usao-dc/pr/proud-boys-leader-sentenced-22-years-prison -seditious-conspiracy-and-other-charges.

US Bureau of the Census. "Money Income and Poverty Status of Families and Persons in the United States: 1984 (Advance Data from the March 1981

Current Population Survey)." US Bureau of the Census, Report P60–149, August 1985. www.census.gov/library/publications/1985/demo/p60-149.html.

US Bureau of the Census. "School Enrollment—Social and Economic Characteristics of Students: October 1985." Current Population Reports, September 1986. www.census.gov/content/dam/Census/library/publications/1986/demo/p20-409.pdf.

US Bureau of Labor Statistics. "Changes in Women's Labor Force Participation in the 20th Century." TED: The Economics Daily, February 16, 2000. https://www.bls.gov/opub/ted/2000/feb/wk3/art03.htm.

Utter, Glenn H., ed. *Guns and Contemporary Society: The Past, Present, and Future of Firearms and Firearm Policy*. Praeger, 2016.

Valentino-DeVries, Jennifer, and Michael H. Keller. "A Marketplace of Girl Influencers Managed by Moms and Stalked by Men." *New York Times*, February 23, 2024. www.nytimes.com/2024/02/22/us/instagram-child-influencers.html.

Van der Kolk, Bessel. *The Body Keeps the Score: Brain, Mind, and Body in the Healing of Trauma*. Penguin Books, 2015.

Vargas, Deborah R. "8. Representations of Latina/o Sexuality in Popular Culture." In *Latina/o Sexualities: Probing Powers, Passions, Practices, and Policies*, edited by Marysol Asencio, 117–36. Rutgers University Press, 2010. https://doi.org/10.36019/9780813548227-011.

Vogels, Emily A. "Teens and Cyberbullying 2022." Pew Research Center, December 15, 2022. www.pewresearch.org/internet/2022/12/15/teens-and-cyberbullying-2022.

Vogels, Emily A., and Risa Gelles-Watnick. "Teens and Social Media: Key Findings from Pew Research Center Surveys." Pew Research Center, April 24, 2023. www.pewresearch.org/short-reads/2023/04/24/teens-and-social-media-key-findings-from-pew-research-center-surveys.

Wailoo, Keith. "Historical Aspects of Race and Medicine: The Case of J. Marion Sims." *JAMA* 320, no. 15 (October 2018): 1529–30. https://doi.org/10.1001/jama.2018.11944.

Watson, Amy. "Top Cable News Networks U.S. 2023, by Number of Voters." Statista, December 13, 2023. www.statista.com/statistics/373814/cable-news-network-viewership-usa.

Waxman, Olivia B. "The U.S. Almost Had Universal Childcare 50 Years Ago. The Same Attacks Might Kill It Today." *Time*, December 9, 2021. time.com/6125667/universal-childcare-history-nixon-veto.

Weale, Sally. "Social Media Algorithms 'Amplifying Misogynistic Content.'" *The Guardian*, February 5, 2024. www.theguardian.com/media/2024/feb/06/social-media-algorithms-amplifying-misogynistic-content.

Weitz, Tracy A., and Susan Yanow. "Implications of the Federal Abortion Ban for Women's Health in the United States." *Reproductive Health Matters* 16, supplement 31 (2008): 99–107. https://doi.org/10.1016/S0968-8080(08)31374-3.

Wells, Chris, Yini Zhang, Josephine Lukito, and Jon C. W. Pevehouse. "Modeling the Formation of Attentive Publics in Social Media: The Case of Donald Trump." *Mass Communication and Society* 23, no. 2 (2020): 181–205. https://doi.org/10.1080/15205436.2019.1690664.

White, Shereen, and Stephanie Marie Persson. "Racial Discrimination in Child Welfare Is a Human Rights Violation—Let's Talk About It That Way." American Bar Association, October 13, 2022. www.americanbar .org/groups/litigation/resources/newsletters/childrens-rights/racial -discrimination-child-welfare-human-rights-violation-lets-talk-about-it -way.

Wilkerson, Isabel. *Caste: The Origins of Our Discontents*. Random House, 2020.

Wilson, O. W. "August Vollmer." *Journal of Criminal Law, Criminology, and Police Science* 44, no. 1 (May–June 1953): 91–103. https://doi.org/10.2307 /1139476.

Wolf, Jacqueline H. "'THEY SAID HER HEART WAS IN DISTRESS': The Electronic Fetal Monitor and the Experience of Birth in the U.S.A., 1960s to the Present." *Icon* 26, no. 2 (2021): 33–61. https://www.jstor.org /stable/27120654.

Yi, Kris. "Asian American Experience: The Illusion of Inclusion and the Model Minority Stereotype." *Psychoanalytic Dialogues* 33, no. 1 (2023): 45–59. https://doi.org/10.1080/10481885.2023.2160171.

Yoon, Soo. "Single Women Can Face a Workplace Penalty Too." *Washington Post*, April 21, 2022. www.washingtonpost.com/business/2022/04/21/single -women-workplace-penalty.

Zhao, Ziyue, Yuanchao Gong, Yang Li, Linxiu Zhang, and Yan Sun. "Gender-Related Beliefs, Norms, and the Link with Green Consumption." *Frontiers in Psychology* 12 (2021): 710239. https://doi.org/10.3389/fpsyg.2021.710239.

INDEX

ABOUT THE AUTHOR

Anna Malaika Tubbs is a *New York Times* bestselling author and multidisciplinary expert on current and historical understandings of race, gender, and equity. With a PhD in sociology and a master's in multidisciplinary gender studies from the University of Cambridge, in addition to a bachelor's in medical anthropology from Stanford University, Tubbs translates her academic knowledge into stories that are clear and engaging. Her articles have been published by *Time*, *New York* magazine, CNN, *Motherly*, *HuffPost*, *For Harriet*, the *Guardian*, *Darling*, and *Blavity*. Tubbs's storytelling also takes form in her talks, including her TED Talk, which has been viewed two million times, as well as the scripted and unscripted screen projects she has in development. She lives in Los Angeles with her husband and their three kids.